The
Godfather
Effect

Also by Tom Santopietro

Sinatra in Hollywood
Considering Doris Day
The Importance of Being Barbra

The Godfather Effect

Changing Hollywood, America, and Me

TOM SANTOPIETRO

THOMAS DUNNE BOOKS
St. Martin's Press New York

THOMAS DUNNE BOOKS.
An imprint of St. Martin's Press.

www.thomasdunnebooks.com
www.stmartins.com

Design by Phil Mazzone

ISBN 978-1-250-00513-7 (hardcover)
ISBN 978-1-4299-5262-0 (e-book)

First Edition: February 2012

10   9   8   7   6   5   4   3   2   1

For my extraordinary aunt
Julia Katherine Santopietro Boyd

And my grandparents
Orazio and Maria Santopietro
Raymond and Helen Parker

Contents

1 Don Vito in Hollywood   1

2 Spring 1992   9

3 Ancestral Voices   15

4 From *La Via Vecchia* to L'America   39

5 The Lure of the Corleones   69

6 Forefathers on Film   97

7 Godfather Cinema   111

8 Frank Sinatra   153

9 *La Famiglia* (di Santopietro, Corleone, *e* Coppola)   169

10 *The Godfather: Part II*   193

11 Patriarchy   205

12 Religion, Death, and Grief   229

13 *The Godfather: Part III*   243

14 The Shadow of *The Godfather*   259

15 *Godfather: Part IV?*   277

16 March 3,1902   281

Acknowledgments   287

Notes   289

Bibliography   307

Index   311

The
Godfather
Effect

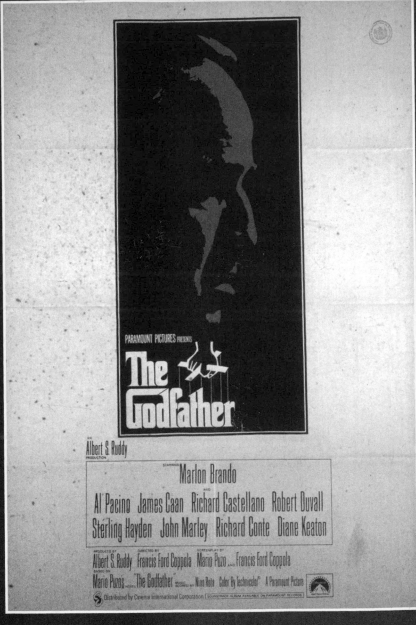

1972 and the start of the phenomenon. Brando on Don Corleone:
"a bulldog: mean-looking but warm underneath." *Photofest*

1 Don Vito in Hollywood

*I am willing to sacrifice my best scene to make the film better . . .
anything . . . I can always put it back. That's the difference with
life—you can't put it back.*

—FRANCIS FORD COPPOLA

WHEN FRANCIS FORD COPPOLA arrived at Marlon Brando's home in
late 1970 to shoot a "makeup test" for the actor's role as aging Mafia
chieftain Don Vito Corleone in *The Godfather,* he had exactly one
thing on his mind: how to conduct what amounted to a screen test
without insulting the world famous Academy Award–winning actor. A legend at age forty-seven, the eccentric Brando had acquired
a reputation for causing on-set difficulties and cost overruns, and
with his recent films having tanked at the box office, no one at Paramount Pictures wanted a temperamental, box-office-poison has-
been to play the role of "the godfather." Time after time, Paramount
Pictures executives had vehemently stated that Marlon Brando
would never play the part. Never.

What those executives had not counted on, however, was the
determination of Coppola himself. Along with his co-screenwriter

Mario Puzo, whose 1969 novel had launched *The Godfather* tidal wave, Coppola had fixated on the idea of the brilliant, mercurial Brando in the title role, and nothing could persuade him to look elsewhere. Forget Burt Lancaster, Ernest Borgnine, Frank Sinatra, Anthony Quinn, and every other Hollywood star who had expressed an interest in the role. For Francis Ford Coppola, budding auteur, only one actor could fulfill the complex requirements of the role. Now he just had to find a way to finesse the test, so that the most acclaimed film actor of the past thirty years did not realize that he was being screen-tested for the consideration of Paramount Pictures executives.

It was actually co-screenwriter Puzo who had originated the idea of casting Brando by sending the actor a handwritten letter couched in the most flattering of terms: "I think you're the only actor who can play the Godfather with that quiet force and irony the part requires." Don Vito Corleone would appear on-screen for only one-third of the movie, but Puzo inherently understood that an actor of Brando's strength, one who could dominate scenes and cast a presence over the entire film, would prove crucial for sustaining mood and texture throughout.

The battle over Brando—upstarts Coppola and Puzo pitted against the collective corporate weight of Paramount Pictures and its parent company Gulf&Western—had dragged on for months. Even when Paramount studio head Stanley Jaffe reluctantly agreed to consider Brando for the role (this after he had already told Coppola: "As president of this company, I say that you are not allowed to even discuss the option of Brando anymore") he set forth a trio of potential deal killers :

1. Brando would not receive any up-front salary.
2. Financial responsibility for any delays caused by the actor's behavior would remain his alone.

3. Regardless of having won an Academy Award and starred in no fewer than twenty-six films, Brando would have to screen-test for the role.

It was with these daunting preexisting conditions in mind that director Coppola, who admitted to being "scared shitless" of Brando, now found himself driving up to the privacy-conscious actor's home. The camouflaged entrance from the road, designed to deter overzealous fans, seemed almost symbolic of the torturous path toward production which lay ahead, and as the director arrived at Brando's front door, one question loomed ever larger: how best to wrangle a screen test out of the film legend without inducing a temperamental explosion?

Having set up the filming with Brando by telling him that he simply wanted to test equipment and "get a take" on the character of Don Vito, Coppola was granted an unexpected gift when the actor himself allowed as how a brief video in makeup would help allay his fears over his suitability for the role of an elderly Italian man. (In later years, Brando would claim he knew all along that he was auditioning.) But—and it was a big but—a test ostensibly made for Brando's own reassurance or to check the makeup he envisioned for the role did not necessarily resemble a screen test suitable to win over studio executives already searching for reasons to summarily reject the actor. With all of these problems running through his mind, the still relatively unknown Coppola stepped through the front door of the legend's home and began work.

Cerebral yet highly intuitive, Coppola instinctively understood the necessity for underplaying all elements related to the "test." Knowing the actor's penchant for privacy and quiet, Coppola had brought along only a skeletal crew. Setting out a cigar and a few props of Italian food in order to inject a bit of proper ambience, the director silently watched as the kimono-clad Brando began stuffing tissues in his mouth to achieve the look and sound he envisioned for Don Vito. Conceptualizing the godfather as a "bulldog," Brando used the tissues to accentuate both a thrusting jaw and a hoarse speaking voice capable of suggesting the effects of aging. Pulling back his long dark-blond hair and applying shoe polish to darken his hair and suggest a moustache, Brando began his metamorphosis into Don Vito Corleone. Rolling back the collar of the white shirt Coppola had brought along (said Brando: "You know those guys, the collar is always bent") and speaking in the gravelly register he felt accurate for a mobster he decided had been shot in the throat, the actor began to move around his home, adjusting his body language, fingering props, and falling deeper into character. Coppola was hooked—or perhaps more accurately—instantly felt vindicated by his choice. Here, in the flesh, stood Don Vito Corleone, just as the director had visualized. Only bigger and better, already a recognizably complex human being.

When the completed test was replayed, even Brando himself, often his own harshest critic, was pleased with the results, feeling that he had successfully captured the look of the aging mafioso—"mean-looking, but warm underneath." Now Coppola had to convince the Paramount studio executives to acquiesce to his artistic vision. With nary a hit to his credit—previous directorial efforts *Dementia 13, You're a Big Boy Now, Finian's Rainbow,* and *The Rain People* had all flopped in the one area that mattered to studios, the box office—Coppola faced a decidedly uphill task. What he had going for him, however, was a bulldog tenacity at least the equal of Don Vito's own, a nearly frightening intensity of belief in his own correctness, and for all of his cerebral nature, a certain street cunning and directorial intuition that allowed him to unveil the screen tests in precisely the fashion that showcased Brando to maximum effect.

When the time came to show the "makeup test" to studio head

Stanley Jaffe and production chief Robert Evans, Coppola and the film's producer, Al Ruddy (who came to call the test "the miracle on Mulholland"), cannily placed Brando's test in the middle of others, thereby heightening its impact. Duly pleased as Evans and Jaffe were—Evans reportedly asked, "He looks Italian—fine. But who is he?"—it was the reaction of the formidable Austrian-born Gulf&Western chairman Charles Bluhdorn that assured Brando's casting. After sitting through the test, Bluhdorn bluntly barked: "Who are ve vatching? Who is dis old guinea?" When told it was Brando, an amused and impressed Bluhdorn signed off on the casting. In Coppola's slightly different yet equally compelling version of that same screening, Bluhdorn "backed away" when he saw it was Brando, but after watching the actor's metamorphosis into Don Corleone, grunted "that's amazing" and approved the casting.

Brando in place, further casting continued, and shooting finally began on March 8, 1971. Such was the anticipation of Brando's performance that in the blitz of publicity undertaken before the film's March 1972 release, Paramount heightened the stakes even further by purposely withholding photographs of the actor in costume and makeup. The studio knew they had a surefire object of audience interest on their hands: here was the world's most famous actor playing a murderous mobster already familiar to millions of readers worldwide. What they didn't know was how the audience would actually react once they sat through the three-hour film.

Upon the film's release, the answer came instantly, in the form of nearly unanimous rave reviews from critics and audiences alike. Coppola and company had created the rarest of species, a truly adult blockbuster film; such was the power of Brando's portrayal that, when combined with the golden-hued cinematography, era-evocative production design, and haunting music, viewers across the nation completely capitulated. They didn't just like the film, they embraced it with a fervor that spoke of a desire to enter the very world of the Corleones—to become guests themselves at Connie Corleone's wedding reception. Suddenly, mobsters or not, Italians were no longer caricatures worthy of derision. They were figures fit for admiration.

Within days of the film's release, comedians, talk-show hosts, and even politicians were not just talking about the film—they were imitating Brando. Jaws thrust forward, voices lowered to bullfrog register, and incessantly repeating the words "I'll make him an offer he can't refuse" until it grew into an instantly recognizable catchphrase, citizens nationwide were already channeling their own version of Don Corleone. Poking fun out of both affection and approval, audiences surrendered to their own visceral reaction; here was a character they found frightening, admirable, and—dare they admit it—reflective of their own innermost fears and desires. In the figure of a Mafia don, Italian-Americans had suddenly gone mainstream.

With this one film, notions of ethnicity in America had been upended in rather spectacular fashion. Mobsters these characters may have been, but in their proud self-assertion, celebration of ethnicity, and love of family lay complex, readily identifiable human beings. For the very first time, Italian-Americans were not just embracing their own story but telling it on their own terms. In the wake of *The Godfather*'s release, it seemed as if the popular Italian-American aphorism might just be true—there did indeed now seem to exist two types of people in the world: Italians and those who wanted to be Italian.

The lasting effect of *The Godfather* ran even deeper, however, because in detailing the saga of the Corleones, author and screenwriter Puzo was examining nothing less than the state of America. His vision filled with an understanding of the fundamental contradictions inherent in all human beings, Puzo's singular achievement lay in his ability to celebrate the virtues of the Italian family while never losing sight of the tragedy lying at the heart of *The Godfather* and America alike. What Puzo and screenwriter/director Coppola delivered—brilliantly—was nothing less than a disquisition on the madness, glory, and failure of the American dream. In exploring that dream in distinctly Italian-American terms, they succeeded in delivering nothing less than the Italianization of American culture.

Even to those who never particularly cared to be Italian. Especially to those who had never cared to be Italian.

Like me.

1918: My father in the arms of his grandmother. Left to right, his siblings Julia, Emma, and Andrew. *Family Photo*

2   Spring 1992

Heroism is the brilliant triumph of the soul over the flesh, that is to say over fear: fear of poverty, of suffering, of calumny, of illness, of loneliness and of death.

—Henri Frédéric Amiel, *Journal*

My FATHER AND I sat in his car, gazing at the fenced-in asphalt space where he had played baseball as a young boy. Turning toward me with a rueful smile, he quietly said, "It's smaller than I remember." Silence ensued for a few brief moments, each of us lost in crowded thoughts. My father was not one given to revisiting the past except in the most playful manner; he'd purposely embellish tales of his youth just to get a rise out of his two children, but a serious contemplation of the past? This was uncharted territory. Then again, there was nothing usual about the circumstances in which we now found ourselves.

Three years earlier, a scant twenty-two months after retiring from his busy medical practice, my father had suffered a series of terrible setbacks, enduring in very short order a stroke, a heart attack, and the amputation of his right leg. So severe were his disabilities that it had taken six months before he would even contemplate a short car trip like the fifteen-minute ride we had just taken across town, traveling from the sprawling modern house my parents had built in 1961 to the tough, now-run-down neighborhood in which he had grown up. Before my father's illness, a trip down memory lane to 1923-era Waterbury, Connecticut, would likely have rated high on my list of things I never wanted to do. Now I was just happy that he felt well enough to go for a ride.

What made my father suggest the drive that day I still don't know. Loading up his wheelchair in case he felt well enough to get out of the car, cushioning the car seat, making sure he would be warm enough, maneuvering him into the car—all the preparations elicited his soft comment, "So much I used to take for granted . . ." We hung a right onto Division Street, stopping in front of the lot where my father's long-since-razed childhood home had stood for decades. Oddly, our arrival felt neither happy nor upsetting. There was nothing maudlin about the trip, and certainly nothing senti-mental: my father believed in honest sentiment but never in forced sentimentality. It simply felt as if he was measuring the distance of his journey: ten miles by car, seventy years in time. Once again he murmured "It's so much smaller"—and I felt immeasurably sad-dened in ways I never had during his entire illness. His world had shrunk to almost nothing as it was; I didn't want his childhood memories diminished in kind.

I tried to make us both laugh with my story of revisiting the fearsome hill I had proudly conquered as a six-year-old on bicycle; returning at age twenty-something, I found myself staring at a barely noticeable gentle slope. My chatter soon drifted away, and we sat together in an uneasy yet somehow companionable silence. I knew my father was remembering his own six-year-old self, won-dering how that baseball-loving youngster had ended up a handi-capped seventy-four-year-old for whom the slightest exertion proved exhausting. In that moment, we both, I think, felt the full weight of time.

Division Street had always been my father's touchstone, the endless stories at family gatherings about how tough life had been causing no end of eye rolling from my sister and me. With each retelling, his walk to school somehow grew longer, his shoes now disintegrating as he trudged through snowdrifts growing higher and deeper, until only Nanook of the North and my six-year-old father were strong enough to brave the conditions. The mere mention of Division Street served, I think, as an affirmation for him, providing a sense of wonder at just how far he had come, and on this day, unspoken, a reminder of how little of his life remained. Division Street brought my father back to the days when his parents were alive and the world lay open before him, the very address signifying both a reminder and celebration of his Italian roots, an underscoring of the strength of his cultural identity. Living in the midst of a fiercely all-Italian neighborhood had brought comfort and pride in an era that found the predominant culture often laughing at the very notion of Italians as bona fide Americans.

Gazing at the site of my father's game-winning home run, I reminded him of his attempts to teach me how to throw a curve ball, the sessions fixed in my mind as a series of hurried instructions before the light faded. I laughed slightly, telling my father that if life were an Andy Hardy movie I would have conquered the curve ball before we headed in to a home-cooked meal. But I was never more than an OK neighborhood ballplayer, a good hitter and poor fielder, who by temperament and talent derived much greater pleasure from sports individual in nature. I liked to figure things out for myself, hated listening to coaches screaming words of advice, and enjoyed the solitary nature of tennis, squash, and swimming far more than team sports. (In cleaning out the family home of fifty years I came across a rather prescient report card from kinder-garten in which my teacher had written: "Tommy is a polite, nice boy who makes friends easily. He plays well with others but is just as happy to go off and play by himself.")

I never quite got the hang of the curve ball, and more than once stomped off, muttering about the dumb game of baseball. My fa-ther laughed for the first time that afternoon—"I remember you banging the front door—and you never even had a temper. That was your sister's department"—but the laugh faded and we sat in the car until dusk fell, lights in the downtrodden neighborhood cutting through the encroaching darkness as I started the car, and, facing away from the past, we slowly drove away. I could tell my father was sad, but I sensed he was still somehow pleased with the visit, as if an unfinished piece of business had been completed. It was the last time my father ever visited his old neighborhood.

Division Street never spoke to me in the way it did to my father. That early-spring visit represented only the second time I had ever visited the neighborhood. In my Waspy upbringing dominated by the Anglo culture of both my mother and school, it had played next to no part in forming my self-identity, resulting in a disconnect I had felt throughout my life. (I here use WASP—white Anglo-Saxon Protestant—as a signifier of ethnicity, but in our supposedly class-less society, it usually strikes me as more a signal of class. Poor white Anglo-Saxon Protestants in the South are never referred to as WASPs—they are called "rednecks," a signifier of class if ever there was one.) Even my full name—Thomas Parker Santopietro—spoke to this disconnect, with my mother's maiden name serving as my middle name. As a youngster trying to figure out where I fit in and who was really like me, I uncomfortably straddled two worlds. In the words of Bill Tonelli's sharply crafted insight: "But you know how it is when you're a kid—you're looking outside, hoping to find some plausible version of yourself already functioning in the world of adults." I couldn't fully understand, much less successfully navigate, the gap between my Italian and Anglo worlds, and if a plausible version of myself was functioning somewhere in the world of adults, I had no idea where he was.

Feeling proudly Italian was the province of the relatives from my father's side of the family, and I paid little attention to the culture, language, or history, groaning in embarrassment at the heavily accented Italian-American caricatures found on television. I didn't feel Italian and actually didn't care about that fact. Italians, according to television and the newspapers, were loud, uneducated, and poorly dressed, and if that's how people perceived Italians, I wanted no part of it.

I had no idea what it really meant to be Italian. No idea, that is, until *The Godfather* came along. Or, more precisely, until *The Godfather: Part II* saw the light of day and turned my world upside down.

I was, courtesy of Francis Ford Coppola and Mario Puzo, about to grow up.

Young Vito on Ellis Island—the promise of L'America. *Photofest*

3   Ancestral Voices

Italian eyes are all dark, with a lot of yesterdays in them.
—GEORGE PANETTA, *VIVA MADISON AVENUE*

IN RETROSPECT, I REALIZE that I had been gathering bits and pieces of Italian identity for years, without really taking any of it on board. As I grew older and the 1970s dawned, my attitude started to change: the portrayal of Italians on television began to grate. The casual use of the slur "guinea wop" rankled with increasing force. I actually began listening to family stories for the first time. But these scattered bits of increasing consciousness still bubbled under the surface, in no way preparing me for the moment exactly ten minutes into *The Godfather: Part II* that struck me with such force that for several minutes I endured the unsettling sensation that time had stopped.

On-screen, nine-year-old Vito Corleone, né Andolini, had arrived in America after escaping from Sicilian Mafia chieftain Don Ciccio, the man responsible for the deaths of his father, mother, and brother. Quarantined for health reasons on Ellis Island, young Vito sits in a chair, gazing out the window of his bare room at the Statue of Liberty standing guard in the harbor. Gently swinging his feet to and fro, he softly sings a song in his native dialect. It's a sequence short in duration, but so powerful to me, so shocking in its unexpected intensity, that I choked up. I didn't sob and didn't even cry, but I was overcome with a personalized emotion I had never before experienced in a movie theater, because to my twenty-year-old self, there on the screen, in the person of young Vito, was my grandfather, Orazio Santopietro, as a young man. My grandfather had come back to life. Time stopping—the hoariest of clichés. But that's how it felt, as if I had been forcibly hurled back seventy years in time.

The power of the image of this solitary boy singing to himself made me realize for the very first time in my comfortable, cocooned, upper-middle-class life just what had transpired in my grandfather's leap to L'America. The guts it took to leave his hardscrabble village of Pontelandolfo in southern Italy, arriving in a new land at age thirteen without family or any knowledge of English. The realization that I, who had never paid attention to being Italian, owed him much I couldn't even explain. And that having died four years earlier, he wasn't around for me to thank. For five minutes I was lost as the images of Ellis Island, circa 1901, flew by. For the first time in my privileged, genetically half, and culturally three-quarters, Anglo life, I felt fully Italian.

What was it about the power of Coppola's vision that hit me with a force that all the years of family stories had never equaled? Granted, I was now older and, as a college sophomore, finally capable of the first glimmerings of perspective. Intellectually I knew that this meticulous re-creation of Little Italy was just that: a fictional re-creation of Italian-American history resulting from the combined efforts of director Coppola, his cinematographer, production designer, set decorator, costume designer, and film composer. I could rationalize all I wanted, but emotionally it didn't matter a bit. I was, as the Brits would say, gobsmacked.

Thanks to Coppola and co-screenwriter Puzo, I finally got it. Well, it would take decades and the loss of both of my parents before I fully understood, but that one image of young Vito and the Statue of Liberty first opened the door to a sense of "Italian-ness" that had heretofore utterly escaped me. Just watching that vulnerable little boy instantly brought to mind the photographs of my impossibly youthful grandfather still dressed in the style of the old country, photographs to which I had never paid much attention. The Santopietro family movie in my head was, for a few minutes, superimposed over Coppola's. In my mind's eye the movie I saw featured my shy, reserved grandfather undertaking the grueling journey to establish a beachhead in America, working ceaselessly to save money before returning to Pontelandolfo years later for my grandmother, Maria Victoria Valletta. Bride in hand, the final voyage to America then began.

At the age of twenty, I had been in private school my entire life, all expenses paid by my parents. By the time my grandparents turned twenty, they had crossed an ocean, started a family, and created a brand-new business, all the while dealing with a new language and an overwhelmingly foreign culture in a city then dominated by the Irish. In my mind, Orazio and Maria somehow blended into Vito and Mama Corleone, and thanks to one bold image of a little boy and the Statue of Liberty, the stories about a tough life on Division Street now began to acquire specificity and texture, landing with an emotional resonance that startled me. Photos of my grandparents working together in their dark grocery store that served the entire Italian neighborhood in the north end of Waterbury filled my head. Was there ever any light in that store? Any ventilation? The work, the unending work. I was grateful and unsettled in equal measure.

What could those Division Street stories really mean to a boy raised in the upper middle class, the son of an Italian-American doctor, Olindo Oreste Santopietro, and a thoroughly English mother, Nancy Edge Parker? President of the Mount Holyoke College class of 1946, my mother had fashioned a life so far removed from blue-collar Division Street that she served as president of the Connecticut Association of Junior Leagues. With her reddish-blond hair and blue eyes, my mother's looks, circa 1962, resembled those of *Mad Men*'s Betty Draper a lot more than Mama Corleone in *The Godfather*. Division Street remained just as much a universe apart for my mother as it did for me, but she reacted in a decidedly different, more accepting, fashion than I.

Not having been raised Catholic, part of the youthful distance I felt from Italian-American culture emanated from the larger-than-life role that the Catholic church played in 1950s and 1960s Italian-American family life. Fearsome priests, weekly catechism, nuns, the pope—it all belonged to another world. My father, a Christian in action, if not church attendance, held a rather jaundiced view of the church, and since my mother did attend church regularly, he was more than happy to have his children raised in her Episcopal faith. My father's disinterest in the Catholic church had been passed on to him from his own father; on my grandfather's first trip to America, he had, with growing dismay and then disgust, watched a priest on board the ship lecturing passengers about the sin of eating meat on Fridays, while surreptitiously helping himself to that very same forbidden fruit.

What also didn't help my father's outlook on organized religion was the squabble over the interfaith aspect of his own marriage. Thanks to the dogmatic insistence of his older brother Andrew's

wife Gert, a more-than-ardent Irish Catholic, my father agreed to
be married in the Catholic church, my mother acquiescing for the
sake of family peace. The church, in its wisdom, ruled that my
parents could not be married at the altar because my mother was
not Catholic. Aside from attending friends' weddings, it would be
a long time before my father once again attended a church service, and, when he did, he ended up saving the life of a man having
an epileptic seizure. Not his idea of either a good or enlightening
morning.

As soon as she returned from her honeymoon, my mother immediately resumed attending the Episcopal church, and did so in
such staunch fashion that three decades later she was elected the
first female warden of the church. Being a fierce advocate of religious ecumenicalism, and given the strong similarities between
the Catholic and Episcopal services, my mother felt very much at
home in the Catholic church, yet even she was nonplussed, decades
later, by her exchange with the neighborhood Catholic priest at the
funeral service of a friend. By force of habit, she had made her way
to the front of the church for Communion, holding out her hand
for the Communion wafer only to be told, in a not so sotto voce by
the priest, "I'm sorry, Nancy. You can't have Communion. You're
not Catholic." As the mourners exited the church at the end of the
service, the priest pulled my mother aside and mournfully stated:
"I'm sorry I had to do that, Nancy. You know, you would have made
a good Catholic." Oy vey, as the Italians say.

Episcopal versus Catholic may have been part of the distance I
felt between the English and Italian sides of my background, but
even that religious difference took second place to the cultural gap
that faced me. Italian-American culture in the early 1960s was not
exactly centered on dancing class for properly brought up young
men and women, but there I was in dancing school every Thursday
night. Decked out in coat and tie and wearing white gloves, I would

bow to my partners, escort them onto the dance floor, and try to master the basics of the waltz and fox-trot under the gaze of our long-suffering teacher, Mrs. Coffee. It was all a long way from Pontelandolfo.

So immersed was I in that white bread, white buck world that when I encountered anti-Italian prejudice for the first time, I remained speechless. Literally. It's not that I was afraid to say anything, it's that the concept of discrimination was so foreign that I thought I had misheard the slur. Standing in the local bank, I finished depositing money earned from teaching tennis (not the traditional summer job in the land of paesanos) and went over to speak to the son of the bank's founder. One of the bank employees, a junior executive feeling his oats, sidled up to talk to the founder's son, and after appropriate introductions were made, the junior executive launched into a monologue about certain bank customers. Taking a look at my blond hair and blue eyes, and figuring he was on safe ground, he capped the commentary by dismissing one such customer with "You know the type—one of those really greasy Italians." The owner's son blanched, and I froze, stumbling out of the bank because I was certain I had heard the man incorrectly. I hadn't. I shouldn't have been so surprised; when my father gained acceptance to the Waterbury Country Club, he was the second Italian-American member allowed to join. Ever. This, in 1961, in a blue-collar city where Italian-Americans outnumbered every other ethnic group. Such were the times that my father's acceptance was preceded by that of only one other Italian-American, another physician who in many ways had served as my father's mentor. I've often wondered if acceptance of the Santopietro application was smoothed by my mother's background and impeccable résumé as the president of every establishment charity in town.

One can only imagine what Don Vito Corleone would have made of dancing class and tennis lessons, yet the image of young Vito on-screen seemed to envelop me both during and after the movie, and I couldn't shake the image. Adding another layer to the mix, the young boy playing Vito possessed a downright eerie resemblance to pictures of my own father as a young boy. In this particular house of mirrors, my grandfather flickered to life in the guise of a ten-year-old, forty feet tall on-screen and looking for all the world like my own father. At the end of the film, when I checked the credits, I was not even startled to see that the name of the boy playing young Vito was Oreste Baldini. I had somehow known in advance that he'd have the same name as my father. The synchronicity of the names made even more sense to me when my father subsequently told me that he was originally named Oreste Olindo Santopietro, but that his names had been reversed by the city registrars—such were the autocratic decisions of the bureaucrats facing down immigrant families in 1917.

Physical resemblances between on-screen characters and my father aside, on another deeper level I connected with the film for a reason I shared with millions of other viewers: it was set in a past that seemed inherently more romantic and orderly than that of 1974 America. The immediate post–World War II world depicted on-screen in the first two films seemed one of logical cause and effect, and for all the violence and treachery displayed, Don Vito Corleone succeeded in bringing order out of life's chaos. The order came at a steep price, but come it did. This godfather provided assurance, and millions responded to that certainty. In the words of Coppola himself: "I think there is a tremendous hunger in this country, if not in the world, for that kind of clear, benevolent authority."

I remained fascinated by the very look of that vanished America on-screen; even as a young boy, the pull of the past had always weighed on me. That, I realize, represented an exceedingly odd state of affairs for a youngster, but exist it did nonetheless. At a very young age I would wonder what my parents had been like at my age. What would I have thought of them if I could have wandered into their third-grade classroom? The thought of time travel endlessly fascinated me, and for someone who possessed no scientific aptitude, I spent a lot of time pondering the possibilities. Waxing aloud in enthusiastic fashion about the idea, I soon learned to keep any such thoughts to myself after my older sister fixed me with a withering glance and muttered: "It can't happen. Don't be stupid," before returning to her magazine.

I'd spend time wondering if reincarnation was possible. I knew I believed in currents of time wafting from past to present, currents that enveloped our lives in similarities too eerie to dismiss as mere coincidence. The pull of the past continued for me in the strangest of manners, often manifesting itself in nighttime dreams that occurred in real time the next day. One such dream threw me for such a loop when it became reality that I discussed it with only one friend, who simply said: "Don't ever tell anyone else. They'll be hooking you up to electrodes for government studies. That dream coming true is too damn weird to even contemplate."

It was not, however, just with my father's side of the family that I experienced these odd time currents, with an increasingly time-warped connection to my mother's Parker side of the family also occurring with some regularity. Always a voracious reader about World War II, over time I reached back even further and became obsessed with World War I. I'd request books on the war for my birthday and Christmas, my parents shooting me odd looks before smiling and saying, "Well, nothing says the holidays like the Battle of the Somme . . ." The battles, the diplomatic figures, and most particularly the poets and novelists whose work read like a sustained howl of rage at the waste and futility—I found them all fascinating. Over and over I'd read works detailing how World War I caused cracks in the English class system, fissures that grew into gaping holes as aristocrats and cockneys fought cheek by jowl in the trenches. Did I find the English class dichotomy similar to the establishment/immigrant clash I always sensed within myself? I'm still not certain.

So familiar did the time period become to me that I would see still photographs or newsreel footage of the time and the scarred landscape would appear instantly familiar on a sometimes disconcertingly emotional level, a strange sense of déjà vu overtaking me. When R. C. Sheriff's classic play of World War I, *Journey's End,* was revived on Broadway early in the millennium, it assumed must-see status for me. Familiar as I was with the material, I was unprepared for the play's end, which found the theater in total darkness, the audience assaulted by a minutes-long aural bombardment that brought home the reality of trench warfare with visceral force. The curtain then rose for a final time and in a startling tableau, the characters we had come to know over the course of the evening appeared one last time, ghosts now dead from the bombardment that had just pummeled the audience. The actors stood motionless in front of a stage-filling memorial wall, hundreds upon hundreds of names inscribed as a monument to heroically futile actions. As the actors silently held their poses, I hurriedly read through the names until I found the one I instinctively understood I'd find inscribed: Corporal Thomas Parker. I have no idea how I knew it would be there or even why I possessed such certainty, but there I was—minus the Santopietro but fixed on the wall. Thomas Parker: killed on the Somme battlefield, November 6, 1916. Royal Welch Fusiliers. The synchronicity became eerier—and yet I wasn't in the least surprised—when I checked out the Web site devoted to the millions of soldiers killed during World War I and found that his was the only picture on the home page, the one soldier picked to symbolize the loss of an entire generation. Age twenty-six and lost forever.

Most dismiss it all as a quirk of fate. It's not an unusual name. I know. But at the same time, I don't. Why the fascination with World War I? Why the endless reading of the history? Why the compulsion to actually stop and look at war memorials in whatever town I'm visiting, trying to scan at least several dozen names and in the process driving my travel companions to the brink of exasperation? What do I think I'll find there? Another name that elicits a frisson of recognition? A silent reminder to those listed that they are not forgotten? The hope that I won't be forgotten?

This non-Italian Thomas Parker version of myself exists in numerous youthful photographs, most particularly in the school snapshots of little Tommy. There I stand, frozen in time in front of a private school so proper that as a third grader I wore a uniform of khaki pants (gray flannels on days of special importance), gray-and-green-striped school tie, and navy blue sports coat emblazoned with a green pocket patch sporting the school motto stitched in Latin. (I'm not sure exactly who that quizzical little boy is, but the prep wardrobe remains, and thirty years later, when attending the humorous Italian-American audience participation play *Tony n' Tina's Wedding,* the "waitress" serving the baked ziti decided I was holding up the buffet line and barked at me "Hey—J.Crew! Hurry it up!") Teachers were addressed as "sir," and school ran every day from 7:45 A.M. until 4:45 P.M., compulsory athletics included. Great and difficult all at once, usually on the same day.

Fresh from this private school atmosphere, at the end of the school day I would occasionally visit my grandparents, running in the door and making a beeline to the stove to see what my grandmother was cooking. Poised to dip into the sauce with a slice of Italian bread in my hand, I knew exactly what was coming next—the same lecture I received every time I'd see my grandfather. Hugging me stiffly, he'd intone: "Tommy, Tommy—how was school? Are you studying? Education is the most important thing." His minispeech resembled a broken record; I knew the words, the pauses, and even his exact cadences by heart, yet it all meant absolutely nothing to me. I didn't regard school as a privilege—I thought of it as a prison sentence. If I had known how to roll my eyes at age eight I would have, so uninterested was I in that particular lecture. School a privilege? I was a good student, but to me school represented a life sentence to the gulag of homework. Even as an adult, particularly during the three misbegotten years spent suffering through law school, I identified with one of the school-hating ten-year-old boys in the Oscar-nominated *Hope and Glory*; toward the end of the film, which is set in the England of World War II, one of the boys glumly arrives for another long, boring school day, only to find that German bombs have destroyed the school. Casting an eye toward the heavens, he jumps for joy and gleefully shouts: "Thank you, Adolf!"

At age ten I held exactly one thought about school: I was trapped until the ancient age of twenty-one. Certainly I held no comprehension of what school meant to my grandfather, a third grader forced to drop out of school in order to help support his family. Thirsting for knowledge, my grandfather grew to be a voracious reader of weighty philosophical tomes, his idea of a fun read being Tolstoy's *War and Peace* or Dante's *Divine Comedy*. My grandmother never read, and I was too young and self-involved to grasp that she remained basically illiterate because schooling for poor young girls in nineteenth-century southern Italy was virtually nonexistent. Even as late as age sixteen I remained surprised—perhaps vaguely ashamed—to see my grandmother signing legal documents after my grandfather's death with a shaky black X.

What did I make of the stories told of my barely five-foot-tall grandmother working side by side in the grocery store with her husband, hoisting slabs of beef onto her shoulder as she walked up the stairs from the store's cellar? I'm not really sure how much sank in, my grandparents' still-potent memories of both the Great Depression and the old country's grinding poverty meaning very little to me. It all seemed impossibly foreign, in other words far too Italian. I was American, and in that age before hyphenated-American nomenclature became the norm, that was enough. Or so I thought.

It wasn't just my grandparents who worked nonstop. I heard stories of my five-year-old father pulling a wagon through the streets calling out "Iceman-Iceman" in the Italian section of town. My sister and I had always laughed at the idea of my father having to pull a wagon filled with ice. I mean, how could those neighborhood people not have a freezer? And why was he born at home? Hadn't my grandparents heard of a hospital? Now, as I looked at *Godfather: Part II*'s re-creation of a Little Italy complete with unpaved roads, I could only wonder, "Is that what Waterbury looked like? Did my father actually pull a wagon through dirt streets? How could he have been strong enough?" Chastened. About my own father.

At the start of his kindergarten year, when my five-year-old father was brought to Slocum Grammar School by his two older sisters, it took approximately sixty seconds for the strict principal to realize that my father did not yet speak any English. Told to learn English before he showed up again at school, my father walked home for another year in the grocery store, bilingual education not being a hot topic in the Waterbury, Connecticut, of 1922. Thanks to his brother and sisters, he arrived back at Slocum School one year later, speaking flawless English.

How could he not speak English, I wondered? What were Grandpa and Grandma doing? I couldn't comprehend that before his first attempt at kindergarten, he was, as the youngest child, still at home, playing in the grocery store while my grandparents worked side by side speaking their native southern Italian dialect. Day care? In 1922? Entrusting a child to a stranger? About as likely in that day and age as the thought of landing a man on the moon. To their dying days, my grandparents, particularly my grandmother, spoke in heavily accented English, and at moments of great merriment or sorrow, my grandmother would revert to Italian, causing me to plead "Grandma—speak English! English!" After my grandfather died, her English dwindled, eroded by the steady drip of her seemingly endless sorrow.

My own Italian remains nonexistent to this day. My grandparents, and even more so my parents, were not particularly interested in my learning the language during the assimilation-crazed days of my youth. Certainly my mother did not speak a word of Italian (in the 1930s, why would a young Nancy Edge Parker have learned Italian?). I suspect that nowadays I'd be enrolled in an Italian language school, bombarded with speeches and stacks of material extolling the greatness of Italian culture. I like to think I'd have the sense to be more than a bit wary, not of all things Italian, but rather of additional schooling. As it was, in grammar school I possessed inordinate jealousy of my Jewish friends, who managed early dismissal one day of each week in order to attend Hebrew school. I coveted their freedom. Coveted, that is, until I realized that their only reward lay in more homework—and in a foreign language to boot. The tip-off should have lain in the fact that never once did any of them exclaim "Oh good, time for Hebrew school . . ."

The closest I've come to speaking Italian, aside from two or three all-purpose curse words, is to sprinkle the phrases I've learned from *The Godfather* into my conversation. It's a tad awkward, but it feels great to toast friends at meals with a not-too-badly-mangled "salud" or "Cent'anni." I've finally embraced the Italian-ness of it all. The topsiders and preppy wardrobe remain (looking back, I was dressed like a little junior prep even at age three, a towheaded blue-eyed boy sporting a commodore's wardrobe), but nothing gives me greater pleasure than to use the word "paesano" when describing a fellow Italian-American. Particularly when speaking with my good friend Mimi, we can, depending on the inflection, use the term in a variety of ways: there are "paesanos" who share our background, "paesanos" who reek of the old country (not an insult, but more an indicator of outlook), and our all-purpose "paesano who wants the free cheese"—in other words, the Italian endlessly searching for a bargain. If my Jewish friends will casually refer to members of "their tribe," I take pleasure in referring to "my paesanos."

Now in my fifties, I think I finally understand. I'm grateful, yet occasionally filled with a glancing but palpable sadness. It's a sadness that never quite lifts, because when I look back, I realize that I felt a certain shame about my grandparents' very foreignness. Never when I was alone with them, and never when with the family, but I felt it often when in the presence of others. I can never undo that fact, and I can never tell my unconditionally loving grandparents that I now understand just how small-minded I was.

What exactly made me so uneasy in my youth? Was I embarrassed by their "otherness"? Yes—upon occasion and at certain times without reservation. Wanting nothing so much as to fit in, I felt downright uneasy that on grandparents' day at my grammar school, Grandma and Grandpa stood out by virtue of their accents and clothing, standing side by side with Anglo grandparents who nodded their approval while murmuring lockjawed pleasantries. I compared my grandparents' third-grade educations with those of the other grandparents, many of whom had attended Ivy League and Seven Sisters colleges, and I felt the lack. I couldn't see the distance of my grandparents' journey and possessed scant understanding of how much they had accomplished. Instead, I remember asking my maternal grandmother, the warm—and notably Anglo—Helen Sarah Norton Parker, to "watch over" my grandparent Santopietros. It's a shameful memory never to be erased.

I was too young, far too sensitive, certainly self-absorbed, and, most of all, too unsure of myself to understand the value of my grandparents' individuality, their insistence on being themselves. Their very Italian-ness, the fierce adherence to the Italian section of town, proved to be their way of coping with an ofttimes hostile world when they first arrived in America. Now armed with the knowledge of what they endured, I find that my youthful embarrassment at their accents has given way to an actual sense of wonder at how much they accomplished and how thoroughly my grandfather educated himself.

Every moment my grandfather could spare from the grocery store he spent reading. Books held his interest, not sports. Two daily and two weekly newspapers, books by the dozen, treatises on economics, the world atlas, investigations into organized religion: all of these opened up my grandfather's world in ways unimaginable back in Pontelandolfo. When he died, and my grandmother's grief seemed bottomless, she drew comfort from a floral arrangement that had arrived attached to a Styrofoam-shaped book. Long after the flowers died, she kept that Styrofoam book, staring at it as she talked about his love of reading. At the time I thought the Styrofoam book was tacky, a gavone's (greenhorn) idea of a tasteful tribute. Now I understand just how much that symbol meant to her.

My grandmother never had a chance to attend school for more than one year, and the memory of her own stunted education weighed heavily on her. She stressed education just as much as did my grandfather, and as a result her daughters Emma and Julia graduated from high school in the early 1930s, an era when such an achievement was not necessarily the norm for the daughters of immigrants. Both of my aunts were smart women, did well in high school, and were clearly capable of college-level work. The Depression, however, dictated that work, not college, would follow high school, and I don't think the thought of their going to college was ever pursued, perhaps ever even discussed. Think Connie Corleone in *The Godfather*: safe to assume the thought of sending Connie to college never crossed her parents' minds. Don Vito and Mama Corleone undoubtedly possessed the same mind-set as other immigrant parents: money for education automatically flowed to the sons. Women, after all, would get married and raise children . . .

Coupling my grandparents' emphasis on education with the fact that higher education remained the province of sons, it seemed preordained that Andrew, born in 1911 and my grandparents' oldest child, became the first in the entire neighborhood to attend college. When he left for his first semester at Niagara University, dozens from the neighborhood went to see him off on the train. His was a victory for everyone in the north end of town.

Decades later I came across letters between my father and his older brother, written just after Andrew left for college. "Dear Brother," they began. I got no further before I said to my father: "Dear Brother?! Why didn't you just say 'Hi Andy'?" It all seemed so hopelessly formal. Two lines later: "My valise survived the trip." A valise, I asked? A valise?! I started to laugh—this four-decades-earlier letter might as well have been written at the time of the Magna Carta, so ancient did it seem to me. Why did I laugh? I think, in retrospect, that it all made me uneasy. Did people think of me as someone this, well, foreign? Did I exude "otherness"? At that young age, laughter distanced me from the foreign nature of it all. I'll never know if my laughter hurt my father. I think he understood; I was a sensitive boy, usually too sensitive for my own good. I just wanted to fit in.

It was actually my father's generation, those first indoctrinated in the American ways, who, when dealing with the simultaneous pull of Italian and American cultures, felt most uncomfortable with the hyper Italian-ness of their lives. Commentator Leonard Covello, born in the United States to immigrant parents, explored this uneasiness in his own blunt memory of schooldays: "We were becoming American by learning to be ashamed of our parents." Dinner at the homes of non-Italian friends often granted a first-time exposure to a culture of WASP reserve, the polite murmured mealtime conversation punctuated only by clinking silverware. Heavily accented English and outsize emotions were nowhere to be glimpsed. In the words of Gay Talese's 1992 memoir *Unto the Sons,* "There were many times when I wished that I had been born into a different family, a plain and simple family of impeccable American credentials—a no-secrets, nonwhispering, no-enemy-soldiers family that never received mail from POW camps, or prayed to a painting of an ugly monk, or ate Italian bread with pungent cheese."

Like Gay Talese and others of his generation, my father wanted to fit in. Starting college at Tufts University in the fall of 1936, he purposely told everyone to call him Sandy, a nickname derived from his surname. Henceforth, no one but family called him Olindo: Sandy it was from 1936 until the day he died in 1992. I asked my father why his three older siblings had such "American" sounding names—Andrew, Emma, Julia—while he, youngest and American born, was given the most Italian name: Olindo. In answer, I was told that my grandparents had named him Oreste Olindo in honor of the man who had helped my thirteen-year-old grandfather emigrate from Italy to the United States. That stopped my teenaged wisecracks about being thankful I wasn't named Olindo Jr.—and stopped them fast. Decades later, I learned that my aunt Emma had been named in honor of Emma Lazarus, the author of the poem found at the base of the Statue of Liberty. Never mind the rather discouraging words actually found in the poem: "give me your tired, your poor, your wretched refuse"—not exactly a rousing welcome to the New World. I still loved the fact that Emma Lazarus was responsible for my aunt's name. To this day

I'm chastened in my realization that my grandparents possessed such heartfelt faith in America. No ironic postmodern worldview for them. It's a faith in their adopted country beautifully rendered in John D'Agata's story "Round Trip"; when characters in the story are asked to list their conception of the seven modern wonders of the world, narrator Joe Miller's Italian grandfather simply says: "Just put down the Statue of Liberty. That's all I want you to put down."

For the first generation born in America, it was only with age and a postadolescent maturity that they grew beyond the attitude symbolized by, in Talese's words, the desire for a "plain and simple family of impeccable American credentials." With adulthood came a dawning realization that the closeness of Italian family life was often envied by others and symbolized America just as fully as did established society. It was these American-born sons and daughters, the Michael Corleones and Frank Sinatras of the world, who eventually came to expect and demand more, insisting on their rightful place at the table and relishing their status as Americans of a decidedly Italian nature.

Ultimately, the conflict in attitude and identity between the original immigrants and their children can be glimpsed in the manner by which each group identified itself. For the original immigrants, identity in the old country proved to be a matter of one's native village or province, and, if asked, immigrants referred to themselves as "Napolitano," never "Italian." It was only upon arrival in the New World, when faced with a suspicious Anglo culture, that they referred to themselves as Italian. By way of contrast, their sons and daughters born in the United States thought of themselves simply as American.

At the start of *The Godfather*, Michael Corleone, the youngest of Don Vito's three sons, embodies this younger generation of self-identifying Americans. He feels a part of mainstream American life in ways unknown to his parents, or even to older brothers Sonny and Fredo. Unlike Sonny, who appears to still have one foot in *la via vecchia* ("the old road/country"), Michael immerses himself in American life, not Italian culture (ironic it is then that he is the one Corleone child who spends time in Sicily). With his Ivy League education and military service during World War II, he initially reads as the one member of the family who can and will escape the insularity of life within the family compound. He has no intention of following his father into a life of crime, and in explaining the divide in thought, culture, and action between his family and himself, confidently tells girlfriend Kay Adams: "That's my family, Kay. That's not me."

Michael is convinced that, unlike his father, he will use his education, not violence, to solve problems. He is, like others of his World War II generation, highly aware of the differences between his parents and those of nonimmigrant Americans whom he encounters; as much as he loves his father, for the first half of *The Godfather*, that is, until Don Vito is shot, one senses that Michael feels separate from his foreign-born father. Even at this early stage of the saga, Michael stands apart.

For his part, Don Vito may belittle Michael's service in the United States military, but he understands the value of his son's schooling. Education equals opportunity, and Don Vito seeks the respectability that education can bring to the family. He does more than hope that Michael will lead a life outside the family business; he envisions a fully American life for his son, one in which Michael's honorary title is not "Godfather" but "Governor" or "Senator."

It's the depiction of changing outlook between generations that grants another level of richness to Puzo's delineation of Michael's corruption, the thread of which forms the backbone of *The Godfather* novel and all three films. Torn between the American world symbolized by education and military service and his family's life of crime, Michael solves his problem of identity once and for all by committing murder in order to avenge the attempt on his father's life. The father-son bond trumps all, a facet of Italian-American mob life matter-of-factly acknowledged in the new millennium by John Gotti Jr. while discussing his own mobster father: "If my father had said 'I don't like this any more—I'm going to be a butcher'—I would have said 'I hope you have a smock for me.'" Never one to miss an ironic comment, Puzo deliberately builds his plot on the premise that after Michael murders his father's enemies, his only means of survival lies in escaping the New World of America for the old country—Sicily. In accepting his family's life of crime and (temporarily) reversing the westward journey of his father, Michael has indisputably chosen *la via vecchia*.

Upon his return to America, Michael embraces his role as heir apparent so thoroughly that he evolves into a don who is simultaneously more American and more fiercely allied with ancient Sicilian codes of peasant conduct than even his own father. He proceeds to achieve the American dream of wealth, success, and power and, through his methods of doing so, plants the seeds of his own destruction.

In puzzling out the strands of Michael Corleone's American saga, Puzo and Coppola did nothing less than create a new template through which to analyze the latter half of the twentieth century. Taking on the biggest themes of all—the American dream, immigrants in the land of the "melting pot," material success and failure, reinvention and redemption—the co-screenwriters managed the unique feat of creating a sweeping epic that nonetheless spoke urgently to the individual.

Over the years I found myself returning to the three *Godfather* films again and again for glimpses of understanding as well as the comforting flights of reverie they inevitably induced. I loved the first film, and instantly surrendered to its opening scene of the raucous, warmth-filled wedding reception, one reminiscent of those held by my own distant relatives. Down the road I came to hold a strange affection for *Godfather III*, a fatally flawed but ofttimes brilliant parable of redemptive failure. It was, however, part II that always spoke most urgently to me, and not just for the primal reconnection to my grandfather's early life. All the darkness lying underneath *The Godfather* burst to the forefront in part II, and this, I knew, was what the *Godfather* saga was really about. *Godfather II* spoke to the youthful cynic in me, the young adult disgusted by Vietnam and upset by Watergate. Fashionably ironic as a twenty-year-old, I couldn't fully articulate such feelings beyond a reflexive and self-conscious expression of disillusionment, but Coppola could and did, pointing out the curdled promise inherent in the reality of America. Major Hollywood films don't come any more tough-minded than *Godfather II*, and unlike virtually all other Hollywood auteurs, Coppola refused to pull any of his punches, condemning every last one of the country's fatal flaws as glimpsed in our collective rush toward wealth and power.

Why was it that *The Godfather* films succeeded in making me feel good about being Italian while presenting an endless array of mobsters on-screen? Bloodletting and explosive violence abounded on-screen, yet what enveloped me was a feeling of warmth and sense of pride. Endless contradictions abounded. I didn't yet have the answers, but I felt certain of one thing: the moment Don Corleone murmured "I'm going to make him an offer he can't refuse," *The Godfather* jumped from popular entertainment into the land of American myth. In those ten words lay the embodiment of my own—any audience's—complicated reaction to the film: I was rooting for the triumph of murderous thugs, strangely compelled by men I knew I'd be afraid to meet, men who plumbed the darkness we all hold within. In other words, surrender I did to exactly what fascinated and frightened me in equal measure.

Whether he wants it or not, a new name for a new country. With one stroke of the official's pen, Vito Andolini becomes Vito Corleone. *Photofest*

4   From *La Via Vecchia* to L'America

There is a new America every morning when we wake up. It is upon us whether we will it or not.

—Adlai E. Stevenson Jr.

THE RING OF AUTHENTICITY found in *The Godfather,* the solid underpinnings that allow readers to relax into the novel with a sigh of "so that's the way it really was," lie in Mario Puzo's thorough understanding of Italian history. What he successfully conveyed was a sense of southern Italy as a land endlessly dominated by foreign powers whose governments were so oppressive in nature that the Mafia arose out of the peasants' desperate need for an agency to help them secure life's merest necessities.

At the beginning of the nineteenth century, the Congress of Vienna rulings (1814–15) divided Italy into eight principalities or separate states, all but those of Piedmont and Sardinia falling under Austrian, Bourbon, or papal domination. Gone were the hopes of liberation and unification that had taken tentative hold in the days of liberal reforms and the French presence. Instead, this consistent

foreign subjugation of the peasantry reinforced a fatalistic southern Italian/Sicilian mentality that life held little promise or personal dignity. In this worldview, pleasures proved fleeting before
disappearing completely, life proving to be nothing more than an
endurance contest. In Jerre Mangione's classic memoir of Italian-
American life, *Mount Allegro,* he sums up the dilemma with the wry
observation that "my father, bonarma, once told me that God must
have once decided to make Sicily the Garden of Eden and then
changed his mind abruptly."

The fact that where poverty exists so too does crime made Sicily the most fertile of grounds for the rise of the Mafia. It's no accident that traditional Mafia figures like Don Corleone, men born in
the latter portion of the nineteenth century, were uniformly Sicilian (the Neapolitan Al Capone proving a notable exception). So
overwhelming was the grinding poverty of Sicily that when Jerre
Mangione traveled there in the 1930s, he did not see a single piece
of modern farm machinery, the farmers he encountered still using
tools a hundred years out of date. Given the traditional antipathy
between the northern and southern provinces, and the reality that
even after unification the center of power remained in northern
Italy, Sicilians remained the last to receive any government lar-
gesse capable of improving farming conditions.

It was in 1850 that Giuseppe Garibaldi and his volunteer army
"liberated" all of the regions south of Rome from Bourbon domination. Garibaldi himself, not to mention his volunteer army, hailed
from northern Italy and possessed scant knowledge of the southern
Italian lifestyle. With his limited northern worldview, Garibaldi
was unable to fully comprehend the hatred held by the southern
peasants for any rulers, be they Austrian or northern Italian. In the
words of historians Jerre Mangione and Ben Morreale, "In effect,
the well-to-do northern leaders believed they were making a revolution for the poor of the South, when in reality they were making

it for themselves." Garibaldi's unification of southern Italy succeeded in doing nothing so much as reinforcing the divide between
the northern Italians who held money and power and the southern
Italians scrambling to eke out a living. So dire did the living conditions remain in the postunification years that over 80 percent of all
Italians who emigrated to the United States hailed from the southern regions known as the Mezzogiorno.

Garibaldi failed to understand that southern Italian peasants,
who identified themselves in terms of region or town, felt no personal connection to the concept of Italy. Having endured centuries
of foreign rule, the peasantry simply regarded Garibaldi and his
army as yet another version of foreign oppression. The postunification government based in Turin never changed the lot of southern
peasants: powerless throughout history, they remained equally
downtrodden in the post-Garibaldi years.

Even after unification was formalized in 1861, the antagonism
between north and south continued unabated. The parliament in
Turin made it quickly apparent that it held no interest in sharing
authority with any of the southern regions; as pointed out by Ben
Morreale, as soon as the Turin government began to issue decrees
imposing new taxes and military conscription, the southerners "simply began transferring their old hatred of the Bourbons to the new
rulers." Paying particular attention to the use and subsequent tax-
ation of farm animals, the government decreed that mules and
donkeys, the backbone of the southern Italian farming economy,
remained taxable, while cows, owned by the wealthy landowners
of the north, were deemed nontaxable. The government in Turin
paid so little attention to the basic necessities of life in the south
that even with numerous railroad lines already servicing northern
Italy, the first railroad built after Italian unification connected Turin with Paris, and not with Naples, the biggest city of the south.

The government in Rome even kept separate statistics regarding southern Italian peasants, as if they remained a different species of human being. No wonder then that when a government report was issued in the nineteenth century regarding the cruelties inflicted upon southern Italians, the author of the report, Giuseppe Massara, stated that "the greatest ill afflicting the southern populations is their lack of faith in legality and justice."

The overwhelming problems facing southern peasants seemed like nothing so much as the outcome of an ancient curse. Poor soil, ancient forms of transportation, outmoded means of farming, and usurious taxes only grew worse under the auspices of the new government, leading to a standard of living so bad that after his visit to Italy, African-American statesman Booker T. Washington commented: "The Negro is not the man farthest down. The condition of the coloured farmer in the most backward parts of the Southern States in America, even where he has the least education and the least encouragement, is incomparably better than the condition and opportunities of the agricultural population in Sicily." Laws written by northern Italians to govern the lives of southern peasants did not differ in any discernible manner or effect from the centuries of laws written by foreign conquerors ranging from the Greeks and Romans to the Arabs, Normans, and Spaniards: the laws on hand continued to favor the rich over the poor and the powerful over the weak.

Worst of all for the southern male peasant, the new postunification Italian constitution demanded that all males serve for seven years in the army, a law that forced men to abandon their land in order to serve a government completely indifferent to their very existence, except as a source of tax revenue. Logically enough, mistrust of government and the military only increased, leading to an attitude of suspicion that made the journey to the United States right along with the immigrants themselves; note the disdainful words of *The Godfather*'s Don Vito Corleone when he sees his son

Michael's World War II military uniform covered in ribbons won for bravery: "What are these? . . . You win these on behalf of strangers?" (One of comedian Jackie Mason's sharpest routines noted the contradiction between Italian street toughness and the inherent Italian dislike of any organized institutions: "Italians are the toughest street fighters in the world. Mean, vicious, ruthless. Jews, on the other hand, are mealy-mouthed accountants and bookkeepers. But look what happens in the army—the Israeli army is the toughest in the world. The Italian army? Feh—If I see an Italian who wants to fight, I throw him a uniform and say, 'OK—fight now!'")

Unable and unwilling to trust police, government, or the military, the peasantry took the next logical step of placing their trust in those outside the legal system, men who could and would grant respect and the enforcement of basic rights. Bitter experience having reinforced their belief that justice and the law were not at all the same thing, peasants ignored written laws and looked to the Mafia as the only means by which justice might be obtained.

As detailed in *La Storia: Five Centuries of the Italian American Experience*, it was in the time following Italian unification that the term "Mafia" (from "mafiosi," meaning a tough, fiery temperament) first began to surface with frequency: "In their paranoia, the [government] agents began for the first time using the term 'mafia' in reports to Turin to summarize any group activity that seemed to impinge on the state's monopoly of authority." Exist the Mafia did, but in order to serve the harsh purposes of a government deeply unpopular in the south of Italy, the specter of the mafia was exaggerated by the northern Italian agents. After all, the reasoning in Turin ran, southern Italians were disorderly, clearly under the sway of the Mafia, and controllable only by the institution of strict laws. To those in power, inflating the extent of Mafia activity seemed the best way to legitimize an unpopular government.

The irony of this situation lay in the fact that while the Mafia may actually have started out as a Robin Hood–like organization with at least a marginal attachment to the notion of helping peasants, over time the Mafia grew to hinder rich and poor alike. As the years passed the Mafia formed alliances with the power elite, thereby gaining new contacts and respectability while simultaneously providing the ruling class with a highly effective means of keeping order. Taken to its logical conclusion, the developing alliance between Mafia and ruling elite finds its ultimate expression in the *Godfather III* partnership between Michael Corleone and the richest establishment group of all: the Catholic church.

and Allied Forces (ILWW)

Faced with unceasingly grim conditions in Sicily, young male peasants faced a further obstacle in the very structure of the Italian family. The time-honored tradition of leaving all property to the eldest son left little room for mobility or advancement among younger offspring, and many younger sons eventually emigrated to America simply for the chance to control their own destiny. One can even speculate as to the fate of young Vito Andolini if his family had not run afoul of Don Ciccio in Sicily; given his status as second son, would Vito still have emigrated to the United States in order to evade his fate? Would his drive, ambition, and native shrewdness have compelled him to escape his "younger son" status by means of voyage to the New World, or would the tradition-respecting young man have remained at home with his family? The only certain answer is that any path in his native village of Corleone would have presented numerous pitfalls simply because of his status as the family's younger son.

The island of Sicily itself often registered as forbidding and something from which to escape. Great beauty abounded, but the dark mountainous regions, replete with cliffs laced by sliding rocks, were harsh in the extreme; it is only toward the coast, near towns like Girgenti, that the influence of the Mediterranean predominates, with groves of olive and lemon trees dotting the land. Life on the Sicilian coast remained immeasurably easier than in the interior regions yet still felt downright harsh compared with the standard of living found in America. Beautiful and bleak all at once, insular yet constantly subject to foreign invasion, the very physicality of Sicily made the island ripe for mass emigration to America. If villagers living on the mountaintops first moved to the flatlands in search of an easier life, their next move came in migration to seaside cities, where ships bearing word of America docked. The final and biggest journey of all then lay in crossing the ocean to the promised land of America itself. Something—anything—had to be better than the bleak *via vecchia*.

America represented hope and a chance to escape the sense of doom and inferiority beaten into the peasants by the rocky soil, grim living conditions, and grinding poverty. Watch the still, reverent expressions on the faces of the immigrants sailing past the Statue of Liberty at the beginning of *The Godfather: Part II*; for these peasants, the statue represents the promise of America, a belief in personal freedom and the future. The actor Ernest Borgnine, born Borgnino (and at one time seriously considered for the role of Don Vito Corleone) relayed in his autobiography that in 1921, as a little boy coming to America on the ship *Dante Alighieri,* he noticed everyone gathered at the railing, gazing in awe at the Statue of Liberty as the ship sailed into New York Harbor. As he continued playing in the ship's sandbox, his mother grabbed his ear and yanked him to the bow of the ship. Slapping her son's rear, she commanded "When you see that lady, you stand at attention." Added Borgnine: "I've been standing at attention for this country ever since, believe me."

As it became ever more clear that unification had brought nothing but additional problems to the southern peasantry, emigration to the United States exploded. In the fifty-year span from 1870 to 1920, Italy lost one-third of its total population, and in 1907, the peak year of immigration, 286,000 Italians arrived in the United States. The southern Italian peasant didn't just want to leave Italy—he wanted to arrive in the United States before the welcoming doors were slammed shut in his face. It wasn't just the fatalistic Sicilian turn of mind that fed this fear. The peasant immigrants held a justifiable concern that the United States government might begin to require a literacy test similar to those mandated by governments in Australia and Latin America. (In fact, the literacy law was finally passed by Congress in 1917.) In an Italian citizenry rife with illiterate men and women, tens of thousands of potential immigrants were incapable of reading the forty words demanded by such tests.

The heavy dose of fatalism that pervaded peasant life in southern Italy had placed little or no emphasis on education. In the peasant worldview, what was the point of books? Books didn't provide food, and all the education in the world didn't matter: *il destino* ("fate") controlled all. A part of the immigrant mind-set wanted to believe in the idea of "freedom, justice, and the American way," but at the same time an across-the-board mantra of older first generation immigrants lay in the words "Whaddya gonna do . . . ," the despairing phrase followed by a weary shrug of the shoulders. This centuries-old peasant mentality was shaped by trying to survive the natural disasters that repeatedly rocked Sicily, catastrophes over which no one possessed control. Ironically, as more than one commentator has noted, it was precisely this "whaddya gonna do" attitude that ensured that, poor though they certainly were, the immigrants to America usually did not come from the very lowest economic rung; it was those poorest of all peasants who, having suffered from a lifetime of *la miseria*, were usually too discouraged or apathetic to make the effort required for the move to America. Lacking the support of any relatives already established in America, the most poverty-stricken peasants stayed in Italy, living out their lives in a silent, bitter acceptance of what they deemed to be their destiny.

Jettisoning lives of poverty, the immigrants who set sail for the United States arrived with genuine belief in their new country. Entering America through the harbor of New York City, these peasants were attracted by the very physicality of the metropolitan skyline: there was freedom and newness in the scale of the buildings, the towering edifices suggesting endless new territories. The very fact of electricity rated as revolutionary for rural peasants who had lived for centuries without even the thought, let alone reality, of artificial light. Like figures in a novel by Ayn Rand, these immigrants appreciated the man-made spectacle of the industrialized New World. It proved, of course, to be a brutal world, one that could and did grind people underfoot in the heedless pursuit of unbounded industrial growth, but the dream of America, or more accurately the desire for it, persisted among the immigrants.

There were, of course, millions of peasants who opted to return to Italy after emigrating to the United States. Generally speaking, these immigrants fell into two categories: those who could not adjust to the radically different lifestyle found in the United States and those whose master plan had always called for a return to the old country once enough money had been saved to afford a comfortable lifestyle in Italy. Money in hand, those who returned to the old country generally proved to be happy with their lot, but for their children, the story proved markedly different: "The American-born children found it especially hard to become acclimatized to the hordes of flies, and open fields used for toilets. All the loving affection of their grandparents could not compensate for the alienation these children experienced in the homeland of their parents, where they felt more American than ever."

For the new immigrants who stayed in America, however, the United States at first proved nothing less than a miracle. Peasants who had been trapped for centuries in a cycle of illiteracy, poverty, and despair now had a chance at economic freedom and individual sovereignty. Such freedom came with a steep price attached—mind-numbing boredom in factory jobs that squelched the human spirit—but economic gains proved possible, and the next generation, that of the immigrants' children, pursued an education capable of catapulting them into polite society. No longer required to leave school at age ten in order to help the family income, the younger generation developed a belief that through education, they, not *il destino,* held the power to shape their own journey. The quintessential manifestation of *la via vecchia*—the centuries-old mentality of low expectations—began to disappear. If, in the old country, one thought of nothing more than survival, food, and some sort of shelter as the best for which one could hope, in L'America peasant immigrants actually developed a sense of expectation. The New World was just that—new. Possibilities for advancement existed, and the very concept of saving substantial money entered daily life for the first time. Life may have been a struggle in L'America, but it also contained moments of surpassing happiness.

The fact that the mass Italian emigration to the United States took place in the late nineteenth and early twentieth century meant that it was already too late for those immigrants to benefit from the U.S. government's nineteenth-century policy of distributing free land to immigrants with previous farming experience. That policy instead benefited the previously arrived Germans and Scandinavians, although it remains doubtful whether Italian immigrants, who held little desire to reenact their Old World dependence on land and the changeable weather, would ever have sought an actual return to the agrarian life. Instead, Italian immigrants gravitated toward cities, most notably New York, San Francisco, and New Orleans, where jobs in construction proved plentiful, albeit low paying, and a support system of fellow Italians already existed.

The very nature of living and working in these cities represented a sea change in the immigrants' mind-set. Working in factories, not farms, meant that they were no longer subject to the whims of nature—fate no longer controlled all. First-generation laborers in factories became second-generation teamsters, a change that resulted in jobs both less grueling and better paid.

Such upward mobility came with a price attached, of course, and the flip side of this advancement from subway builder to teamster came in the workers' realization that in many ways they now controlled their own work even less than they had as farmers. Instead of battling just the elements, they were now faced with foremen and factory owners, men who controlled every part of their working lives, from hours and pay to hiring and firing. It was the laborers' feeling of helplessness when faced with all-controlling bosses and anti-Italian prejudice that gave rise to the Don Corleones of the world, men who helped supplicants by providing protection, albeit for a price. Part of the appeal of Vito Corleone's rise in *Godfather: Part II* lies in his impatience at having to play by the rules; smart as he was, it wouldn't have taken him long to figure out that in early-twentieth-century America, the harder the physical work, the less the job paid. Fired from his own job because of neighborhood boss Don Fanucci, and having watched his fellow immigrants trade in one form of oppression for another, he began to consider the solution found in a life of crime, and his decision to bypass the traditional decades-long wait for advancement resonates with every viewer who ever felt overworked and underpaid.

Immigrants living in urban ghettos learned to depend not just on the Don Corleones of their world but also on each other. Metaphorically speaking, the support system of fellow Italians proved to be a New World version of huddling around the campfire, safety in numbers ensuring that hardcore cultural values could be defended against "others." (The shortcoming of this inherent Italian reliance on family and friends to solve problems lay in the fact that Italians did not readily avail themselves of the limited government solutions that actually did exist.) Italians were and are a social people by nature, and tough and filthy as city conditions proved to be, the fact that the newly arrived immigrants were still living among their own kind brought psychological relief, a bona fide feeling of "I'm not alone."

Just as in the old country, *la famiglia* came to constitute the true center of life, and incessant family gatherings, on any and all pretexts, helped, in the words of Jerre Mangione, to "celebrate the existence of one another." It was as if the constant socializing with one another reanchored family members' corporeal being in the New World. So ingrained was this constant socialization that, as pointed out by Thomas Ferraro, the Italian language at the time did not even possess a word for "privacy."

Before extended families were scattered in the flight from city to suburbs, this constant intrafamily socialization served to ensure that 99 percent of Italian-Americans remained law-abiding, God-fearing citizens. How could one indulge in theft, cheating, or acts of violence with aunts, uncles, cousins, and grandparents continually keeping watch over a never empty house? Such familial closeness may have proved a detriment (insularity) as well as advantage (support), but the advantages did in fact prove substantial: when Daniel Moynihan and Nathan Glazer wrote their sociological landmark *Beyond the Melting Pot,* they posited that the strong family unit found with immigrant Italians actually gave the first generation children the physical and, even more important, emotional strength to forge their way into the economic and professional heart of American life. It was left to the Corleones of this world to successfully invert this equation, with their own family closeness proving to be precisely what ensured their success as criminals. Their tight-knit family proved quintessentially Italian; their life of crime did not.

With or without the Don Corleones of the world, it was not long before the sky-high expectations of newly arrived immigrants collided with the reality of life in America. The conditions and prejudices facing Italian peasants as they struggled to gain a toehold made for a reality markedly different from the promised land myth of L'America. The Germans, Irish, and Scandinavians who had settled in America one generation earlier felt threatened economically by the waves of newly arrived Italians and, just as the original English settlers had done to them, erected economic and political barriers against Italians. Used to the domination of Sicily by foreign powers, the older immigrants ceased to be surprised by their lack of acceptance in the United States, the controlling American WASP establishment registering as a new iteration of the old social stratification. The Don Corleones of the world decidedly fought against it, and the newly arrived immigrants didn't like it, but many simply shrugged their shoulders in what amounted to a collective peasant sigh.

It was observing this Old World shrug of the shoulders and its accompanying world-weary incantation of "Whaddya gonna do" that could cause my always-smiling mother to erupt in utter frustration. Because she was loathe to criticize anyone, much less a relative, it was genuinely shocking to hear her loudly exclaim "I hate listening to that. Hate it." This from a woman who considered "shut up" unspeakably vulgar. In my mother's view, there was "always plenty that can be done. This is America. Roll up the sleeves, tackle the problem head-on, and face forward." There's a reason my mother's favorite entertainer was the always positive, endlessly energetic Doris Day. Episcopalians could be every bit as tough as Italians—just in a slightly different way.

The more established Anglo-Saxon and Celtic immigrants of the time viewed the newly arrived Italians with disdain, or, more precisely, as inferior "dagos." Frank Sinatra, born in Hoboken, New

Jersey, to immigrant parents in 1915, and a man who often seemed to carry the hurt of every Italian-American insult on his own thin shoulders, characterized the prejudice thus: "Then I discovered at—what? Five? Six? I discovered that some people thought I was a dago. A wop. A guinea. You know, like I didn't have a fucking name."

Anti-Italian sentiment remained so pronounced that even in the Hoboken of the 1920s, a city replete with Italian immigrants, Frank Sinatra's father, Martin, a part-time prizefighter, found it necessary to disguise his Italian origins by fighting under the name "Marty O'Brien." When Sinatra's parents opened a bar, they adopted the same strategy and used Martin's alias as the name of the bar. The lesson was not lost on Sinatra himself, who, early in his career, refused a requested name change to Frankie Satin with the terse comment "The name is Sinatra. Frank Fucking Sinatra."

These "dark-skinned, garlic-smelling dagos" inspired fear and mistrust among Anglos and were looked upon as occupying the same low rung on the social ladder as that of "the coloreds." What African-Americans and southern Italians shared, in fact, was the look of being "different." The very foreignness of Italians—the dark skin and particularly the use of foreign dialect—made it easy for American authorities to disproportionately blame them for any crime, whether real, exaggerated, or imagined. Anti-Italian prejudice increased so rapidly, and with such ferocity, that in 1891, eleven Sicilians previously exonerated in the murder of a corrupt police captain were lynched by a White Defense League mob in New Orleans. As pointed out by Thomas Ferraro in his book *Feeling Italian,* this action was condoned by "such distinguished arbiters of national public opinion as Senator Henry Cabot Lodge and the editors of the *New York Times.*" The *Times* published not one but two editorials about the lynchings, both of which justified the actions, while reasoning that Sicilians were "sneaking and cowardly . . . the descendents of bandits and assassins, who have transported to this country the lawless passions, the cut-throat practices and oath-bound societies of their native country, [who] are to us a pest without mitigations." In this opinion, the *Times* reflected a national sentiment found in other newspapers, one of which featured an editorial writer matter-of-factly describing Italians as "a horde of steerage slime." Hand in hand with such editorials came repeated press invocations of the word "Mafia," an Anglo explanation of Sicilian otherness and a convenient, ready-made justification for the New Orleans lynchings.

Although most newspapers blamed the rise of urban crime on the newly arrived Italian immigrants, some did raise voices of reason. Writing in 1908, the historian James Adams posited that blaming the crime problems in cities on the "foreigners" constituted faulty reasoning, pointing out that these same foreigners had been largely law abiding in their native country. Expounding on his theory that it was, in fact, the overcrowded, filthy urban conditions facing Italian immigrants that prompted the turn to crime, Adams wrote: "There seems to me to be plenty of evidence to prove that the immigrants are made lawless by America rather than that America is made lawless by them." Framed in the much blunter terms of famed muckracking journalist Lincoln Steffens, the same message hit with even greater force: "The foreign element excuse is one of the hypocritical lies that save us from the clear sight of ourselves."

Factories routinely maintained strict quota systems to limit the number of Italian employees, and while salaries for urban Italian workers certainly ran higher in the United States than they had in the old country, it was also true that Italian-Americans still earned decidedly less than any other ethnic group in the United States, with the exception of African-Americans. A 1910 study of southern Italian immigrant families undertaken by the U.S. Immigration Commission showed that the average Italian family income for the

year amounted to $688, a full $112 below the $800 considered sub-
sistence level for a family of five.

Italians were routinely denied positions in government agencies, and so extreme was the anti-Italian prejudice of the time that
of the thirty thousand men in the Irish-dominated New York City
police force in 1906, only eleven possessed even a rudimentary
understanding of Italian. The police force's dislike and distrust of
Italians was returned in kind, resulting in a cynicism among the
immigrants so profound that many cast a jaundiced eye at the mere
presence of any law enforcement official. Writing in *Mount Allegro*,
Jerre Mangione details that in the Rochester, New York, of the
1930s, when his Uncle Stefano had jewelry stolen from his business,
"None of my relatives considered it strange that Uncle Stefano
should have gone to a Mafioso for help; nor did they doubt that if
the police and the press had not interfered he would have recov-
ered the jewelry . . . Eventually he and the rest of my relatives were
to make a distinction between the American police and the blatantly corrupt police system they had known in Sicily. But at the
time all policemen were regarded as obstacles to justice."

Consistently belittled and treated as third-class citizens by politicians and police alike, Italians were dealt a further, and rather
conclusive, blow by the passing of the Immigration Act of 1924. By
setting quotas, the act slowed immigration to a trickle and made it
crystal clear that non-Anglo-Saxons (i.e., Italians) were no longer
welcome in the United States. At the same time, the tide of immigration was further stemmed by the rise of fascism in Italy, with
the Fascists passing new laws that prohibited emigration. Oddly
enough, or perhaps not oddly at all, Fascists were perceived as fervent enemies of the Mafia, yet their modus operandi proved just
the opposite: the Fascist method of combating criminal activity
was to pick up any known anti-Fascist who happened to be in the
area where a crime had been committed, charge him with the

transgression in question, label him a member of the Mafia, and sentence him to jail. The pursuit of these anti-Fascists left the true mafioso free to roam and plunder.

If there was one single incident that inflamed Italian-American passions and caused a widespread doubt about the viability of justice in America, it was the guilty verdict handed down in the case of Sacco and Vanzetti. In a trial that garnered worldwide press attention, two Italian immigrants, Nicola Sacco and Bartolomeo Vanzetti, were charged with the murders of a factory paymaster and guard during a robbery that took place in 1920. Standing trial before a decidedly biased judge who willfully ignored prima facie evidence while allowing blatantly prejudicial statements to stand, Sacco and Vanzetti were tried and found guilty, spending nearly seven years on death row before being executed on June 1, 1927. In the view of Sacco and Vanzetti supporters in the United States, as well as a growing worldwide audience, the guilty verdict resulted from the defendants' Italian background and admittedly radical political beliefs, and not from actual commission of the crimes. Confronted with the unjust execution of Sacco and Vanzetti, Italian immigrants began to think that justice in America was proving to be as illusory and elusive as it had been in southern Italy. The godfather who protected his own began to look better and better.

It was at just this time of Sacco and Vanzetti that my grandfather had his own unexpected encounter with the United States government. Being a voracious reader of newspapers, English and Italian alike, tales of the injustices facing Italian-Americans weighed on him; while he remained grateful for the opportunity to run his own grocery store, the phrase "liberty and justice for all" seemed, in his estimation, to have begun disappearing from the scene when it came to Italian-Americans. Gravely disappointed in the Sacco and Vanzetti verdict and determined to read further about the issues, he subscribed to a Socialist newspaper. Some months after subscribing, the FBI came calling, and after a few pointed questions about his political beliefs, my grandfather got the message and canceled his subscription. No man who journeyed to America on his own as a teenager is timid, but neither is he impractical. After that my grandfather kept his opinions to himself.

Given the scope of legal and governmental indifference to the fate of Italian immigrants, it seemed inevitable that certain Italian-Americans would turn to crime as a means of acquiring status, power, and, if necessary, revenge. Without ever condoning a turn toward crime, those with a clear eye understood the storm of conditions that gave rise to this criminal class; writing of the immigrant's world, one commentator of the time reasoned that "changing a man's language, upsetting his moral and social conventions, altering his inherited tradition of conduct, unsettling his ancestral faith, these are the very best means possible for making him a disbeliever in all established institutions including those of the United States."

It's the juxtaposition of the immigrants' original, unfettered belief in their new country with the reality of life as they found it that lends additional layers of poignance (and irony) to the very first words heard in *The Godfather*: "I believe in America," says undertaker Amerigo Bonasera (a name that translates, intentionally, as "America Goodnight"). Immigrant Bonasera (played by Salvatore Corsitto) had arrived in America full of hope, and part of him still believes in the promise of the country, but the wealthy young men who beat his daughter have received nothing more than the proverbial tap on the wrist from the American courts. Justice has not been served.

Hearing Bonasera's bald statement constitutes a startling opening to the film, and not just because of the shadowy lighting that heightens the mystery as to whom he is speaking; underneath the grave dignity of his words, it is clear that he no longer believes in the American judicial system. He has run smack into the reality of the limits imposed on law-abiding Italian immigrants. "Liberty and justice for all" has turned out to mean that only the rich, Anglo, and powerful have full access to the dream. Bonasera's American dream has soured, or, perhaps more precisely, is now suffused with sorrow, and in order to achieve justice, the undertaker finds it necessary to humble himself before Don Vito Corleone, a murderous mobster and head of a powerful crime family. In asking for justice from Don Vito, Bonasera is, in effect, hoping that the godfather will grant him the ability to once again believe—in America and in the future.

In many ways, Bonasera and Don Corleone personify the conflicted attitude toward America that immigrants developed after facing the reality of life in the New World. The economic opportunities afforded in the United States existed side by side with the continued exploitation of Italian-Americans, and grateful as they remained for conditions far superior to those found in southern Italy, the immigrants oftentimes held a disdainful opinion of what they deemed a too-liberal American culture and family life. How, they asked, could you trust a system where parents allowed their children to act in the reprehensible manner of the young men who attacked Bonasera's daughter? *Mannagia l'America.* Damn America. Says Bonasera: "I raised my daughter in the American fashion. I gave her freedom . . . She found a boyfriend—not an Italian. She went to the movies with him; she stayed out late." In the view of Bonasera, it's the loose social mores that are to blame. Such New World permissiveness is contrasted later in the film with the presence of multiple chaperones when Michael Corleone and his bride to be, Apollonia, take a walk in the countryside of Sicily. The presence of chaperones is there so overwhelming that in order for Michael and Apollonia to even touch, she must pretend to stumble on their walk, allowing him to steady her by his hand.

It's the very conundrum at the heart of the immigrant experience that is addressed in the first minutes of *The Godfather* film. The
breakdown of the social order can be restored (and ironically then
further broken) only by the godfather ordering an even more violent act of retribution, one aimed at those who harmed the undertaker's daughter. For Bonasera and all those like him, the lessons of
the old country have been reinforced in the new: trust in friends
and family, not the government. "Ahh," the immigrants reason,
"America or Sicily, it's all the same."

The old Sicilian mind-set had crossed the ocean, donned a new
set of clothes, yet arrived at precisely the same destination, leading
to difficult and enduring questions about America itself. Since Sicilians had in fact emigrated all over the world, not just to the United
States but also to Argentina, Chile, and Australia, why did the mob
develop with such extraordinary force and power only in America?
It is, in fact, Francis Ford Coppola himself who most presciently
analyzed this very question; in an interview published in 1975, the
year after *The Godfather: Part II* was released, Coppola conveyed his
conviction that the Mafia needed America in order to fully blos-
som: "America was absolutely ripe for the Mafia. Everything the
Mafia believed in and was set up to handle—absolute control, the
carving out of territories, the rigging of prices and the elimination
of competition—everything was here. In fact the corporate philosophy that built some of our biggest industries and great personal
fortunes was a Mafia philosophy."

Frank Sinatra sounded a similar note in his stated belief that
Prohibition caused the rise of the mob in America: "Prohibition
was the dumbest law in American history . . . It was never gonna
work, not ever. But what it did was create the Mob. These dum-
mies with their books and their investigations, they think the Mob
was invented by a bunch of Sicilians in some smoky room some-
place. Probably in Palermo. Bullshit. The Mob was invented by all

those self-righteous bastards who gave us Prohibition. It was invented by ministers, by Southern politicians, by all the usual goddamned idiots who think they can tell people how to live. I know what I'm talking about on this one. I was there."

Crime, of course, had been a part of American life since the very beginning of the country, but Sinatra was right: it was the Prohibition Act of 1920, coupled with the Great Depression, that brought mobsters much greater power and influence over the public imagination. Thanks to the combination of larger-than-life newspaper headlines and the proliferation of radios, mobsters and their attendant notoriety were brought directly into American living rooms. Some criminals wrapped themselves in the cloak of respectability—Joseph P. Kennedy made his fortune in bootlegging but presented himself as a respectable financier—while others, like Al Capone, thrilled with the very vulgarity of their criminal activity. Capone's message was singular: crime paid and it paid bigtime. Even while middle-class Americans were "tut-tutting" about the Capones of the world, many lower-class Americans experienced vicarious satisfaction by following the criminal exploits of such men, the gangsters' smashing of social and economic barriers thrilling the public through its raw power. It's an appeal that continues to resonate today in the attitude of twenty-first-century gangsta rappers, who represent nothing so much as another manifestation of the self-assertive voices of ethnic pride demanding to be heard.

When viewed in conjunction with the real-life behavior of gangsters like Capone, the widely popular on-screen exploits found in *Little Caesar* and *Scarface,* films released at the same time the United States definitively shifted from an agricultural-based economy to one founded on industrial production, created a nationwide image of violence that both reflected and exploited the inherently imbalanced American social system. Power through profit—what could be more central to the American culture of corporate capital-ism? Not much, as it turned out, and it's a very big reason why Coppola's metaphor of *The Godfather* as an indictment of American capitalism succeeds. His vision is based on historical reality.

Although the most extreme forms of anti-Italian bigotry like the lynchings in New Orleans disappeared as the century progressed, the image of Italian-Americans as mafiosi retained its power, a problem heightened by the reassertion of anti-Italian sentiment at the outbreak of World War II. The wartime "enemy" status of Italian-Americans is recalled much less frequently than that of the Japanese-Americans who were interned in camps; easily forgotten is the fact that during World War II, over six hundred thousand Italians living in the United States were classified "enemy aliens," with thousands of them imprisoned in camps. So casual and wide-spread was the dismissal of Italian-Americans that President Franklin D. Roosevelt, looking down on Italians from his lofty patrician perch at the start of World War II, explained that he did not find it necessary to intern all Italian aliens because "they're just a bunch of opera singers." In reality, Roosevelt was only restating the preju-dices first formulated by another upper-class WASP, novelist Henry James, who wrote of being appalled by Manhattan's Lower East Side and its "great swarming of Italians and Jews."

As Bill Tonelli points out in his introduction to the *Italian Amer-ican Reader,* such was the tenor of the war years that Joe DiMaggio's father was forbidden to fish in Northern California, his years of work as a fisherman ignored in the atmosphere of fear and suspicion that gripped the nation. Even with the DiMaggio name attached to this insult, press attention to the incident remained rather mini-mal; perhaps it was the studied insularity of the Italian-Americans that kept such injustices out of the public eye, the events seldom recorded even by Italian-Americans themselves. Has there ever been another ethnic group that recorded their suffering less frequently? In this deliberate silence lay the worst possible manifestation of the old peasant bleat "whaddya gonna do?"

The Italian-American response to this shoddy World War II–era treatment lay in the record number of Italian-Americans who enlisted in the armed services after the outbreak of war, my father (U.S. Navy) and his brother Andrew (U.S. Army) among them. It's as if Italian-Americans tried to outdo one another in attempts to prove their essential American-ness, wanting to fit in and be looked upon as "real" Americans. Serve in the armed forces and you belong. Die for your country, with a military honors burial, and you're an American. Forever.

Ironic it was, then, that America's überpatriot, the longtime head of the FBI, J. Edgar Hoover, insisted for years that the Mafia did not exist in the United States. It was only after realizing that ongoing investigations into such a criminal organization would result in millions of dollars flowing toward the FBI that Hoover quickly became a rather enthusiastic hunter of mafiosi. His newly found passion for sniffing out mobsters did in fact dovetail nicely with the postwar years; as the 1940s turned into the red scare years of the 1950s, the idea of Italian Mafia families reappeared on the national radar screen, courtesy of the U.S. Senate investigations chaired by Senator Estes Kefauver in 1950. Like Hoover, the senators on Kefauver's committee realized that the mere mention of the Mafia carried great political currency and that it gathered both money and attention. Wrote Ben Morreale and Jerre Mangione: "All crime could now be blamed on a foreign conspiracy, and investigating organized crime opened up routes to the highest offices." One need look no further than Robert Kennedy's career in order to realize that his relentless pursuit of the mob in general, and of Sam Giancana in particular, garnered him continuing national press attention. So all-encompassing was Kennedy's headline-making "war on crime" that in American politics it has been matched in terms of media attention only by Rudolph Giuliani in his premayoral days as attorney general for the City of New York. Chasing gangsters, it seemed, equaled the highest form of patriotism, not to mention continued media coverage and political power.

It was the Kefauver committee hearings, broadcast on national television, that first presented charts of Mafia family trees to the American public, thereby ensuring a widespread belief that Mafia tentacles reached into every facet of American life. These very same family trees, prominently featured in *Godfather: Part II*'s Senate investigation of Michael Corleone, provided a literal manifestation of an organization previously cloaked in shadows and whispers. Few people ever denied the existence of organized crime in the United States, but given the status of the Kefauver committee meetings as hearings, not court proceedings, hearsay evidence proved admissible and resulted in sensationalistic testimony tailor-made for page-one headlines. The Kefauver committee, convinced of the Mafia's widespread existence, and perhaps even more certain of plum press opportunities, issued a statement that "there is a criminal organization known as the Mafia operating throughout the country with ties in other nations in the opinion of the committee. The Mafia is the direct descendant of a criminal organization of the same name originating in the island of Sicily."

Exist the mob did, but the reality of its reach, size, and influence proved to be somewhat different from that assumed by the committee. In writing about the Kefauver-led investigation, Baron Turkus, a prosecuting attorney in the Murder Inc. trial, stated that after the committee's investigation had lasted over one year, traveled coast to coast, listened to six hundred witnesses, and cost $250,000, not one single member of the Mafia had been found. Nary a witness admitted to even knowing a member of the mob, but newspaper publishers and television news producers had leapt at the ability of the hearings to generate moneymaking headlines, and as a result remained loathe to follow up with any accurate in-depth analysis. A stereotype that "Italian equals mobster" had been created and confirmed.

Twelve years after the Kefauver hearings, the McClellan investigation brought Mafia family charts back to the attention of the public. This investigation, chaired by Senator John McClellan from Arkansas, brought hoodlum Joseph Valachi, the first publicly known Mafia informer, to the attention of a nationwide audience. Valachi, a self-admitted murderer, had been born in the Bronx, could not speak Sicilian, and functioned as such a low-level hood that he was dismissed by another gangster, Vincent Teresa, as "a nothing," but he became an instant source of fascination in the country, and his use of the phrase "cosa nostra" as a synonym for "Mafia" was instantly adopted by the general public. Making numerous contradictory statements that proved difficult to decipher, let alone verify, his testimony nonetheless registered so strongly that, in the words of British historian Christopher Duggan, it was "largely on his evidence that the Godfather image of Mafia became embedded in the mind of bureaucrats with the law enforcement establishment." Originally published in 1968, one year before Puzo's *The Godfather*, *The Valachi Papers* received the Hollywood big-screen treatment in 1973. The film, starring the decidedly unconvincing and Lithuanian Charles Bronson as the Bronx-bred Italian-American Joseph Valachi, nonetheless proved a box-office winner.

Hollywood film or not, Valachi's actual importance lies in the fact that his testimony opened the floodgates for Mafia turncoats. With the shattering of *omerta*, the mob's heretofore inviolable code of silence forbidding any talk about "the Family," it soon seemed as if mobsters could not stop talking. Mafia members willing to testify on the record abounded, and the witness-protection program moved into high gear. As a result, insider Mafia testimony ceased to surprise.

Just how much styles had changed became evident in the 2011 testimony of longtime Bonanno crime family boss Joseph C. Massino. The only official boss of a New York mob family ever to cooperate with federal authorities, Massino became the first Mafia chieftain to testify against a former cohort, in this case the family's former acting boss, Vincent Basciano. Massino, who began cooperating with the government after being convicted of seven murders in 2004, was asked to specify his powers as the longtime boss of the Bonanno crime family, and in reply matter-of-factly rattled off: "Murders, responsibility for the family, made captains, break captains." If any testimony could truly shatter the lingering public image of honor and loyalty among mobsters, Massino's could and did; asked by Basciano's defense lawyer Richard Jasper if mob members often lied to one another, Massino bluntly stated: "All the time. It's a way of life in the mob."

In the new millennium, it isn't just the mobsters themselves who easily break the code of silence—members of their own families all but elbow one another out of the way for their chance in the spotlight. While one could spend the better part of the millennium trying to imagine Mama Corleone signing up for the has-to-be-seen-to-be-believed reality television show *Mob Wives,* that 2011 VH1 show, equal parts *Sopranos* and *Real Housewives,* finds four Staten Island Mafia consorts happily flaunting their public and private lives for the home viewer's consumption. For these women (three Italian—including Sammy Gravano's daughter Karen—and one Albanian), the personal is business, and their willingness to open their homes to camera crews grants them the measure of fame they rather desperately seek. No revelation proves too personal if it ensures more screen time; screaming, crying, fighting, and tough talking their way through personal dramas both real and manufactured, these thirty-something women represent an Italian-American stereotype come to life. Tough, profane, and armed with industrial-strength New York accents, the four mob princesses in question are unlikely to appear as guest hosts of *Masterpiece Theatre* anytime soon.

By its very nature, the United States of America, and Hollywood in particular, subverts the entire idea of *omertà*: America celebrates the individual over the group and the present over the past. Given the nature of the late-twentieth-century era of tell-all, one that began in the 1960s and accelerated with the early 1970s advent of *People* magazine, it therefore made perfect sense that Puzo himself set his post-*Godfather* mob novel, *The Last Don*, in Hollywood, the holy seat of self-revelation and media spin. It therefore proved all the more ironic that as the decades passed, the changes in mob protocol and media coverage only served to make Don Vito and his Old World code of silence all the more alluring, representing, as he did, a last and increasingly venerated vestige of secrecy.

The revelations arising in the post-Valachi era ensured that the public's perception of Italian-Americans grew increasingly distorted, perpetuating stereotypes that equated an individual mobster's life with an entire nationality's propensity for crime. Tape recordings made public years after the fact reveal that in the 1970s, President Richard Nixon agreed that while it would be a smart political move to appoint an Italian-American to a top government post, he wondered aloud, "where would we find an honest Italian-American?" (Unfortunately for Nixon, the answer came in the person of the Watergate judge, John J. Sirica; it also proved ironically fitting that it was the president's own attorney general, John Mitchell, who—for fear of offending Italian-Americans—instructed the Department of Justice to cease using the term "Mafia," and instead utilize the phrase "organized crime.")

Mobster or man on the street, by the 1970s it seemed as if not just Hollywood but also an increasing number of Americans were, in the parlance of the times, "letting it all hang out," a state of affairs that meant that the stage was now set for the counter-emergence of Nixon's fabled "silent majority." Here was an audience buffeted and confused by unceasing social change who hungered for what their rose-colored nostalgic view of decades past deemed a simpler and more decent America. This longing for the past underlay a substantial portion of *The Godfather*'s appeal, the audiences seduced by the warmth of the on-screen gatherings easily forgetting that the passing of the Old World way of life lay embedded in the very act of emigrating to L'America.

Inevitably, the most important conflict in *The Godfather* came to center on the clash between the Old World lifestyle of keeping a (multigeneration) family together and life in a new country that forsook the family in the name of individual advancement. It's a conflict framed by Puzo in the unlikely form of a highly successful mob family, but in holding up this particular mirror to the American psyche, Puzo was fitting, indeed helping to define, the zeitgeist of the times. His stated goal may simply have been to write a financially successful novel, but his actual achievement lay in successfully mining the deepest of veins: self-definition for Americans of all ethnic stripes

A saga of father and sons: "I never wanted this for you." *Photofest*

5   The Lure of the Corleones

Writing itself is a form of grieving, of trying to preserve what will otherwise be lost.
      —LORI SODERLIND, *NEW YORK TIMES BOOK REVIEW*

Italians have a little joke, that the world is so hard a man must have two fathers to look after him, and that's why they have Godfathers.
      — TOM HAGEN IN *THE GODFATHER*

LONG BEFORE FRANCIS FORD Coppola arrived on *The Godfather* scene, Mario Puzo had toiled for years on his epic novel about mob life in the United States. The author of two critically acclaimed novels (*The Dark Arena* [1955] and *The Fortunate Pilgrim* [1965]) that had sold poorly, a deeply-in-debt Puzo had decided that his next book would be a bestseller; critics be damned—sex and violence would prove the order of the day.

In the recollection of Paramount Pictures executive Robert Evans, Puzo, who had received a mere $5,000 advance from his Putnam & Co. publishers, appeared in Evans's office with only fifty-odd pages having been written yet nonetheless asking for film option

money. Without giving the matter much thought, Evans paid a
$12,500 option fee for film rights, said fee to be applied toward a
$75,000 payment if Puzo actually completed the book and found
a publisher.

In later years Puzo disputed this recollection, and former *Variety*
publisher Peter Bart, then Evans's vice president in charge of creative affairs, claimed that the pages first landed on his own desk,
courtesy of a conversation with William Targ, an editor at Putnam.
Whatever the book's actual provenance, Puzo did indeed expand
the initial pages into a 479-page novel that was published in 1969, its
title changed from *Mafia* to *The Godfather*. At which point the tidal
wave hit. With enthusiastic word of mouth propelling sales ever
upward, and critics acknowledging, if somewhat grudgingly, the
novel's irresistible mixture of sex, violence, and criminal power,
the novel landed on *The New York Times* Best Seller List for a stay of
sixty-seven weeks. Italian-Americans, the novel's intended target,
took to the book in the tens of thousands, but so too did readers of
every ethnicity. Selling one million copies in hardcover and a staggering six million copies in paperback, *The Godfather* proved so successful that in its wake over one hundred fifty books of fiction and
nonfiction concerning the mob were published, an industry-wide
phenomenon known as "*The Godfather* industry."

Which leads to one question: Why? What was it about this tale
that hooked readers who ranged across all boundaries of race,
creed, color, and age? As sales soared, it grew readily apparent that
The Godfather had morphed into a cultural phenomenon much larger
than the sum of its parts; by blending an irresistible myth about
family with an epic saga of mobsters pursuing the American dream,
Puzo had actually succeeded in painting a bone-deep, warts-and-all
portrait of America in the second half of the twentieth century and

in the process delivered nothing less than a tragic American romance.

Mixing elements both larger than life (watch Michael wreak havoc on his enemies) and recognizably small (see Don Vito play tenderly with his grandson), Puzo used the panoramic background of organized crime to position a mob chieftain as a recognizable everyman, an immigrant pursuing his own twisted version of the American dream.

Puzo himself may not have known any gangsters, but thanks to his research and storytelling skills, readers now understood, and even sympathized with, the attraction of the Mafia for immigrants denied justice through official channels. With his research guaranteeing that audiences would accept the basic premise of the novel, Puzo was granted a freedom to range far and wide in the structure of his plot, and the resulting epic entertained readers with fantasies of empowerment and, most of all, revenge. If, as a novelist, Puzo understandably indulged in poetic license from time to time, readers still wanted to believe that every aspect of the story was authentic, and decades after the novel's publication, his characters continued to resonate with the American public in ways unheard of for all but the most iconic of books. Vito and Michael Corleone now live on in the collective consciousness of America in the same way as do Rhett Butler, Scarlett O'Hara, and Jay Gatsby.

The Godfather returns over and over to the themes of money, big business, and corruption, but fierce as Puzo's condemnation of American capitalism was, he was smart enough to avoid giving a history lesson on why Italian immigrants disgusted with their mistreatment by American business briefly succumbed to the appeal of socialism. Few remembered that over one thousand Socialists held political office in the United States of 1911, and fewer still that the young Benito Mussolini had once been a committed Socialist; Puzo knew that such emphasis in a novel would prove a non-starter. Instead, emphasizing family and the human urge for revenge, he laid in devastating critiques of the American dream with deft understatement, resulting in a novel that has a level of commentary easily glimpsed for those of a mind to dig beneath the surface yet one never so blatant as to turn off those for whom the surface elements of family and murder sufficed.

Puzo fills *The Godfather* with a realistic, indeed cynical, understanding of the American political and business establishment, with Michael Corleone, at one point in the saga, bluntly stating that Italian-Americans "must learn from the philanthropists like the Rockefellers: first you rob everybody, then you give to the poor." In adroitly acknowledging the reality of systemic political corruption—Vito Corleone's rise to mob boss is aided by his holding of politicians and judges "in his pocket"—Puzo correctly reasoned that audiences would respond with a "so what—they're all corrupt" shrug of the shoulders when faced with the godfather's nefarious activities. Don Corleone is portrayed as a loving if exacting avenger on behalf of everyday citizens and, in the apt words of actress Talia Shire (Coppola's sister who portrayed Connie Corleone in all three *Godfather* films), remains a "decent man on the dark side, who is struggling to emerge into the light and bring his family there. That's what makes it dramatically interesting."

It's not that Puzo sugarcoated just how corrupt the Corleone family could be. It's that audiences willingly accepted it all. The Corleone family's control of labor unions? "Doesn't matter," said the audience. Don Vito's involvement with unions made sense to readers, especially those armed with the knowledge that most of the original Italian immigrants had joined labor unions precisely in order to secure protection of their jobs. Readers simply found it logical that corruption in the union would prove endemic, and if Don

Vito enriched himself at the expense of the union, well, in their view, a corrupt union proved better than no union.

Don Vito's refusal to engage in the trafficking of drugs put the audience even more squarely on his side. What, readers seemed to ask, is a little union racketeering when drugs are so much worse? By basing Don Vito's refusal to deal in drugs on the well-known early-immigrant aversion to any involvement with the narcotics trade, Puzo grounds the story while simultaneously heightening audience acceptance of the family's criminal involvement with unions and gambling. If, according to Gay Talese's *Honor Thy Father,* 75 percent of the money taken in by organized crime before the explosion of the drug trade emanated from gambling, an activity with which most of the public had at least a nodding acquaintance, it seemed logical that audiences would look upon the mob's control of gambling with some dispassion.

Criminal activity established and accepted, Puzo next insisted that readers consider the reality behind the image put forth by all characters, Italian or not. In the character of studio head Jack Woltz, the avowed enemy of the Sinatra-like singer Johnny Fontane, Puzo created a Hollywood chieftain whose public persona as benevolent producer lay at decided odds with the reality of his life as a pedophile who beds a preteen girl with the cooperation of her own mother. Compared with Woltz, a paternalistic don who grants favors out of compassion for those who pay him respect doesn't seem so bad. Faced with a choice between the two, audience members in effect shake their heads as if to say, "These businessmen are worse than the Corleones." Puzo is stacking the deck, but, faced with Woltz's amoral behavior, the audience wants revenge—Corleone style.

Upon publication, the impact of *The Godfather* proved to be so powerful that it changed not only how real-life mobsters interacted with one another but also the very vocabulary with which both

law enforcement agencies and the general public discussed organized crime. For the purposes of his novel, Puzo actually invented the
term "godfather" as an expression of mobster respect; forty years after publication, even the FBI now uses the term to describe the heads
of crime families, an appropriation of his fictional term that proved to
be a source of much amusement to Puzo during his lifetime.

Such was the power of Puzo's fictional universe that, particularly after the release of the film, real-life mobsters started speaking with the same phrases and inflections as their on-screen
counterparts, while further appropriating such *via vecchia* customs
as kissing the "godfather's" hands as a sign of respect. Renowned
mob hitman Salvatore "Sammy the Bull" Gravano actually acknowledged that *The Godfather* had an effect on how he conducted business: "It made our life, I don't know, it made our life seem honorable.
I would use lines in real life like 'I'm gonna make you an offer you
can't refuse.'" This, of course, from a man who went on to add that
the movie caused him to commit a total of nineteen murders: "I
only did, like, one murder before I saw the movie." Indeed, the
speech patterns of more than Italian-American mobsters were affected: thanks to Puzo, talk of crime families, "caporegiemes," and
"consiglieres," began to trip off even the most Anglo of tongues.
Italian-American idioms and values had gone mainstream.

Given that Puzo invented the idea of a "godfather" and thereby
further popularized the term "crime family," it's worth noting that
the word "Mafia" was not even used during the 1920s heyday of
mobsters like Al Capone; such men were simply referred to as gangsters. Capone never belonged to a so-called crime family, and, far
from being exclusively Italian, his criminal organization included
"seven hundred to one thousand men from every ethnic group in
New York and Chicago." Criminals of all ethnicities may have
composed Capone's gang, but as the decades passed the media

conflation of Italians and crime fit the purposes of newspapers and politicians alike. Wrote one Italian historian: "The mafia image of the 1890s was resurrected by the politicians after World War II. This image served the interests of those who revived it; just as Americans drove out their Italian and American-born Italian competitors on the New Orleans docks in 1891, so Attorney General Edwin Meese, in 1988, found a Sicilian drug ring to capture while himself under suspicion of corruption."

With character and plot established, Puzo began work on the thematic underpinnings of the novel, hitting on the idea of the multigenerational family saga as a prism through which to view American history, specifically that of post–World War II American business. Indeed, the gargantuan aim of the novel (and three *Godfather* films) is nothing less than a depiction of the parallels between Michael Corleone and the United States of America. If Michael registers as a man who has lost his way, betraying those closest to him in his headlong pursuit of money and unquestioned power, then in Puzo's view the United States has just as decisively lost its way in pursuit of corporate profits to the exclusion of all else. In Mario Puzo's America, crime flourishes precisely because it's another form of private enterprise.

Puzo intentionally drew further parallels between Michael's increasing immersion in a life of crime and the American involvement in Vietnam. Just as Michael pursued a life with no way out, so too, at the time of the novel's publication, was America enmeshed in a war with no exit strategy. Fifty-five thousand Americans and hundreds of thousands of Vietnamese died, while munitions companies grew rich and the manufacturers of napalm prospered. (As the national mood continued to darken, so too did the story of the Corleones, and the Michael Corleone found at the end of part II, seeing enemies everywhere and remaining convinced he is above the law, resembles Richard Nixon at his worst.) Puzo's pitch-black take on American big business, an authorial viewpoint even more cynical than that of Don Vito himself, represents an unrelenting and lacerating attack on the corrupt nature of corporations that hold themselves above the reach of the law. The Corleones, Puzo posits, could indeed be vicious, but no more so than corporate America; just as big businesses focus on the bottom line in order to please shareholders, the purpose of the Mafia proves to be exactly the same: making money. In the blunt words of Francis Ford Coppola: "Both the Mafia and America have their hands stained with blood from what it is necessary to do to protect their power and interests. Both are totally capitalistic phenomena and basically have a profit motive."

At its most fundamental level, *The Godfather* manages the extraordinary feat of criticizing the mob while simultaneously reinforcing the very idea of it, a duality made possible by the novel being set in a recent America that had already nearly vanished. Puzo condemns the mob's destructive force, its violence and disregard of all accepted ethical norms, yet at the same time cleverly casts the world of *The Godfather* in, if not a rose-colored worldview, then at least a golden-hued patina of nostalgia. It's the lure of the past that brought in readers and struck a chord. Those who were not fully at ease in the present, dissatisfied professionally and personally, looked to the past with a glance that smoothed away all of the grit; even real-life mobsters succumbed to the lure of Puzo's fictionalized bygone world. In Gay Talese's *Honor Thy Father*, a masterful nonfiction account of Mafia life in the Bonanno family, Talese notes that when Bill Bonanno, son of the Bonanno family boss, read *The Godfather*, he identified with the vanished world of Michael Corleone: ". . . he became nostalgic for a period that he had never personally known." For the Bill Bonannos of the world, the past was more than just a different country—it was a better one as well.

It was this shimmering lure of the past that informed the very look of *The Godfather* film, and, in the carefully constructed palette of Coppola and cinematographer Gordon Willis, even the extraordinarily poor Sicily of the time looked unendingly beautiful. Life was fondly recalled through a haze of nostalgia; in effect, what's remembered is the eating of fresh figs while cosseted in the gentle breeze of a warm summer day, and not the harsh scratching out of a living through the farming of rocky, unforgiving soil. Coppola and Willis carried this lyrical look forward into the scenes in *The Godfather: Part II* set in New York City's early-twentieth-century Little Italy, the determinedly soft-focus lighting bathing the neighborhood in the literal glow of nostalgia. Presenting the young Don Vito as a Sicilian don in the guise of Robin Hood, the film allows the viewer to grasp the chaotic, crowded conditions of the time, but always through a filter of golden-lit warmth. (So realistic is the re-creation of New York's Little Italy circa 1917 that it comes as a bit of a jolt to read that the interior scenes of Vito's apartment were shot on a studio set in Los Angeles.)

The very look of the films is so convincing that the reality of Vito's murderous acts is nearly lost amid nostalgia for a well-ordered past. It's a longing pervasive in the extreme, transcending America to become nearly universal: in his encyclopedic *Godfather Legacy*, Harlan Lebo quotes Japanese critic Tadao Sato as explaining that *The Godfather* appealed to Japanese audiences because of the hierarchical nature of the mob boss/subordinates relationship: "Behind the popularity of the movie, I can see Japanese nostalgia for the old family system . . . which modern Japanese society has lost."

If, in the words of F. Scott Fitzgerald, "So we beat on, boats against the current, borne back ceaselessly into the past," it is this constant pull of our collective yesterdays that underlies the annual pilgrimages of suburban Italians to New York City's Little Italy;

these wanderers from the outlying environs, driving up in their tinted SUVs, are searching for a past that never was, one created in their mind's eye and in the three *Godfather* films. Trying too hard to enjoy themselves, they walk the crowded streets in which their grandparents and great-grandparents first lived upon arrival in the United States, streets from which those immigrants tried to escape. (One can only imagine the original immigrants' reaction to the news that in 2011, the rental price on an eight-hundred-square-foot one-bedroom apartment on Mulberry Street, in the heart of Little Italy, reached $4,200 a month.)

What exactly are these suburban men searching for? A link to roots? A connection of any sort away from the sterile suburbs? Mythologized as the historical center of Italian-American life, Little Italy retains a permanent place in the national imagination of Italian-Americans, but these suburban pilgrims are searching in a Little Italy that is constantly shrinking, one now limited to a few square blocks and surrounded by an ever-growing Chinatown. (The December 2010 census revealed that the proportion of Italian-Americans among the 8,600 residents in the two dozen square blocks traditionally referred to as Little Italy had shrunk to five percent.) The Feast of San Gennaro may draw thousands to the neighborhood each year, but there now exists a nearly mournful unease in the area. One is hard-pressed to find the truly authentic amid the "Kiss Me I'm Italian" T-shirts.

Lacking any direct immigrant experience themselves, latter-day generations of Italian-Americans seem to perceive their past through the refracting lens of Hollywood, responding to the *Godfather* films as received wisdom. These twenty-first-century Italian-Americans know nothing of the real Little Italy of decades past, their constant searching representing the final act in the conflict between preservation and assimilation—assimilation has won, as it always must. "Ahh," the pilgrims think, "this is the way it really used to be," persisting in their search for a sense of the heroic absent from their tidy but often empty lives. They are retracing the steps of ancestors like my grandparents, those serious men and women (the myth of jolly Italian peasants singing "O Sole Mio" is just that—a myth) who married, left their homeland, crossed an ocean with neither education nor knowledge of English, and forged a brand-new life for themselves. The courage, singleness of purpose, and heroism displayed by these pioneers loom ever larger in a modern age bereft of heroes.

To a large nationwide audience, the Corleones themselves displayed just such heroic qualities. Using their own code of honor, they defied the governmental and business establishments, viewing those institutions as controlled by moral outlaws—a view of political America shared by millions of United States citizens at the time of the book's publication during the Nixon administration. In the Corleones, audiences saw what they perceived as a justified and legitimate use of force to solve problems. By managing the neat trick of symbolizing the antiheroes so in vogue in the early 1970s, the Corleones spoke to the all-pervading sense of anxiety that dominated the national cultural landscape. Outlaws they may have been, yet the Corleones' "otherness" only served to increase their oddly heroic stature. This honorable, respectful, and by the way murderous family did more than fit the zeitgeist of the time—it helped define it.

If, in the propagandistic words of President Calvin Coolidge, "the business of America is business," then the business of Don Corleone remained that of power, a power that allowed him to grant favors to family, friends, and politicians, but always on his own terms. "Well," Puzo seems to imply, "amass enough money and you too can say 'fuck you' to anyone and everyone. It's the

American way." Cynical perhaps, but an increasingly skeptical American public understood and accepted just such a worldview.

In a nation dominated by pervasive media coverage of the abuses of power found in both Vietnam and Washington, *The Godfather*'s focus on the exercise of just such power struck a nerve. Said Puzo: "It's about what power does to you. Who survives. I think it's a tragedy." In other words, in corporate and political America, whoever controls the money manipulates the media, and whoever manages the media defines both public image and what is deemed newsworthy. Those who wonder why politicians hungry for power have close yet continually uneasy relationships with the artists who present them to the public need look no further. In Coppola's own take on the issue: "Want to know who controls the world at any time? Just check who's employing the artists." It's a lesson learned well by, among others, Adolf Hitler, who employed director Leni Riefenstahl to film Nazi Party rallies in an exalted light, the resulting stylized iconography presented as the overwhelming will of the people. In Hitler's own words: "By the clever and continuous use of propaganda, a people can even be made to mistake heaven for hell, and vice-versa."

On either conscious or subliminal levels, nearly everyone understood that the Corleones represented the triumph of capitalism in all its glory and dishonor. Money equaled power, and big business/ big money, criminal or not, held the keys to the kingdom. Regardless of how high one climbed up the ladder, whether in politics (part II) or religion (part III), money ruled and corruption reigned. Near the start of part II, Michael matter-of-factly tells the corrupt Senator Geary: "We're all part of the same hypocrisy, Senator." In a wonderfully cynical touch designed by screenwriters Coppola and Puzo, part II's opening scene of young Anthony's confirmation party depicts Senator Geary as full of disgust and condescension toward Michael, intentionally mispronouncing Italian surnames and casually spewing anti-Italian slurs of "greaseball"; later in the film, when the philandering senator is, courtesy of the Corleones, caught in bed with a dead girl, his complete and utter cooperation with the Corleone family is assured, especially in his role as a committee member delving into Michael's criminal empire. No longer disrespectful of Michael, Senator Geary rises during the committee meetings to deliver a stirring ode to the millions of hardworking Italian-Americans who help to make America great. The business of America isn't business—it's hypocrisy.

Mafia and big business are bluntly depicted as two sides of the same coin: both are corrupt, tell the truth selectively, and do exactly as they wish. When, in *Godfather II,* a contingent of Americans arrives in 1958 Cuba in order to set up shop with the government of the dictator Fulgencio Batista, the line up of this uniquely American contingent consists of gangsters, elected officials from the United States Congress, and CEOs of America's biggest corporations. Thugs, businessmen, and politicians are united by one common aim: making money for themselves.

This message of financial corruption particularly resonated with my father, who started out in life as an admirer of Socialist Henry Wallace and veered progressively rightward with age until he supported Ronald Reagan. Increasingly conservative he may have grown, but he never lost his capacity to see through government hypocrisy, and in one memorable political discussion during my teenage years, matter-of-factly stated: "Of course dozens of countries hate us. We support every corrupt right-wing dictator who comes down the pike, if it helps our economic interests." He had no problem in flatly acknowledging that the North American continent had been stolen from Native Americans, that southern agriculture had in large part been built on the backs of African-American slaves, and he sardonically commented that our need for oil resulted in governmental support for the House of Saud at the expense of the Saudi population. This, from a man who earned his MBA before his MD and happily passed hours reading about the stock market. He was a firm believer in the capitalist system, but an equally firm believer in facing up to the reality of our national shortcomings. It was this refusal to sugarcoat that made my father so admire the first two *Godfather* films; if he reveled in the Old World feeling permeating so much of the first film, he responded even more strongly to part II's magisterial evocation of the immigrant's journey to America ironically juxtaposed alongside the sight of big business running amok. The fact that the United States of the twenty-first century composes less than fifteen percent of the world's population yet consumes half of the world's resources would leave my father shaking his head in dismay.

The genius of *The Godfather*—and genius it is—lies in the fact that Puzo (and Coppola in the films) successfully delineates so much more than the central metaphor of the Mafia as another manifestation of American capitalism (a notion actually first raised in Robert Warshow's 1948 essay "The Gangster as Tragic Hero," in which he considered the on-screen gangsters' greed and relentless push for money and success). Within the framework of one atypical yet quintessentially American family, Puzo considers the national move from city to suburb, the trek of the populace from east to west, and the changing nature of the national socioeconomic base. In its skillful melding of all of these themes, *The Godfather* provides a rare Sinatra-esque feeling that popular culture can be just that: possessed of broad appeal yet capable of delivering a cultural statement packed with considerable heft.

The Godfather's Italianization of America, a state of affairs referred to by Thomas J. Ferraro in *Feeling Italian* as "two sides of the dialectic—the secularizing of Catholicism among the Italians versus the Italian Catholicizing of secular America," allowed Americans of every conceivable stripe to see themselves and their families reflected in the Corleones' weddings, baptisms, and funerals. These fictional Italian-American gatherings grew into a type of national measuring stick against which nearly all immigrants measured their own journey toward assimilation. In its emphasis on proud ethnicity, *The Godfather* changed not just the way Italian-Americans saw themselves, but how Americans of all backgrounds viewed their individual and national self-identities, their possibilities and attendant disappointments.

Right beneath the surface appeal of the Corleones lay the not-so-hidden irony that the warm, family-oriented culture to which audiences responded so fervently was disappearing in unceasing increments with each passing day. The industrial manufacturing base of the first half of the twentieth century that had codified the blue-collar values informing so much of the Italian-American experience of the time began to fragment in the face of the nationwide change to a service economy. As Italian-American immigrants moved to the suburbs right along with the rest of America, the cultural hold of traditional values, which had been reinforced by close proximity to neighbors, began to dwindle: the suburbs demanded assimilation, which meant that ultimately all that remained of the original culture were scattered fragments. As the original immigrants aged and died, they took with them the last genuine vestiges of a culture overrun in the rush to assimilation.

Which leads to a rather large question: in the supposedly post-ethnic era of the twenty-first century, why does Italian-American culture still continue to hold such interest for non-Italians? After all, Russian and Asian mobsters proliferated in late-twentieth-century New York City without any blockbuster films or novels springing up around them, yet the appeal of *The Godfather* continues to grow in exponential fashion with each passing year. What made readers not just accept the Corleones but also root for them with such ferocity?

The actual answer seemingly goes to the heart of what it means to be an American: audiences loved the Corleones because they fought over the very issues that the entire United States population fights over: money, power, control, lust, and social status. (The only twenty-first-century American desire missing from this list is the ever-increasing, shrill demand for fame.) Cross the Corleones and they'd get even. Try to stop the Corleones and they'd continue their climb, right over one's literally dead body. Audiences understood these actions, in effect admitting "I might not kill anyone, but as to wanting revenge—that I understand." When the Corleones succeed, they allow viewers to experience a fantasy life of what existence would be like if lived outside the law: a life of taking—or more accurately grabbing—what that individual decides is rightfully his own. Conversely, when the Corleones fail, the reader/viewer is still allowed the luxury of disassociation: "That's the Corleones. I'm not like them."

Coppola himself supplied one smartly reasoned, slightly less murderous explanation for the saga's appeal on his DVD commentary to "the Coppola restoration" of all three films, wherein he positioned the *Godfather* saga as "our Dickens or Trollope." As such, through the Corleone family's public/private dichotomy of criminal activity/family life, audiences caught glimpses both flattering and sobering of twentieth-century America's evolution.

When placed in relief against the audience's suburbanized world of the 1970s, the Corleones represented danger and violence, a sought-after and ironic antithesis of the security and comfort the original immigrants longed to give their children and grandchildren. Having scrimped and saved in order to move their descendants to the suburbs, the immigrants exhaled in relief upon arrival, only to realize years later that their grandchildren found the suburban environs overly sanitized and lacking in authenticity. Admiring the world of the Corleones and reveling in it from a remove represented the easiest and best way by which audiences could escape their own stultifying lives. (In the twenty-first century, one can see the same appeal of the forbidden in the allure of gangsta rappers for comfortable white teenagers in the suburbs.) Frustrated by their own lives, audiences inherently understood the Corleones' turn to crime as a means of circumventing dead-end jobs with few benefits and little future.

At the most basic and overriding level, the Corleones represented power in the eyes of those who traditionally lacked it. For readers and viewers faced with a world that made less sense to them with each passing day, a world wherein political and legal bureaucracies seemed to reward wrongdoers and punish the innocent, the Corleones made sense, their appeal proving seductive and reductive in equal measure. By the time of the film's release in 1972, the sense of controlling one's own destiny had begun to disappear; bigger corporations didn't prove to be better, they just destroyed family businesses and the sense of belonging to a community—but the Corleones decided their own fate.

Against the background of the overly analytical, increasingly feminized, let's-discuss-our-feelings world of the late 1960s and early 1970s, it was, for many, the Corleones who symbolized courage and manhood. The ferocious Sonny shoved back fast and hard, just as Michael exacted revenge no matter how long the wait. Faced with the increasingly unstable world of late-twentieth-century America, audiences found the certainty of the Corleones ever more attractive.

Even with complex financial deals worth millions in play, the Mafia depicted in *The Godfather* remains centered on personal relationships and a sense of honor that, once lost, can never be regained. Don Corleone controls a multimillion-dollar financial empire, but when he chastises Amerigo Bonasera, it is not over money but for disrespecting his friendship, for never inviting the don to his home. Just as in the Old World, social status centered on personal relationships and small but significant actions. In effect, organized crime, here headed by an all-powerful patriarchal figure, re-creates southern Italian village life in the New World, with the don representing the one person capable of successfully bridging the world of the Italian village with that of the non-Italian power structure. Here were concepts that audiences of all ethnicities not only understood but came to admire.

At the same time, however, Puzo took great care to ensure that audiences never lost sight of the fact that underneath his gentle exterior, Don Corleone brandished his friendship as a weapon, using violence, when necessary, in order to reinforce his own exalted sense of honor. In his 2001 novel *Lucchesi and the Whale*, Italian-American author Frank Lentricchia employs the memorable phrase "the ice-pick of conversation"; in the case of Don Vito Corleone, the accurately rendered phrase would be "the ice pick of friendship." He instills fear by withholding his love, yet at the same time inspires love because of a willingness to take on his supplicants' own worst deeds and fears. In Don Vito's hands, the distance between fear and love proves infinitesimal.

Don Vito appeals because he has stayed true both to himself and to his culture. He has adapted to American life but never surrenders his Italian instincts. In the atmosphere of burgeoning ethnic pride that characterized America in the second half of the twentieth century, this resolve struck a chord, particularly resonating with an aging male audience in the same way as did Frank Sinatra's singing of "My Way."

For all his millions, what comforts Don Vito at the end of his days are the eternal verities of Italian life: a glass of wine and the tending of a small vegetable garden. He has returned to nature and stands apart from the endless human machinations of which he was a past master. It is as if Vito has stripped away everything extraneous, and he strikes readers as a man who understands what is important in life. That wisdom is in fact part of his continuing appeal; in the twenty-first century, he continues to represent the rare mass media older male who actually seems mature, the antithesis of Hollywood's cartoonish, grumpy old men with bucket lists, figures at whom one pokes comedic fun. In a new millennium filled with sixty-year-old men wearing backwards baseball caps while greeting friends as "dude," Don Vito seems like a wise old man—murderous to be sure, but wise nonetheless.

By masking his violence under an ofttimes gentle demeanor, Don Corleone enhances his connection with the audience. Readers and movie audiences alike were riveted by the fact that his violence was never arbitrary but rather sprang forth in order to preserve the law and order of his own universe, most notably on those occasions when an "offer" of friendship had been refused. Every action he takes, whether ordering the severed head of Woltz's prize stallion shoved into Woltz's bed or making sure an elderly woman can keep her dog, serves, in his estimation and that of the audience, as a means of restoring the proper balance in life.

Even Don Vito's first murderous act, one depicted on-screen in *Godfather: Part II,* is delivered in a fashion that gains audience sympathy; Don Fanucci, the don of early-twentieth-century Little Italy, is a bully and a thief, and when, after shooting Fanucci, Vito seamlessly blends in with the roaming crowd of a street festival, the cheers that explode make it seem as if the cheers are not just a part of the festival, but rather for Vito himself. Murder of Don Fanucci completed, Vito returns to his family, the very picture of a contented family man, as he strokes the head of his baby son Santino while the plaintive sound of an old Italian song whispers on the soundtrack.

It is these everyday details, the touching simplicity of the young Don Vito presenting a piece of fruit to his wife as a present, that grounded the film in a universality of family. Vito's understated on-screen presentation of the fruit instantly brought me back to my own grandparents, who would end meals with a piece of fruit, oftentimes peeling and cutting the fruit for each other. So caught up was I in the warm feelings generated by the image of young Vito as family man that it took me several moments to actually focus on the fact that Vito had just committed his first murder. With the shooting of Don Fanucci, young Vito had become the head of a new crime family and, by extension, godfather to the entire neighborhood of Little Italy. What had resonated with me was not the murder of Don Fanucci, but the melding of *Our Town* with Italian immigrants, and in that response I suspect I was not alone.

Vito appealed to men and women of all ethnicities because, regardless of his soft-spoken demeanor, he is a man of action. There will be no mind-numbing, day-after-day assembly-line routine for Don Vito. He has recognized and seized his main chance, shooting Don Fanucci when the opportunity presented itself. For audiences trapped in their own dull routine, Vito's aggressive independence read as quasi-heroic. Like Frank Sinatra, he took the leap, serving as an identifiable figure through whom audiences could live vicariously.

Vito and his paesanos Tessio and Clemenza grasped the fact that in a New World hostile to Italian immigrants, the new family of the gang, one headed by an all-powerful, beneficent godfather, could substitute for and even replace one's own blood family. In the old country, men surrounded by a large extended family of multiple generations had a villagewide support system, but in the United States, Clemenza, Tessio, and their fellow newly arrived immigrants relied on Don Vito, the head of their chosen family. Even with the steep price involved, Vito Corleone made one feel protected, and audiences instinctively clung to that sense of protection as the seductive weapon it was. Just as a sense of connection and well-being resided in the comfort of food and a shared meal, so too was there comfort to be found in the enveloping, if potentially murderous, embrace of a godfather who took care of all problems.

In very important ways, audiences projected their own needs onto Don Corleone, regardless of the character's reality. When he dies onscreen playing in the garden with his toddler grandson, he is impersonating a monster, the better to entertain the youngster (Shana Alexander characterizes Brando's on-screen death as a lesson: "In dying the way we all expect to die—unexpectedly—he teaches the difference between death as titillation and death as terror.") Director Coppola felt the scene added to the reality of Don Vito as a real-life monster, but audiences tended to skip right over that reading, concentrating instead on the heartwarming image of Vito as a kindly grandfather. Sweet and cuddly he isn't, not by a long shot, but the audience had grown to admire, indeed love, him, and a wise, warmhearted family man is what they were determined to see. With his fierce defense of family and his righting of the wrongs that society inflicts, Don Vito inspires a sense of audience identification. Nowhere present is the traditional stereotypical figure of the on-screen Italian, an exotic figure who only served to reinforce the audience's sense that such an outsider could never be considered a true American.

The canny structure of both novel and film allows audiences to overlook the fact that they are cheering for murderous thugs; *The Godfather* plays out not so much as a battle between the Corleones and the forces of law and order, but rather as a series of escalating conflicts between the five major crime families. When the Corleones do in fact tangle with the representatives of law and order, the battles inevitably feature corrupt lawmen who seem to prevent, rather than aid, the serving of justice. No one in the audience roots for a man like police captain McCluskey, who, far from helping to protect Don Vito in the hospital, actually aids in his attempted murder.

By the smart use of adroit parallels, Puzo and Coppola further mitigate any sense of collective audience guilt at rooting for killers. After Don Vito is shot, Clemenza rationalizes the soon-to-occur murders of Don Corleone's would-be assassins by linking those murderers to no less a figure of evil than Hitler: "You know you gotta stop 'em at the beginning, like they shoulda stopped Hitler at Munich. They shoulda never let him get away with that. They were just askin' for big trouble." After all, Clemenza reasons, by avenging his father's near death through the act of murdering McCluskey and Sollozzo, Michael Corleone is just preventing another Hitler . . . who knew the Corleones could so neatly assume the mantle of Winston Churchill?

With the Corleones' wrath focused on competing crime families and corrupt law enforcement officials, *The Godfather* did not have to concern itself with the ordinary citizens who are, in reality, the prime targets of mobsters' violent shakedown tactics. With no ordinary citizens depicted as victims of the family, then with whom would the audience of readers and moviegoers identify? The paternalistic criminal/godfather. In the well-chosen phrase of the film's production designer, Dean Tavoularis: "[Coppola] wanted the audience to see that these guys were in many ways like us—that's the paradox of it. Like Hitler holding a party . . . You can't relate to a guy blowing someone's brains out, but you can relate to a guy making spaghetti."

For all of the surface adherence to Catholic dogma found among the Corleones, the Christian concept of turn the other cheek did not exactly gain much traction with the family members, a state of affairs audiences found eminently satisfying. Viewers wanted the Corleones to emerge victorious precisely because they represented audience members' own desire to exact revenge. Unable and unwilling to break the social contract by killing, the audience in effect found release by living vicariously through the Corleones.

Particularly in part II, key changes that co-screenwriters Coppola and Puzo made from novel to screenplay further heightened audience affinity for Vito. In Puzo's novel, the change in Vito's surname from Andolini to Corleone (the name of his village) is his own idea: he switches his name in order to preserve some tie with his native village. Writes Puzo in the novel: "It was one of the few gestures of sentiment he was ever to make." By way of contrast, in *Godfather II*, the scenes of Vito's arrival at Ellis Island make it clear that the youthful Vito Andolini's surname is changed to Corleone by an uncaring official. The change in reasoning between book and film represents a crucial edit, underscoring audience rapport with the character by increasing the perception that Vito has been insulted by Anglo society beginning with his very first day in America.

Contrary to public memory, the novel does in fact include sections dealing with young Vito's life in Sicily, but these sections were notably and smartly altered for the purposes of part II's screenplay. In the novel, Vito's mother sends him to America to live with a friend, while in the movie, young Vito witnesses his mother's murder by Don Ciccio's bodyguards, and as a result must literally run for his life. Caught up in the little boy's bid to escape, the audience roots for and identifies with the youngster on his journey to America. In the apt words of Vera Dika in her essay "The Representation of Ethnicity in *The Godfather*," "Vito's mother had been brutally murdered before his eyes, and the violent propulsion of her body in response to the gunshot blast was the force that catapulted him into the new world."

With the one key change of Mrs. Andolini's murder, Puzo and Coppola have simultaneously sketched in the psychological underpinnings for Vito's subsequent actions, as well as heightened audience sympathy. From this point forward, Vito's anger is directed outward. He is ready for revenge, and the audience, identifying with a young boy forced to watch his mother's murder, is eager for him to seek that retribution.

In similar fashion, Don Vito does not avenge his father's murder in the novel, but in *Godfather: Part II*, the twenty-something Vito travels to the old country and avenges both parents' death by killing Don Ciccio. The fact that Vito undertakes this Old World–style meting of justice upon his return to Sicily makes sense to the audience. Vito has waited fifteen years before retaliating, and the bases of his character, understandable and thrilling, if still frightening, are now in place: Power. Silence. Control.

Puzo and Coppola do, of course, take further well-considered liberties in the film in order to ramp up the saga's themes of retaliation and reprisal. When, in the first film, Michael hides in Sicily after murdering McCluskey, he asks, "where are all of the [village] men?" and is told that they have all been killed by vendetta; this answer may convey heightened excitement and danger, but as pointed out by several commentators, in reality the men would simply have "all left looking for work in Germany and other more industrialized areas of Europe." Industrial work in Germany does not an Italian-American epic make, however, which is why, during Michael's exile in Sicily, his protector Don Tommasino is heard to tell him: "Sicily is a tragic land . . . There is no order. Only violence and treachery in abundance."

Liberties and all, it's the manner in which Coppola and Puzo delineate the metamorphosis of Michael from faux-naïf to ruthless killer that largely drives the first two films. Perhaps their greatest feat lies in the ability to make his rise and reign exciting and off-putting in equal measure, in the process delivering both sides of his character. If, in the first film, audiences root Michael on, wanting him to avenge the attempted assassination of his father, by the time of the second film these same audiences want to keep Michael at arm's length. They remain fascinated by him but, at the same time, repulsed by a man who could order the killing of his own brother; Fredo Corleone holds no power, but he has betrayed his brother, and for Michael the need for revenge overrules even blood ties.

In the novel, Vito's last words are a wondering "Life is so beautiful," but his son and successor Michael is not a man who will ever be able to utter those words. He lacks his father's compassion, and for all his Ivy League education, his vision extends no further than in undertaking whatever action will best serve Michael Corleone. In Coppola's view, "Vito kills with his own hands, Michael by remote control, while waiting in a dark room. I think most everyone would agree that Michael's is the more terrible violence." Michael can't keep his business separate from his family life, and the corruption of his business dealings inevitably taints his family, until he not only orders the murder of his brother, but inadvertently causes the death of his own daughter. Michael may say that everything he does is for his family, but at heart his actions further only his own perverted brand of justice. The real tragedy of Michael Corleone lies in the fact that his mania for revenge destroys his own family from within.

Money trumps all in the universe of the mob, and it is Michael Corleone, even more than his father, who personifies American capitalism run wild. When confronted with the figure of Michael, both on the page and especially forty feet high on the screen, the audience is forced to ponder just how closely he epitomizes the greed inherent in the American system. The figure of Michael even resonated, metaphorically speaking, years before the go-go Reagan era of deregulation brought unfettered capitalism to the forefront of the nation's consciousness. Much as he might protest the fact, Michael Corleone would recognize his spiritual brother in the "greed is good" *Wall Street* protagonist Gordon Gekko. In his quest to gain ever greater riches, the hole inside Michael remains bottomless, expanding, not shrinking, with each passing year.

Michael may be the most forward-looking of Don Vito's off-spring, yet he's the one Corleone who can't outrun the past. The college education that at first pushes him away from his father in the end brings him back to his roots, his education ultimately serving as just another tool to be used in his life of crime. He begins *The Godfather* with a sense of separation from his hyper-Italian family, but, by the end of the film, his true alienation lies in his distance from the mainstream society he had at first embraced, every last one of his expectations now upended.

Over the course of the original novel and first two films, the audience had developed a passionate, rooting interest in Michael Corleone, and when, by the end of part II, he stood alone as king of the mob, the screenwriters had actually boxed themselves into a corner that undercut the appeal of the sixteen-years-later part III: There were no longer any obstacles for Michael to overcome except those of his own making. With the ruthless precision of a true artist, Coppola, in part III, lay bare the very nature of power, microscopically examining how and why such power corrupts. Complete with larger-than-life operatic trappings and a refusal to sugarcoat the horrible deeds undertaken in the name of survival, *Godfather III* aspired to the realm of out-and-out tragedy. In large measure, Coppola achieved precisely what he intended, but it was not what audiences wanted, and the film suffered at the box office as a result. Tragic overtones were acceptable to viewers when diluted with the seasonings of rooting interest and revenge, but in *Godfather III*, the downward spiral of the Corleones proved incessant. Haunting and powerful it was, but in its unrelentingly grim tone, *Godfather: Part III* proved a tough sell. Absent a softening nostalgic gaze, and without Vito to provide a touch of humanity, here lay the one Corleone offer America could and did refuse.

1932 and the Italian as "other." Paul Muni as Scarface, the most famous gangster in film history—until Don Vito Corleone. *Photofest*

6   Forefathers on Film

---

*The [gangster film] genre speaks to not merely our fascination/re-
pulsion with aspects of our socioeconomic milieu that we prefer to
shut our eyes to but also to our fascination/repulsion with the most
haunting depths of ourselves.*

—Jonathan Munby, film scholar

Upon arrival in America, Italian immigrants found solace in a con-
tinuation of the storytelling tradition that had defined the essence
of village life in the old country. Gaining psychological comfort
from the kitchen table conclaves that centered on tales of *la via vecchia*, stories composed of equal parts wine and nostalgia, newly
arrived immigrants gathered family members together on the
slightest of pretexts. First Communions, promotions, graduations,
the purchase of a new television—all became reasons for a gathering of the clan.

Although a rich visual tradition centered on the artistic mas-
terpieces of DaVinci and Michelangelo had always informed the
Italian culture and folkways, no ongoing written tradition existed
as a complement to that of storytelling. Until very recent years, one
would be hard-pressed to name more than a handful of prominent

Italian-American novelists because, while the talent was present, the custom of writing was not. Gay Talese has actually pointed to the tight-knit Italian-American family's incessant interaction as a key reason why Italian-Americans have not flourished as authors. In his view, the essential state of a writer, one who stands apart while observing those around him, runs antithetical to the Italian instinct for socialization. In a dislike borne out of centuries of oppression by a succession of foreign conquerors, Italians inherently distrust loners, in other words, those, like writers, who behave differently.

Writers, Talese further posits, must be willing to discuss personal matters of an emotional and familial nature, a requirement that runs contrary to centuries-old Italian codes of privacy regarding the sanctity of *la famiglia*. The end result of such purposeful cultural isolation lies in the decided scarcity of well-known Italian-American authors, a lack that has continued into the twenty-first century. As several commentators have pointed out, one need only look at any recent compendium of American literature, including the field's standard bearer, the *Norton Anthology*, to test the validity of Talese's observation; while the anthology may run to well over one thousand pages, one will search in vain for either literature centering on Italian-Americans or a single word written by an Italian-American.

As the years after the arrival of the original immigrants passed, the traditions of family socializing and storytelling began to disappear. People moved to the suburbs, and as the sense of belonging to a larger, less insular suburban community took hold, the constant need for the company of one's own family lessened. The hours of storytelling around the dining room table dribbled away, firsthand knowledge of the old country fading right along with the fast-disappearing tales themselves.

The flipside of this change, however, lay in the fact that new methods of Italian-American storytelling—namely, those found in film and television—replaced the old by drawing on Italy's rich visual tradition. (In the bluntly accurate phrase of Jerre Mangione, the tradition of oral storytelling had disappeared because "television by then had reared its voracious head and seemingly swallowed their tongues.") It therefore came as no surprise that in the New World, trailblazing Italian-American artists like Frank Capra and Vincente Minnelli came to prominence not as writers, but as directors in the visual medium of the film industry.

Extraordinary artists though they were, Capra and Minnelli still had to work within the confines of a studio system that, in the forty years of sound films before *The Godfather* debuted, had fixed the image of Italian-Americans on-screen in the form of either Chico Marx's dimwitted con man or mobsters with decidedly Italian accents. The opening salvo in this parade of Italian gangsters came with the 1930 release of *Little Caesar,* a film that presented the Jewish Edward G. Robinson (born Emmanuel Goldenberg) in the role of gangster Rico Bandello. It is, in many ways, a first-rate film, and represented the first salvo in the portrayal of the American dream gone sour. Centering as it does around a compelling antihero, the film lays the groundwork for the sympathetic treatment of gangsters that fully flowered in 1967's *Bonnie and Clyde.* In the classic closing line of *Little Caesar,* Edward G. Robinson's Rico actually looks surprised as he lays dying from bullet wounds and utters a wondering "Mother of mercy—is this the end of Rico?" It's a fascinating film, and Robinson turns in a highly compelling performance, but don't look anywhere for an Italian-American with even a scintilla of goodness. Italian equals bad—end of story.

Shortly after the release of *Little Caesar* came the 1931 real-life slayings of Joe "The Boss" Masseria and Salvatore Maranzano, murders engineered by "Lucky" Luciano. Luciano's rise was chronicled in the press as the "Americanization of the mob," because

with these slayings, he had killed two members of the older generation of mobsters, the so-called Moustache Petes of old country
demeanor. In this real-life generational shift, one akin to young
Don Vito murdering the old neighborhood chieftain Don Fanucci,
Luciano assumed power and became a media star.

The groundwork for Luciano's larger-than-life public persona
had actually been laid with the realistic reporting of Roaring Twen-
ties crimes engineered by Al Capone and his strongman Frank
Nitti; such reporting had caused circulation and profits to soar, but
figuring that nothing succeeds like excess, newspapers now began
engaging in wildly inaccurate reporting, trumpeting headline-
making news about a nationwide spree of mob killings that had
ended in the death of forty Sicilian gang leaders. The reality behind
the headlines proved to be far more prosaic, however, and a perusal
of newspapers in twelve large U.S. cities in the last three months of
1931, shortly after the murders of Masseria and Maranzano, revealed exactly one killing associated with the mob. The public paid
no attention to this boring reality. Who cared about accuracy?
Italians as killers made for good copy. With Edward G. Robinson's
Rico Bandello blazing his machine guns forty feet high onscreen,
the image of Italian-American mobsters grew larger than life.

When, two years later, Robinson's portrayal of Rico Bandello
was followed by Paul Muni's turn as mobster Tony Camonte in
the wildly popular *Scarface*, Hollywood's portrayal of the Italian-
American male as mobster was fully fixed. Onscreen and larger
than life, *Scarface*'s gangsters spoke with impossible-to-miss, talk-
a-like-a-this-a accents that reeked of immigrants freshly arrived
from the old country. No one ever pretended that there were no
Italians in the mob, but it was all a matter of proportion: By the
lights of these films, if you were Italian there was a good chance
you'd turn into a criminal. Even more certainly, if you led a criminal life, you had to be Italian.

In these classic gangster films of the 1930s, from *Little Caesar* to *Scarface* and *Public Enemy* (the last named featuring not an Italian hoodlum but rather James Cagney's Irish Tom Powers), the gangster's lust for power proved attractive and exciting, but, given the moral climate of the times, his pathological grab for power was simultaneously depicted as the cause of his downfall. Criminals had to be punished for their misdeeds, and with *Little Caesar*'s depiction of pride and arrogance as the fuel for Rico's rise and fall, the action-packed movie at times resembled a quasi-morality play: the American dream may have faltered, but Rico's murder-fueled grab for riches must of necessity result in the ultimate punishment— death. Similarly, before the final release of *Scarface*, Howard Hawks was forced to add the subtitle "The Shame of a Nation" and insert a clunky scene of citizens demanding government action against mobsters. In film after film, the fall of the gangster was shown to be his own fault, with society saved once he had met his demise. Audiences, who were simultaneously attracted to and afraid of the on-screen gangsters, had their resistance to following in the hoodlums' footsteps rewarded: in all of these films, a life of crime equaled certain death.

The Godfather, on the other hand, constituted a revolution in the portrayal of mobsters; the Corleones represented equal parts excitement and evil, but, at the end of the day, society was not saved. The Mafia proved no worse than the crooked forces of the governments and big businesses with whom it battled, and just as the soft-spoken Don Corleone occupies a space worlds removed from the titular characters of *Little Caesar* and *Scarface,* so too does *The Godfather* itself constitute a revolution in genre.

Scarface's screenplay certainly skated into the territory of caricature with its portrayal of the title character, but, whatever those excesses, they paled in comparison to the wildly exaggerated ethnic appearance and cartoon accent of his on-screen mother. In order to appreciate just what a departure *The Godfather* proved to be from these caricatured figures, one need only compare *Scarface*'s Mrs. Camonte and her fresh-off-the-boat, over-the-top accent with the very first words heard in *The Godfather*, the "I believe in America" plea for justice delivered by undertaker Amerigo Bonasera. Bonasera is clearly an immigrant, but his speech is lightly accented and devoid of all histrionics. He is a recognizable human being. Throughout the entire *Godfather* saga, none of the characters speak with exaggerated immigrant accents, and the film's only notable use of a stereotypical accent occurs when Clemenza purposefully teases Michael that he should tell Kay "I love-a you with all-a my heart!"

For an eighty-year-old film, *Scarface* holds up very well—it's nigh unto impossible to resist images like a machine gun blasting away the months of a calendar—but it wins no prizes for its depictions of Italian-Americans. Talented though the director (Howard Hawks), writer (Ben Hecht), and actors (Paul Muni, George Raft, and Boris Karloff) were, it is clear that these filmmakers looked upon Italians as "others"—immigrants who somehow weren't "real" Americans. In the course of an eighty-eight-minute film, the viewer is presented with a simple-minded organ-grinder complete with monkey, Scarface's own wildly over-the-top suits as representative of an Italian's notion of class, and a heavily accented gangster/sidekick so dumb that he's not just illiterate, he holds the phone upside down yet can't understand why he doesn't hear anyone.

It was only with the 1933 advent of the Hays Code, a movie-production code that effectively severed the overt on-screen connection between organized crime and Italian heritage, that criminals with non-Italian surnames began to appear. In the end, however, the lack of a vowel at the end of a surname didn't matter greatly, because in all other ways, the Old World Italian background of the gangsters continued to be stressed. Years later, when the power of the Hays Code began to diminish, the overt link between mobsters

and ethnicity returned, the gangsters on-screen remaining cartoonish in a decidedly Italian fashion.

Just as Westerns traditionally tended to treat Native Americans
as "others" against whom order must be maintained, with the advent of *Little Caesar* and *Scarface*, the gangster film began to present
Italian mobsters as the ethnic others, men and women who did
not deserve recognition as true Americans. Faced with the caricatured Italian-Americans presented on-screen, non-Italian audiences
found no common territory with the characters, the gangsters'
looks, actions, and identity all reading as impossibly foreign. Dark
of skin, heavy of accent, and decidedly neither Anglo nor Protestant, Italians proved tailor-made to play the role of "other." Dark-
haired, voluptuous, plump women and hairy, primitive men—such
were the conceptions of Italians presented in popular media throughout the twentieth century, and the inevitable result of such a disconnect between reality and media image lay in the sense of moral
superiority that those in the heartland felt toward Italians.

As Madison Avenue advertising in the 1950s and 1960s made
clear, blonde remained the national ideal, blue-eyed blondes most
of all. Nothing, the nation was told, could ever be better than a
woman being granted status as "A Lady Clairol blonde—a silky,
shiny blonde." Blue-eyed blondes might have existed in great number in northern Italy, but in the American public's imagination, all
Italians remained dark, swarthy, and untrustworthy.

Constantly told that their differences equated with inferiority,
Italians, like Jews, suffered damage to their own self-image. Hair
was straightened. Noses were fixed. It's why Sinatra meant so much
to Italians and Streisand to Jews: here were stars who reveled in
their otherness, proud of their ethnicity and certain that their talent
could provide the key to any door through which they wanted to
pass. If the gatekeepers didn't want them, well, their attitude seemed
to say, "screw 'em." They'd form their own clubs and exercise their

own power. Like the Corleones, these stars of the highest rank possessed the power to live by their own rules.

As the decades passed, the power of gangsters on-screen continued unabated, but this time in the guise of television programs like *The Untouchables*. These television gangsters, clearly of Italian heritage, earned respect through their power and spoke to boys of all ages. It didn't matter that the G-men always triumphed—everyone knew that the mobsters were the characters with juice. Writing of his childhood, Italian-American commentator Fred Gardaphe mused: "In my Chicago neighborhood, we never played cowboys and Indians. Inspired by television programs like *The Untouchables*, we played cops and robbers, and none of us ever wanted to be the cops. While there might have been Italian-American cops in our town, there were none on television. It is no wonder then that many of us young Italian-American boys became so infatuated with the attention given the Italian-American criminals, that we found our own ways of gaining that notoriety and power."

When my then-forty-year-old physician father would come home from an exhausting day in the office and hospital, he liked nothing better than to forget his patients' problems through an hour with *The Untouchables*. My mother would glance at the television and sigh, "I don't know why you watch that. It always turns out the same." Which is, when you think about it, a succinct critique of the genre's plusses and minuses. In this case, familiarity bred not contempt but contentment. It took the release of *The Godfather* some fifteen years later to permanently rewrite the rules of this particular genre.

In the wake of *The Untouchables*, as the countercultural 1960s gained force, otherness of character now became an asset rather than liability. Gangsters came to hold the screen in sympathetic, oftentimes near-heroic fashion, and by the time of *The Godfather*, the Hays Code edict that the lawman, not the gangster, be the central figure on-screen had long since faded. This evolution in the portrayal of on-screen mob figures was mirrored by the gangster film's emerging status as a genre unto itself, one replacing the Western as both quintessential American frontier story and cornerstone of popular American mythmaking.

The ascension of the gangster film was aided by the fact that in the postwar years, Western films began to switch focus from the search for justice to the demand for revenge, the same quest that underpins all modern mob films. In Vito Corleone, *The Godfather* presented a leading man who is an ethnic variation of the traditional Western hero: he is strong, demands respect, and silently keeps his own counsel. (By way of contrast, his twenty-first-century descendant, fictional New Jersey mob boss Tony Soprano, can't stop talking, especially to his female psychiatrist.) Even with all of their surface differences, the methods of Don Corleone and Western heroes remained notably similar: don't tip your hand, and never let the enemy know what you are thinking. If, in the figure of Don Vito, Puzo and Coppola present an ethnic version of the strong, silent Western hero, then Michael Corleone represents an even more modern version of the same. Like his father, Michael, a supreme master of indirection, disguises all. He is, in theatrical terms, all about subtext, which is why such a repellent character fascinates. "What is he thinking?" audiences wonder. "What's next?" Michael hooks audiences precisely because he reveals so little.

If the mobster film has come to replace the Western as the quintessential on-screen form of American self-expression, it is also no accident that so many Italian-Americans helped settle the western town of Las Vegas and make it the adult playground it is today. Brought up on a steady diet of Western films, which featured strong silent men, wide-open spaces, and the carving out of new identities, many second-generation Italian-American men, raised in the East, looked upon the West as the "real" America. If Italian-Americans weren't going to be considered true Americans by the eastern establishment, well, the paesanos' reasoning seemed to run, they would follow the route of "reel" Americans and reinvent themselves as authentic Americans out west.

The endless, flat landscape and limitless horizons of the West represented the literal manifestation of living in a wide-open world, one only imagined by the tenants of crowded urban neighborhoods. When, at the end of *The Godfather,* Michael Corleone moves the family west to Lake Tahoe, he is undertaking a journey far greater, in both geographic and psychic terms, than the earlier family move from Little Italy to the suburbs. He is, in effect, following Horace Greeley's exhortation to "Go west, young man." The Corleones will build a brand-new family compound in the sprawling western spaces while pioneering the new frontier of desert gambling.

It was this late-1950s westward trek of the urban paesanos that greatly hastened the crumbling of the old urban neighborhoods. As the majority of the original immigrants died off, their children refused to live in city neighborhoods rapidly being taken over by African-Americans and Puerto Ricans. Bewildered by the swift changes in their old stable neighborhoods, the few surviving original immigrants who held on to their dwellings did so with a grim determination, their confusion over changes in L'America fed by a sense of self- and racial righteousness composed of equal parts discouragement and iron will. (When faced with immigrants who did not want to sell their property, politicians were not above using eminent domain in order to force a sale of the property, all such activities carried out in the name of supposed urban renewal.) As vandalism increased, the houses were either sold to slum landlords, or, on occasion, the immigrants' children themselves became slum landlords. The potent cocktail of politics, aging, race, and the newly arrived scourge of drugs destroyed the character of the old neighborhoods. Buildings crumbled, race riots ensued, and the last vestiges of urban peasant life vanished. The Corleones, like so many others, hitched up their wagons and headed west to their promised land.

This unraveling of America was reflected in films of the late 1960s, like *The Graduate, Easy Rider,* and *Five Easy Pieces,* all of which were released shortly before *The Godfather.* In these films, standard American mythology was undercut, and it's symptomatic of their time that each of these films ended without providing any clear-cut answers. These were sour, tough films made for a disturbed, changing audience. In the wake of Arthur Penn's *Bonnie and Clyde* (1967), a landmark film that found audiences rooting for and identifying with the titular outlaws, audience reaction to the fundamental antagonism between mobsters and the law was officially up for grabs. As a result, viewers were now primed for a new and much tougher depiction of violence, one that Coppola himself has traced from Kurosawa ("the father of violence on film") to *Bonnie and Clyde* (the film's climax, which found the couple killed by a fusillade of bullets, provided the direct inspiration for Sonny Corleone's massacre at the tollbooth) and on to Sam Peckinpah's *The Wild Bunch,* before landing at *The Godfather* itself.

The Godfather opened on March 15, 1972, only months after the smash-hit success of Clint Eastwood's *Dirty Harry.* Highly controversial and roundly criticized by many critics, most notably Pauline Kael, as a quasi-fascist lament for law and order, *Dirty Harry* (and its four sequels) seemed to empower the exhausted audiences of the time, who felt trapped in a country they found devoid of honor and justice. When, at film's end, *Dirty Harry* shot a serial killer who had escaped through legal technicalities, viewers were not disturbed: instead, they cheered. Audiences found themselves rooting for men who refused to play by a set of laws that only served the ruling class. The time for Don Corleone and the on-screen Italianization of American culture had arrived.

Favors requested and granted—for a price. *Photofest*

7   Godfather Cinema

I believe that when you make a film it's like asking a question, and when you finish the film you maybe know—a little bit—the answer.
                                                        —FRANCIS FORD COPPOLA

This is the joke of the movie business . . . no one knows anything.
                                                        —FRANCIS FORD COPPOLA

FRANCIS FORD COPPOLA MAY now seem like the only man who ever could have directed *The Godfather,* but at the time of the film's production, he proved no one's first choice to shepherd the property from page to screen. Those who turned down the film because of what they considered its dubious commercial prospects read like a who's who of Hollywood directors circa 1971: Richard Brooks, Arthur Penn ("I've seen the movie before"), Peter Yates, Fred Zinnemann, Franklin Schaffner ("It glamorizes the Mob"), and even Coppola himself all turned down the film, with Coppola initially rejecting the job because he had not particularly enjoyed his first, cursory reading of the novel. Turned off by the lengthy subplot concerning Lucy Mancini's vaginal surgery and subsequent romance with her surgeon and finding the character of Johnny Fontane's childhood friend Nino Valenti to be superfluous, Francis Ford Coppola was not very interested in the job.

In the recollection of Peter Bart, he was the first to mention the idea of using Coppola as writer and director, telling Robert Evans, "He's a brilliant writer and he loves telling stories about his Italian family." Said Coppola himself: "I'm fascinated with the whole idea of a family. In the things I'm writing that is constant." It is this very focus on family (what Sicilian novelist Leopardo Sciascia terms "the agonizing religion of family") that informs Coppola's particular achievement in the film: the abilty to movingly portray intimate, personal concerns within the framework of a sprawling, larger-than-life epic.

Whether the catalyst for Coppola's participation was Bart or Evans himself, the director rather quickly ditched his reservations about signing on for the simplest of economic reasons: his independent company, American Zoetrope, conceived as a production center for younger filmmakers wanting to work outside Hollywood, was broke and owed $600,000 to Warner Bros. Given that rather dire situation, Coppola could ill afford to turn down the proposed payment of $150,000 plus 6 percent of the net profits. In addition to his need for money, Coppola's qualms were further overcome when, upon rereading the novel, he conceived the idea of using the Corleone crime family as a metaphor for unbridled capitalism. Here, the writer/director thought, was subtext worth exploring: just as the post–World War II United States grew into a superpower nation where money ruled all, so too did the Corleone family's criminal pursuit of wealth corrupt them from the inside out.

It is fortunate for everyone involved that even before Coppola changed his mind, Brooks, Zinnemann, and other directors turned down the film, because the essential Italian-ness of the piece would have eluded each of those prospective directors to a greater or lesser degree: they could never have understood the material in their soul and sense memories in the same way as did Coppola. (Producer Al Ruddy was not Italian, but his job required more drive and street smarts than it did a creative Italian background.) One need only look at a film like John Huston's *Prizzi's Honor*, a mob film directed by a great, but non-Italian, director to gain further understanding as to why Coppola's direction (and screenplay) proved so key to the success of *The Godfather*. Throughout his extraordinary career, Huston directed many a first-rate film (*The Maltese Falcon, The African Queen*), but *Prizzi's Honor* is overpraised, and Huston's understanding of Italian-American life negligible. The world of James Joyce's *The Dead* represents terra firma for Huston, but not so that of the two-dimensional figures found in *Prizzi's Honor*. Even a cursory comparison of Huston's ham-fisted portrayal of Italian life to Coppola's mosaic of dialogue, action, and setting underscores the differences in clarity and vision. Coppola understood the Italian-American lifestyle in the very fiber of his being, and it's safe to say that no other director would have thought to insist that only Italian plum tomatoes be planted in Don Vito's vegetable garden in order to ensure authenticity.

In addition to his directing duties, Coppola signed on as co-writer of the screenplay with Puzo, who bluntly stated: "The kid understands structure and I don't." The two men quickly became fast friends, and their shared love of food and cooking helped cement their budding friendship. Realizing that events and characters must of necessity be compressed in the process of screen adaptation, Puzo agreed to Coppola's excising of Lucy Mancini's romance with her surgeon, the elimination of Nino Valenti, and the limitation of Johnny Fontane to four brief scenes.

In operating from a bone-deep familiarity with Italian-American life, Coppola was able to improvise on his extraordinarily thorough preparation with the telling details that spoke to the essence of the

Corleones' world. His instinct for the correct phrase, the silence that spoke volumes, and the sheer Italian-ness of the characters on-screen lent credence to his self-description as a "writer who directs." In accurately depicting how these characters lived, loved, murdered, and celebrated their rituals, Coppola bulldozed decades of cartoon depictions of Italian-American life into oblivion; speaking to actor Abe Vigoda (Tessio), Coppola forthrightly stated: "I want to look at the Mafia not as thugs and gangsters but like royalty in Rome."

Reshaping the genre of the crime film in modern terms, Coppola examined the headlong rush of the "American century" through the lens of the Corleone family, and in Michael Corleone's rise and subsequent fall, he saw the downfall of America: "Like America, Michael began as a clean, brilliant, young man endowed with incredible resources and believing in a humanistic idealism. Like America, Michael was the child of an older system, a child of Europe. Like America, Michael was an innocent who had tried to correct the ills and injustices of his progenitors. But then he got blood on his hands. He lied to himself and to others about what he was doing and why. And so he became not only the mirror image of what he'd come from but worse."

Crucial to Coppola's vision was his insistence that the film be set in the immediate aftermath of World War II, and not in the 1970s, as urged by Paramount Pictures for cost-saving purposes. Paramount's era-switching idea was born out of a financial desperation so acute that in 1970 its parent company, Gulf&Western, made five times more money selling cigars than it did from movies. Indeed, before production on *The Godfather* began, the Gulf&Western board had ordered Charles Bluhdorn to "sell Paramount or shut it down," the movie studio being saved only by a quickly made twenty-minute film (directed by Mike Nichols) in which an impassioned Robert Evans managed to convince the board of the all-but-guaranteed glories to be found in the forthcoming *Love Story* and *Godfather*.

The financial failure of Paramount's 1968 mob movie *The Brotherhood*, directed by Martin Ritt and starring Kirk Douglas, had made the powers that be all the more uneasy, yet Coppola stuck to his demand for the more costly period setting. He understood the power of placing the film in the immediate post–World War II era, a time when America, still regarded as the world's "good guy," fully believed in the validity of its self-appointed task to "make the world safe for democracy." Americans had just fought "The Good War," and in the words of Vera Dika, the immediate postwar years found "American pride and moral purpose intact." Using a nation at its zenith as his background, Coppola never shortchanged the violence and corruption underpinning the Corleone empire, yet at the same time he crafted an extraordinarily personal and authentic look at the realities of Italian-American life in the mid–twentieth century.

Certain of his artistic vision for the film, Coppola fought his next major battle of the production over the casting of Marlon Brando. This showdown over casting represented a gutsy move by a director lacking box-office clout, and while it paid off in countless ways, with Brando's extraordinary performance granting the film a decided and all-important gravitas, financial repercussions from Paramount's reluctance would be felt for years. All talk of Brando putting up a bond as a hedge against financial overruns had been forgotten once the actor had signed for the role, and Coppola even managed to wrangle a $50,000 upfront salary for Brando after being told that none would be forthcoming, but to this day the director feels that Brando's lower-than-normal salary rankled the actor throughout filming and beyond. Originally offered scale plus 5 percent of the gross receipts over $50 million, Brando, through his lawyer Norman Gary, ultimately received a salary of $100,000 by giving back his points. Given the film's extraordinary success at the box office, it was a decision that ultimately cost Brando $11 million in lost profits. That shortfall, in Coppola's view, remained the single biggest reason why terms could not be reached for the actor's cameo appearance in part II. That "guest appearance" may only have been scheduled for one birthday party sequence at the film's end, but oh what a scene it would have been . . .

Battle after battle loomed for Coppola during the film's preproduction, and, contentious as the disagreements over Brando had been, the fights over the casting of Al Pacino in the pivotal role of Michael proved no less acrimonious. A well-regarded but unknown stage actor at the time of filming, Pacino was not originally favored by any of the Paramount executives, with Robert Evans bluntly stating: "A runt will not play Michael." Convinced that Pacino was the one actor who could successfully navigate the tortured and complex journey of Michael Corleone, Coppola eventually wore down the Paramount executives' resistance through a combination of his own persistence and the inability of the front-office executives to find anyone they disliked less than they did Pacino.

Ironic it proved, then, that when production executive Robert Evans finally offered the role to Pacino, he found that the actor had already signed with MGM for a different mob film, the comedic *The Gang That Couldn't Shoot Straight*. MGM, owned by billionaire Kirk Kerkorian, and run by the notoriously ruthless James Aubrey, refused to let Pacino out of his contract in order to film *The Godfather*. In the recollection of Robert Evans, he then called attorney Sidney Korshak, a man long rumored to be a mob lawyer, for help with the situation. According to Evans, shortly after he spoke with Korshak, MGM's Aubrey called Evans back, and after a storm of profanity said, "I'll get you for this . . . The midget's [Pacino's] yours" (for a fee of only $35,000). When Evans subsequently asked

Korshak how he achieved this turnaround so quickly, Korshak replied that he had simply called Kerkorian and "asked him if he wanted to finish building his hotel" (the hotel in question was the enormous MGM Grand in Las Vegas). Life imitating art imitating life—and an offer the powerful Kerkorian could not afford to refuse. (Perhaps fearing the image this projected, a Kerkorian spokesperson bluntly stated of this story: "There's no truth to it.")

Coppola's exhaustive preproduction planning included the creation of an immense notebook in which he placed cutout pages of the novel annotated with his own copious notes regarding character and motivation, a document so encyclopedic in nature that he came to regard the script itself as almost superfluous: "I wrote the script from this notebook. The script was really an unnecessary document and I could have made the movie just from the notebook." Yet even with this extraordinary preparation, further bits of principal casting evolved through a combination of forethought, caprice, and occasional dumb luck. It was producer Al Ruddy who discovered Lenny Montana, then serving as bodyguard to one of the young dons observing the filming, and helped cast him in the role of Don Vito's murderous henchman Luca Brasi. The untrained, gargantuan Montana, a former professional wrestler who checked in at six foot six, 320 pounds, could not remember his lines, a potential problem that in the end led to the invention of one of the film's more memorable scenes: rehearsing a speech thanking Don Vito for the invitation to Connie's wedding, the hulking Brasi, much like the actor portraying him, paces and sweats in a desperate attempt to recall the proper words. Montana's real-life insecurity at the prospect of acting with the world-famous Brando infused the scene with an additional element of good-natured humor, while adding another layer to the audience's perception of Don Vito's power.

If Montana was cast by virtue of standing near the set during filming, Simonetta Stefanelli won the role of Michael's first wife, the young and beautiful Apollonia, in a different yet similarly unexpected fashion; at the end of her film test, Stefanelli unthinkingly skipped away, an unplanned action Coppola thought symbolic of her character's naïveté. One skip and the plum role was hers.

A relatively obscure Diane Keaton was cast as Michael's second wife, Kay Adams, because after watching her performance in the film *Lovers and Other Strangers*, Coppola "thought maybe Diane could bring some eccentricity to it." Robert Duvall, still rather unknown but highly regarded ever since his turn as Boo Radley in *To Kill a Mockingbird*, remained Coppola's first and only choice for the role of Don Corleone's adopted son and consigliere, Tom Hagen. In the most interesting casting possibility of all, before James Caan was cast as the violent, hot-tempered Sonny, Coppola conducted a startling screen test of the not-yet-famous Robert DeNiro. Included among the DVD extras for Coppola's full-scale restoration of the trilogy, the resulting test registers with a vividness that jumps off the screen. (Paramount spent $420,000 on screen tests for dozens of actors, yet in the end cast the three actors—Duvall, Pacino, and Caan—whom Coppola had long ago tested on his own at virtually no cost.) The scarily intense DeNiro may not have been quite right for the role of Sonny, but he would go on to contribute an extraordinary Academy Award–winning performance as the young Don Vito in *Godfather II*. (Coppola actually did cast DeNiro in the role of Caporegieme Paulie Gatto for *The Godfather* but acceded to the actor's desire to replace Pacino in *The Gang That Couldn't Shoot Straight*.)

As it turned out, Caan, who had also tested for the roles of Michael and Tom, proved a particularly inspired choice for the role of Sonny, yet even his casting was fraught with the problems that seemed part and parcel of making *The Godfather*. Carmine Caridi had actually won the role of Sonny, but in the standoff over casting

between Coppola and Evans, Evans announced that he would accept Pacino in the role of Michael if Coppola would agree to the
casting of Caan as Sonny. Writing in his 1994 memoir *The Kid Stays
in the Picture,* Evans bluntly summed up the multiple casting problems by observing: "The war over casting the family Corleone was
more volatile than the war the Corleone family fought onscreen."

In the end, Caan proved a near-ideal choice, his broad-shouldered
physique, curly hair, and manic energy fitting the volatile Sonny
to a T. Caan downplays the acting skills required for his portrayal
("What fucking transformation? . . . I grew up in the neighborhood"), but he spent time and care developing Sonny's manner of
speech, hitting upon the inspired idea of channeling comedian
Don Rickles's "do anything–say anything" vocal approach. (It was
this rapid-fire speech pattern that inspired Caan's memorable ad
lib of, "You gotta get up close, like this—and badda bing! You blow
their brains all over your nice Ivy League suit.")

Caan's Sonny may be the one Corleone who fulfills the stereotype of the hot-blooded southern Italian male, but his portrayal of
such a larger-than-life character is remarkably subtle, informed by
both inspired improvisation (smashing the camera of the photographer taking pictures at Connie's wedding, and then disgustedly
throwing dollar bills at him) and myriad details gleaned from real
life: "I noticed how [the gangsters] are always touching themselves.
Thumbs in the belt. Touching the jaw. Adjusting the shirt. Grip-
ping the crotch. Shirt open. Tie loose. Super dressers. Clean. Very,
very neat." Caan's characterization dovetailed beautifully with Sonny's all-id approach to life and formed a fitting contrast to the controlled passions of Michael and Vito.

Granted, novelistic detailing of a character's inner life must of
necessity be sacrificed on film, but it's worth noting that through
no fault of Caan's, Sonny emerges as a more fully rounded and in-
telligent man in the novel than he does in the film, registering on

the page as far more than just a hot flash of temper. To wit: in Puzo's novel, it is Sonny who most thoroughly understands Michael, saying to him: "I was just laughing at how funny things turn out. I always said you were the toughest one in the Family, tougher than the Don himself. You were the only one who could stand off the old man." On-screen, even in James Caan's enormously effective performance, Sonny's cunning and insight are shortchanged in favor of temperamental explosions; in the case of his death, the explosions are literal, his massacre at the tollbooth engineered by the sewing into Caan's clothes of over one hundred squibs filled with gunpowder and fake blood. Said Caan: "[They all] had to point outward, because they would blow a hole in you otherwise, which would really be fun . . . All I remember was A. D. Flowers, the effects guy, going, 'You know, I've done I don't know how many pictures, and I've never put this many squibs on anybody before.' I was really happy to hear that."

Finally, after months of controversy, Coppola had succeeded in landing his ideal cast, but new obstacles surrounding the projected start of filming seemed to arise every day. Given the sensitivity of millions of law-abiding Italian-Americans to the prevailing mass media image of the Italian as mobster, it's no surprise that the biggest such problem of all originated within the Italian-American community itself. In the wake of *The Godfather*'s overwhelming success as a novel, many Italian-American activists balked at the very idea of a *Godfather* film, fearing that such a movie would only serve to further spread the stereotypical murderous image around the globe. As a result, pressure was brought to bear on Paramount by a number of civil rights organizations, an ironic state of affairs given the difficulties heretofore faced in molding any Italian-American antidefamation organization into a unified force possessing actual political heft.

It had, in fact, taken the fictional *Godfather* mobsters to overcome the ingrained Italian-American reliance on family, not social organizations, for the solving of problems. Thanks to distress over the possibility of Don Vito Corleone being immortalized on film, membership rolls for the various Italian-American civil rights organizations rose dramatically, achieving levels long dreamt of by organizers. For the first time, traditional rights organizations such as the National Italian-American Federation (NIAF) and UNICO began to muster a degree of the sociopolitical strength long exhibited by organizations like the NAACP. Suddenly, Italian-American organizations were front-page news, their protests reaching a fever pitch with the announcement that the Italian-American Civil Rights League would organize rallies to shut down the film.

League president Joseph Colombo Sr., reputed crime boss and self-styled "real estate salesman," had announced the formation of the league with a stated goal of unifying Americans of Italian descent into a group that celebrated Italian culture while defending/monitoring the rights of Italian-Americans. Colombo also held the not-so-incidental goal of striking back at the FBI for what he perceived as harassment and persecution and made the league's first official action the picketing of FBI offices on March 30, 1970.

It was, however, with the announcement of *The Godfather*'s filming that Colombo lay claim to a publicity bonanza, the controversy over the film raising league membership to 45,000, a figure further buttressed by the estimated 250,000 people attending the organization's first public rally. In lashing out at the proposed filming of *The Godfather*, the league sent letters en masse to every member's representative in Congress: "A book like *The Godfather* leaves one with the sickening feeling that a great deal of effort and labor to eliminate a false image concerning Americans of Italian descent and also an ethnic connotation to organized crime has been wasted."

From the perspective of Paramount Pictures, Joseph Colombo's power over unions instantly made him a force with which to be reckoned, and in fact the league had immediately flexed its muscle by threatening to withhold crucial Teamster cooperation during location filming. The league next strong-armed merchants located in the heart of the film's Little Italy locations into displaying league decals in their shop windows—Colombo and company meant business. It was at this very time that, according to his autobiography, Robert Evans, staying in a New York City hotel with wife Ali Mac-Graw and their young son, received a raspy-voiced phone call in which the caller threatened, "Take some advice. We don't want to break your pretty face, hurt your newborn. Get the fuck outta town. Don't shoot no more about the family here, got it?"

Tensions ran high and tempers flared. The first victim of the brewing violence aimed at *The Godfather* was producer Al Ruddy, whose car windows were shattered by a shotgun blast. (So concerned had Ruddy been about possible violence that he had purposely switched cars with his assistant, Bettye McCartt. When his car windows were destroyed, Ruddy's automobile had actually been parked by McCartt in front of her own house.) It all made for a rather unpleasant reminder of Ruddy's own vision for the film: "I want to make an ice-blue terrifying movie about people you love . . . There had to be a real terror to the piece, a real fear to this thing, because this was the world in which these people lived, no matter how you coated it over."

It was at this point in the decidedly shaky proceedings that Evans ordered Ruddy (a man characterized by writer Nicholas Pileggi as someone who had "always been able to talk his way through obstacles") to meet with Joe Colombo himself, a meeting that took place at New York's Park Sheraton Hotel. Refusing the league's request to replace the characters' Italian-American surnames with blander names that sounded more "American" (correctly noting that *The Godfather* without Italian surnames simply made no sense),

Ruddy did offer the league's executives the right to read the script and thereby reassure themselves that the movie would not denigrate Italians. None of the executives took the time to read the script, but, if they had, they would have noted that the word "Mafia," the use of which caused them their greatest concern, was uttered only once in the entire film. Not having read the script, the league actually felt that Ruddy's willingness to delete all references to the terms "Mafia" and "Cosa Nostra" constituted a major victory.

Reassured that the film would neither stereotype nor demean Italian-Americans, the league backed off from further protests. Evans promulgated an additional reason for the ensuing peace, recalling that after receiving the threat of violence against his family, he had phoned Sidney Korshak and "within 72 hours, every door was open." Colombo and his partners were further pacified when Ruddy promised them the proceeds from the film's premiere (although that deal was subsequently nixed by the Paramount execs). With a canny sense of public relations, Colombo then invited Ruddy to a press conference, claiming that the sight of the two men together would send the message to league members that the movie need no longer be boycotted. What the press conference also provided, of course, was a major publicity forum for Colombo and the league; major television networks as well as dozens of print reporters came to the press conference, and, in Ruddy's words, as a result, "There was an article in the *Wall Street Journal*—MOB MOVES IN ON GULF AND WESTERN. The stock plummeted." Worse, however, was the next day's *New York Times* featuring a front-page, three-column article headlined "Godfather Film Won't Mention Mafia," complete with a photo of Ruddy and Colombo standing side by side. Upon seeing the page-one article, Bluhdorn exploded; furious that he did not know about the press conference and aware that in the public's eye Ruddy had caved in to the league, the volatile Bluhdorn held Ruddy fully responsible for the appearance of an additional *New York Times* piece, an editorial headlined, "Yes, Mr. Ruddy, There Is a. . . ." (The headline was inspired by the words of New York State senator John Marchi from the heavily Italian Staten Island. Having termed Paramount's agreement with the league "a monstrous insult to millions upon millions of loyal Americans of Italian extraction," one that "makes it look like the League came home with some prize," Marchi insisted that the filmmakers unequivocally denounce the mobsters in the film, sarcastically observing, "Yes, Mr. Ruddy, there just might be a Mafia.") Terming Ruddy's deal with the league a "hypocritical, craven act," the *Times* editorial writer went on to quote Marchi, who bluntly stated: "The League could render its most constructive service if it were to join with Americans of all nationalities and races in opposing the Mafia, instead of trying to render it invisible by making it unmentionable."

Embarrassed by such publicity, Bluhdorn fired Ruddy, with the producer's job saved only when Coppola stepped in and demanded that he be retained. In the midst of this onslaught of publicity, it was, interestingly enough, Ruddy himself who accurately pointed out that the media, in its stories about the film's problems, blurred the lines between the league and the mob, reporting as if the two were interchangeable. Although actual mob figures represented a minute percentage of the league's total membership, the problem of perception was exacerbated by the reality of Colombo's status as a mob chieftain.

In the end, all parties involved settled into a relatively peaceful truce, and Ruddy came to accept the fact that without the Mafia's help, the film could not have been made: "There would have been pickets, breakdowns, labor problems, cut cables, all kinds of things. I don't think anyone would have been physically hurt. But the picture simply could not have been made without their approval and if the boys hadn't helped us . . ." In Ruddy's recollection, Colombo came to appreciate his good-faith efforts, eventually telling the producer: "'You didn't bullshit us, you've been straight up with us. Anything I can do to help you, I'm gonna help you.' And they helped us on a number of occasions . . . The guys were great to us." As pointed out by Nicholas Pileggi in a *New York Times* article published seven months before the film premiered, this deal ensured that Paramount not only became "the first organization in the world to make money on the Mafia, but [one that] will also have conned Mafiosi into helping them do it."

When all was said and done, a big aid to Ruddy lay in the simple fact that the American love of show business came to take precedence over ethnic pride. With everyone in the country beginning to demand his own fifteen minutes of fame, it's no surprise that at the height of prefilming tensions, when Ruddy "pointed to [league] members, suggesting they could be extras . . . the group broke out into cheers . . ."

The final chapter in the league controversy occurred when, as the filming neared completion, Colombo himself was shot on June 28, 1971, at an Italian-American Unity Day rally (falling into a coma, he clung to life for another seven years). In a twist worthy of both *The Godfather* and Lee Harvey Oswald/Jack Ruby, Colombo's assassin, the African-American Jerome Johnson, was killed instantaneously, but the man who killed Johnson was never found. Rumor held mobster "Crazy Joe" Gallo responsible for ordering Colombo's shooting, and less than ten months later, on April 7, 1972, Gallo himself was shot while celebrating his forty-third birthday in a restaurant on Mulberry Street, his assassination seemingly carried out in retribution for the shooting of Colombo.

With well-known mob figures a near-constant presence throughout all location filming, the actors inevitably interacted with their real-life counterparts, and James Caan in particular evinced a fascination with the real-life mafiosi, most notably Carmine "The

Snake" Persico. Intently observing the men as they interacted with one another, Caan absorbed mannerisms and speech patterns, perceptively noting that the combination of embraces and kisses with toasts of "cent anni" and "salute a nostra" resulted in a package "of this marvelous old world stuff from guys who were born here and don't even speak Italian."

Caan was not alone in his observation of the local wise guys. Even Brando interacted with the mobsters, recalling in his autobiography that "several members of the crew were in the Mafia and four or five mafiosi had minor parts." Taking such interaction/observation one step further, Brando actually based part of his characterization on the brother-in-law of actor Al Lettieri (Sollozzo), one Pasquale "Patsy Ryan" Eboli, a "reputed capo in the Genovese crime family" according to *The New York Times*. In the recollection of Eboli's daughter Giovannina Bellino (a self-described "real life Meadow Soprano"), Brando, Caan, Morgana King, Gianni Russo (Carlo Rizzi), Al Ruddy, and Lettieri all came to dinner at the Eboli family home in Fort Lee, New Jersey (with a federal agent tailing Eboli parked right up the block). Sitting down to a meal of homemade eggplant parmigiana, the actors talked and observed, the evening proving such a success that some weeks later, in order to learn the Italian dialogue necessary for the Sollozzo/McCluskey restaurant shootout, Al Pacino journeyed to the Ebolis' home (and proved so short of funds that the family paid his cab fare). In an eerie sychronicity between the fates of the Eboli and Corleone families, on July 16, 1972, Patsy's brother, Tommy Eboli, was found dead on the streets of Brooklyn with five bullets to his head and neck. Patsy Eboli himself disappeared in 1976, never to be heard from again.

When it came to real-life mafiosi, it wasn't just the Ebolis with whom Brando interacted. During location shooting on Mott Street in Little Italy, alleged crime boss Joe Bufalino asked to meet the actor, who obligingly gave Bufalino a tour of the set for Don Vito's Genco olive oil company. Brando's encounters with mobsters continued during the filming of 1990s *The Freshman*; when asked to meet with John Gotti, Brando complied, performing a card trick for the mob chief. (It says everything about the ever-shrinking and changing character of Little Italy that by the year 2010, the Ravenite social club in which Brando met Gotti had morphed into a shoe and handbag boutique.) If mobsters reacted in this starstruck fashion in 1971, one can only imagine their behavior in the reality-television-obsessed America of the new millennium.

Master psychologist that he is, Coppola made sure that the very notion of family began to take hold among cast members even before filming began; given that his cast did not yet know one other, Coppola arranged a meet-and-greet "family" dinner at Patsy's restaurant in the East Harlem section of New York City, and as the dinner progressed, the essence of each character began to emerge. Assuming the role of paterfamilias, Brando opened the wine to begin the celebration, while Talia Shire, the lone female among the leading characters, began to circle the table serving the pasta. (Coppola's only reservation about Talia's casting lay in the fact that after her first-rate screen test, he thought she looked too beautiful for the role of plain jane Connie. Robert Evans's enthusiastic reaction to the test cinched the deal for Talia.) All the actors felt awestruck in the presence of Brando, but a more relaxed relationship ensued once filming began; as a sign of the burgeoning friendships, Caan and Duvall began dropping their pants and mooning Brando, preferably at highly inappropriate moments on set. Brando went his costars one better by mooning no fewer than five hundred extras during the filming of Connie's wedding reception. In recognition of Brando's efforts, at the end of filming Caan and Duvall presented him with a belt reading "Mighty Moon King."

After more than a year of preproduction, and a good five months later than the originally planned start date, filming of *The Godfather* began on March 8, 1971, with Coppola directing a scene of Michael and Kay exiting Best & Company after Christmas shopping. Even after filming began, however, Coppola's job remained far from secure, and word began circulating that Evans felt the movie did not contain enough excitement and required the addition of an "action director" to beef up the on-screen battles. To stave off the possibility of any usurper, Coppola spent the next weekend on an interior set with sister Talia and his nine-year-old son Gio, blocking out all of the action for the no-holds-barred fight between Connie and her husband Carlo (Carlo was played by the intense Gianni Russo, whose screen test had proved so ferocious that it scared his test partner). Safe to say, it is decidedly odd to picture the director's nine-year-old son helping to block out a soon-to-take-place violent confrontation between his aunt Talia and the thuglike Carlo, and in voice-over commentary on the DVD restoration, even Coppola himself admits that it proved very difficult to direct a scene depicting his own sister as the victim of a brutal beating. Forty years later, regardless of how radically on-screen violence has mushroomed, that fight between Connie and Carlo still makes for startling viewing, welling up, as it does, with a ferocious, character-driven, feral quality.

Given *The Godfather*'s present-day standing at the top of polls listing the greatest American films of all time (not to mention the three films' staggering cumulative worldwide gross of one billion dollars), it is surprising to learn how often director Coppola was nearly fired. While continually fighting with the Paramount executives off the set, Coppola also found himself arguing on the set with cinematographer Gordon Willis, who loudly told the director in front of cast and crew: "You're not using your actors right." Coppola found himself the constant subject of innuendo and doubt, with faith in his abilities remaining so low that while using a stall in the men's room during filming, he overheard crew members discussing what a terrible director he was; embarrassed, as well as concerned that the crew members would recognize his shoes, Coppola's response was to lift his feet off the floor until the coast was clear.

As relayed by Jenny Jones in *The Annotated Godfather,* further reasons for Coppola's near dismissal ran the gamut from casting decisions to finances:

1. Paramount executives remained annoyed that the very young Coppola (thirty-two) had dogmatically insisted on Brando's casting. (So impassioned had been Coppola's plea for Brando that, upon completing his pitch in front of the executives, Coppola fell to the ground, clutching his chest. The Paramount brass thought he was having a heart attack; Coppola maintained he had intended the action as a joke. The Paramount executives were not amused.) Front-office reaction to the actor's actual performance was not helped by what the executives termed his "mumbling" during the first week's dailies. (According to Peter Bart, after viewing the early dailies, even Coppola's champion, Robert Evans, had sarcastically said: "I can't understand Brando and I can't see the actors—other than that the work is great.")
2. Displeasure with the first week's footage featuring Pacino
3. Coppola's demand for a location shoot in Sicily
4. Consistent budget overruns throughout filming; Coppola fell one day further behind schedule during every week of shooting, and inquiries were actually made as to Elia Kazan's availability to take over as director.

Exaggerations and distortions about Coppola's near firing have grown with the hindsight of four decades, but there is no doubt that at the start of production his position remained tenuous. During the earliest stages of filming, the film's editor, Aram Avakian, told Evans that the film "wouldn't cut" and that Coppola didn't understand the concept of continuity. At the same time, Jack Ballard, Paramount's head of physical production, said on a conference call that the director "wasn't up to the job" and that he wanted Avakian to take over as director. Although that idea gained little traction, Evans was concerned enough about Avakian's charges that he asked editor Peter Zinner (*In Cold Blood*) for his opinion of the dailies; assured by Zinner that the footage was first-rate, Evans fired Avakian and hired Zinner (in some versions of the story, it is Coppola himself who fired Avakian. When, years later, Coppola discussed the events of that third week of shooting, he stated: "So on that Thursday, I fired five guys, because I was still the director. I just did a preemptive strike.")

Even granted the mythology about the filming of *The Godfather* that has now taken hold, what does ring true is Coppola's own recollection that it was Brando who saved his job by bluntly insisting, "If you fire Francis I'll walk off the picture." With filming already under way, Paramount could ill afford to replace their much-ballyhooed star, and in Coppola's own grateful words: "Brando saved my neck." (On a further pragmatic level, Coppola in later years reasoned, "I think they [Paramount] decided it would be more trouble to fire me.") Director and star proceeded to forge a solid working relationship, and if Brando's refusal to learn lines and insistence on cue cards exasperated Coppola, the director also knew that Brando's belief that such a technique increased a sense of spontaneity never harmed his characterization. (In an amusing side to the issue of cue cards, Peter Bart actually asked Brando on set why he wanted all of the words printed out in such a fashion. Brando's clipped answer? "Because I can read them that way." End of discussion.)

With his job somewhat secured, Coppola turned his attention to the staging of the film-opening wedding reception. The decision to begin the film with this lengthy scene was an inspired one, the canny, bifurcated structure of the sequence allowing the audience to be instantaneously enveloped in two different yet simultaneous worlds. On the exterior lay the warm, happy outdoor wedding reception: Italian-centric and dominated by Old World customs, it's a romantic celebration of family, complete with dancing guests, platters of food, and an all-embracing sense of community. Concurrently, through the adroit use of cross-cutting, the audience is brought into the dark, mysterious, yet intriguing world of Don Vito's study, a hub of quiet favors given and exchanged.

As designed by cinematographer Gordon Willis, the look of the film serves both worlds, with the wedding reception deliberately shot in a "kind of bright Kodachrome with a 1940's feeling. I introduced the yellow-red of these scenes which gave it an orangey period look. I made that particular sequence much brighter so that we cut from there to the dark interior of the study . . . and then bang you cut back outside to the wedding, in that orange color." As a result, within the first ten minutes of the film, audiences have already been exposed to the public/private split between what is seen and what is known, between mystery and openness. Hooked by such storytelling, spectators ask the most basic of all questions: what happens next? So skillful is this first extended sequence—an aria for all intents and purposes—that it is minutes later before viewers realize that through a minimum of dialogue and a maximum of visual storytelling, they have now been introduced to, and provided with insights into, every single one of the film's major characters.

Transmitting texture through his visual imagery, Coppola allows audiences to feel a part of the film's action, to viscerally experience the events on-screen as if they too were guests at Connie

Corleone's wedding reception. In this participatory gusto lay a big reason why the appeal of *The Godfather* crossed all ethnic boundaries: everyone reacts with a smile to the warm tones and look of Connie's wedding. Italians in the immediate post–World War II era knew how to celebrate with abandon, and the movie audience responds to this sense of bygone communal enjoyment. This is not polite Anglo society standing by while Lester Lanin plays a fox-trot and passes out beanies. Here the dancing and singing are filled with joyful abandon, the celebration of love, family, food, drink, and music passing from fun into a secular religious experience.

In the disconnected electronic new millennium, people of all stripes yearn for the sense of belonging displayed at the wedding, and one of the sadnesses inherent in the loss of *la via vecchia* is that it is just such gusto that has passed from Italian weddings. Right alongside the higher education that has become the norm for men and women alike resides a sense of assimilation too buttoned-down for such displays of abandon. If the original Italian immigrants changed simply by virtue of their arrival in the United States, then with the passage of generations, their community's essential Italian-ness has been radically watered down as well. Sing and dance the tarantella like fat Clemenza at Connie's wedding? Order towering wedding cakes in a more-is-more display of having arrived? Never. We're too tasteful and refined for that now. The loss is ours.

With this first extended wedding reception, Coppola has also set the standard against which all future Corleone family celebrations will be compared, from Anthony's baptism at the end of *The Godfather* to his First Communion at the start of part II and on through Michael's investiture as part III begins. All of these celebrations are measured against the warmth of the original wedding celebration and are found to be lacking. The Corleone family will never again be as united as at Connie's wedding, and through the course of all three films, these ostensibly happy celebrations come to serve as beautifully calibrated instruments for measuring familial and societal change through the decades.

The cleverness of using the public celebrations of *la famiglia* as tentpoles for all three films lies in the fact that these public occasions simultaneously reveal private behavior. For every scene celebrating, as it were, "family values," there exists an opposite and equal sequence exposing corruption and treachery. Such dichotomy is purposefully extended through both sequels: in part II, young Don Vito kills Fanucci during a boisterous street festival, the sound of the fireworks in the background notably contrasted with Vito's quiet return home. Part III opens with the public ceremony and family celebration of Michael's papal decoration, but the revelry is interrupted by the arrival of Sonny's illegitimate son Vincent, who attacks rival mobster Joey Zasa in Michael's private office. In this contrast between the public and the private, Puzo and Coppola add multiple layers to the films, the duality of structure and purpose echoing the film's central assertions that political, business, and religious institutions all hide a dirty underbelly of corruption and greed. The Corleones simply represent the face and logical outcome of American capitalism at its most extreme, and, as such, the message of *The Godfather* rings ever clearer forty years after its first iteration.

At the time of the first film's release in early 1972, President Nixon had ordered the mining of Haiphong Harbor, the antiwar movement had grown to encompass the middle class, and citizens of all ages had grown extraordinarily cynical about their government. While American families seemed endlessly racked with disputes over Vietnam, Nixon's government, feminism, and the black power movement, Coppola and Puzo presented the rarest of all species on-screen: a united family. OK, it was a family of killers, but, audiences seemed to say, at least they're happy . . . The Corleones might have been murderous thugs, but they valued family and loyalty, and as corporate America in the late 1960s turned remarkably indifferent to the fate of its longtime workers, the search for profit overcoming any sense of allegiance, the Corleones registered as a paradigm of loyalty. Discipline and adherence to the patriarchy remained the coin of their realm, and at a time when every institution from the military to the church was being loudly questioned, the appeal of Corleone certainty, discipline, and family unity loomed large in the public consciousness.

From a purely technical standpoint, a big reason why Don Vito's world so effortlessly seduces audiences lies in Coppola's and cinematographer Gordon Willis's decision to use low lighting levels for the indoor scenes, the purposefully flat lighting produced by a Willis-designed set of inverted overhead lights that "bounced into diffusing frames." The overhead lighting may have originated in order to disguise Brando's makeup, but it served a greater artistic purpose by helping to delineate Brando's character. In Willis's own words: "It put his eye sockets into the back of his head and gave it a sinister feel . . ." The technical here merged with the psychological, deepening the audience's visceral reaction to both action and characterization. Continued Willis: "Point, counterpoint; light, dark; big, small—using contrasts can achieve a desired emotional response. This could be as simple as manipulating where characters appear on the screen or lighting a dark room with sunlight." Comparing prints of *The Godfather* pre- and postrestoration is to see exactly how much Willis contributed to the film's appeal. Because of *The Godfather*'s overwhelming popularity in its original release, so many prints were struck that the original negative was virtually destroyed, and the subtleties of the color scheme, the muted browns and golds that so enhanced the movie, devolved into an overall murkiness. As film archivist Robert Harris described the process, it was "like making a Xerox of a Xerox of a Xerox," and the seductive power of Don Corleone's world dissipated into a wan gloominess. Postrestoration, thanks to Willis's artistry, Don Vito's shadowy world of power registered with more subtlety than ever.

Willis's approach with lighting affects the audience on both conscious and subliminal levels. Faced with the film's opening image of Amerigo Bonasera intoning "I believe in America," the audience collectively asks one question: to whom is he speaking? It's Don Vito Corleone himself, but the decision to hide Brando's face in planes and shadows only emphasizes his status as a man of mystery. Audiences wanted more information, but explanation was deliberately withheld, the cool shadows in Don Vito's study presented as simultaneously threatening and inviting. The images found in Don Vito's world actually counted for more than did the discussion at hand; viewers intuitively understood from the mere look of the film that the godfather was a man of extraordinary power, his despotism exercised in the form of paternalism.

All audiences thrill to the idea of eavesdropping on big deals, and the more secretive, the better, but throughout *The Godfather*, it wasn't just the secret nature of the deals that fascinated—it was the casual brutality of it all. When, at Don Vito's funeral, it is made clear that longtime aide Tessio has betrayed Michael, audiences are intrigued by how calmly Tom Hagen and Michael take the news. There are no histrionics, no stereotypical Italian emoting. Instead, Hagen simply turns to Michael and murmurs "I always thought it would be Clemenza, not Tessio." Translation: Tessio is now a dead man. In this one line of dialogue Puzo and Coppola sum up the clinical brutality of the Mafia, one that simultaneously horrifies and titillates. Every single meeting in *The Godfather*, no matter how close the participants, holds the potential for betrayal.

Caporegieme Tessio has betrayed Michael, but it is, he claims, nothing personal—just business. Except, of course, it's all personal, a philosophy outlined in the novel by Michael himself: "Every piece of shit every man has to eat every day of his life is personal. They call it business. OK. But it's personal as hell . . . The godfather. If a bolt of lightning hit a friend of his, the old man would take it personal. That's what makes him great. The great Don. He takes everything personal. Like God."

For his part, the hotheaded Sonny doesn't even attempt to pay lip service to the concept that it's just business, bluntly rolling over Tom Hagen's counsel and shouting out: "They shot my father—business my ass!" In framing Sonny's response, Puzo and Coppola have actually underscored the universal; it is, in fact, personal for all of us, and in Sonny's cut-to-the-chase rationale for starting the five-families war, we all find echoes of our own lives. In the brilliant television series *The Sopranos*, Tony Soprano still attempts the "it's business, not personal" rationale, explicitly stating, "It's business. We're soldiers. We follow codes . . . orders." However, even as he espouses this philosophy, he reacts in a blisteringly hot-tempered fashion, taking every slight, perceived or real, in highly personal fashion. With a mother who puts out a contract on him, how could it ever be otherwise?

Brilliant *The Godfather*'s storytelling may be, but it is certainly not flawless; one misses the novel's nuanced explanation that Michael can return home from Sicily because a Bocchicchio family member already on death row has been paid off to take the rap for the murder of McCluskey. The Bocchicchio family will now be handsomely rewarded for its help, the underlying reasoning running along the lines of, "He's going to die anyway. Might as well let him take the rap and make some money for the family in the bargain." It's a display of ruthless peasant logic that dovetails nicely with the novel's prevailing ethos, and in its satisfying toughness this byzantine plot twist provides a textured cynicism that could only have added to the film.

This is, however, a small caveat. For the most part, Coppola and Puzo have crafted an engrossing screenplay that streamlines the sprawling novel with a slick professionalism. Even with the constant shifts and turns of the plot, the screenwriters still manage to add the smallest of details, which simultaneously heighten and undercut the allure of the Corleones at the most unexpected of moments. When the hulking Luca Brasi straps on his bulletproof vest before meeting with Sollozzo and the Tattaglia family, the strains of "Have Yourself a Merry Little Christmas" play softly in the background, an ironic melding of Christmas music with expected violence. Having glimpsed the bulletproof vest, the audience is now anticipating gunplay, but when Brasi meets Sollozzo, he is stabbed in the hand and killed by garroting. It is, in the words of Coppola's own notebook, a "beautiful piece of misdirection."

After ensuring that audiences empathize with Don Vito throughout the first half of the film, the screenwriters then proceed to upend all expectations with a near-fatal assassination attempt, causing this favorite audience character to promptly recede into the background. Such plotting constitutes a bold move on the writers' part, yet audience interest is actually now heightened because of Michael's unexpected emergence as his father's heir apparent. It's a dynastic succession handled by a simple but astutely judged piece of dialogue, with Michael visiting his father in the hospital and literally standing over him while murmuring a comforting "I'm with you now—I'm with you."

The torch has been passed, with an entirely new set of mob dynamics put into play. Equally compelling as his father, but more complex and certainly colder, Michael Corleone represents the Cinderella story so beloved by audiences, but one here recast in distinctly Italian-American terms. The nearly forgotten "different" son has turned into the family king, a Cinderella-like rise granted a noticeable twist: far from being rewarded for goodness, by the end of *The*

Godfather, this underdog has morphed into a powerful, unprecedented personification of evil.

Coppola's streamlined storytelling is matched by his unadorned visual style and technical mastery. Rarely if ever calling attention to his own directorial touches, he uses camera placement in service of story and revelation of character, employing the trademark Hitchcock technique of overhead camera shots only at the moments of greatest tension. When Michael arrives at the hospital to visit his father after the attempted assassination of the don, he notices—as does the audience—that the hospital is unnaturally quiet, the only sign of life a half-eaten sandwich left at the nurse's station. As he walks down the empty corridors of the hospital in anxious search of his father, everyday objects begin to acquire an aura of menace, the tension growing with each stride. Combining the ominous sound of footsteps echoing down deserted corridors with the overhead shots that heighten the sense of foreboding, Coppola achieves a Hitchcockian level of audience response, part dread and part excitement, until Michael opens the door to his father's room and finds . . .

Although Coppola has publicly stated that he does not particularly enjoy violence on the screen, he managed to film each of *The Godfather*'s dozen-odd murders in unique fashion. The climactic murders of Michael's enemies prove gruesome and exciting in equal measure, with the sequence neatly capped by the garroting of brother-in-law Carlo as he sits in the front seat of his car. It's a measure of Coppola's skill as a filmmaker that, repulsive as the murder of Carlo is, it remains mesmerizing from start to finish, right down to the artfully detailed touch of Carlo's feet crashing through the front windshield of the car as he draws his final breaths.

The quieter scenes in the film are staged in just as memorable a fashion, the lighting and framing that create the different playing areas of the don's shadowy study never calling attention to themselves, the characters existing on-screen as near-unmoving figures fixed in time and space. When taken together, such technical elements add another level to the intended contrast between the seductive environment of the don's study, and the terrible deeds set in motion therein. Nothing excites an audience more than characters balanced on a knife's edge, and in the don's mysterious study, characters' fates teeter on the edge of the abyss.

Although Coppola's collaboration with Gordon Willis grew into a harmonious one during the shooting of parts II and III, the interaction between the two on the first film often proved contentious. Willis's painstaking, time-consuming methods produced shots of great beauty but frustrated Coppola by cutting down on the time available for additional takes. For his part, Willis chafed at what he deemed the director's chronic indecisiveness, with Coppola's constant last-minute changes necessitating continual relighting. In the end, however, their joint striving for perfection resulted in a unified visual style that conveyed volumes of detail about each different on-screen locale.

The look that the two men crafted for the Sicilian sequences is deliberately gentler than that found in the shots of New York City, the lighter visual palette representing a manifestation of love for the old country and *la via vecchia*. By using different exposure levels for the Sicilian location shoots, Coppola and Willis created landscapes that seem suffused with Michael's romantic love for Apollonia; the harsh Sicilian countryside remains bathed in a glow so shimmering that one half expects an Italian shepherd to wander by warbling, "There's a bright golden haze on the meadow."

So smoothly do the talents of Coppola, Willis, and gifted production designer Dean Tavoularis mesh throughout all three films that the finished movies seem to unspool as the product of a single vision. Building on Tavoularis's prodigious research of photographs and historical settings, the first film succeeds in crafting a nigh onto perfect, eerily accurate re-creation of midcentury American life. If, in the words of Stephen Sondheim, "The art of making art is putting it together . . . bit by bit . . . every little detail plays a part," Tavoularis here succeeds in creating film art. It is his design of the settings for all of the five-family meetings that reinforces Coppola's central metaphor of the mob as another facet of American capitalism. It's more than the meetings being conducted in the cool tones and understated words found in any board meeting of a major American corporation; it's the very look of the boardrooms that underscores the message, the tables, lights, and fixtures right out of mid–twentieth century corporate America. (The look of such meeting rooms even changes throughout the three films, the increasingly impersonal look reflecting Michael Corleone's chillier, less personal—indeed faceless—style.) Careful viewers can even sense the passage of time simply by noting Tavoularis's planting of one telling detail: in the later sections of the first film, Don Corleone's study features a television set in the corner. Ten years have passed since Connie Corleone's wedding reception, and Don Vito, like most Americans, now owns a television set. By just such details was the character-specific look of the Corleone compound painstakingly achieved.

Coordinated by Tavoularis, art director Warren Clymer, set decorator Philip Smith, and costume designer Anna Hill Johnstone, the physical production, complete with period-accurate hospital equipment, cameras, clothes, books, magazines, and appliances, achieved a verisimilitude that viewers found irresistible. It's not just the obvious props like automobiles that read as period specific; it's also the utensils, glassware, and dishes, right down to the frying pan used by Clemenza as he prepares his tomato sauce. Street signs, posters pasted onto the side of city buildings, overhead streetlights—taken together, the endless details all combine to create the very feel of the Corleone world.

Even Don Vito's Genco olive oil offices were carefully stocked with period-looking cans of olive oil; all it took was one quick pan of the Genco premises, and I felt as if I were inside my grandfather's grocery store on Division Street. For my father, the sense memory triggered by the film proved much more profound, the interior shots of the Genco premises instantly recalling his own childhood. For me, as for so many, Coppola's film supplied missing bits of sense memory, providing a near-palpable feel for the grocery store I knew only from family photographs. Here, in these fleeting frames, lay my equivalent of the trips down memory lane undertaken by suburban paesanos visiting Little Italy. Like them I was in search of authenticity. They sensed it in the remnants of the old neighborhood. I found it in the visions of Francis Ford Coppola and Dean Tavoularis.

Full credit for the film's success must also be granted to editors William Reynolds and Peter Zinner, who allowed scenes to unfold at a relaxed tempo that mirrored the tone and pace of this bygone world. The deliberate rhythm of the extended sequences granted audiences the time to slowly immerse themselves in the complex world of Don Corleone (it is Zimmer whom Coppola credits with the highly effective decision to add organ music to the climactic frenzy of crosscutting between the baptism of young Michael Rizzi and the violent murders of Michael Corleone's enemies). Viewers watching the film in the new millennium are likely to be struck anew by the smooth editing and measured pace, styles so unlike the unceasingly frenetic style of quick cuts that sprang to prominence after the birth of MTV in the 1980s.

Stunning as it is to look at, *The Godfather* provides just as extraordinary a listening experience, thanks to the beautiful and now iconic score composed by Nino Rota. Hard as it may be to credit, that haunting music was actually deemed "terrible" by Robert Evans when first he heard it, his dislike proving so severe that he demanded the entire score be thrown out. It was only after a test screening for a group of forty viewers elicited raves for the music that Rota's soon-to-be Academy Award–nominated score was saved. (His nomination was subsequently dismissed because he had previously used several minutes of the same music in the Italian film *Fortunella*.) *From "Don Pasquale" (Donizetti opera)*

Never overblown, indeed often spare and subtle, Rota's melancholy score conveys layers of Old World attitudes that haunt not just the ear but, even more significantly, the emotions of the audience. Performed on solo trumpet, the film opening "Godfather Waltz" suggests the sound of *la via vecchia* all by itself, the sad music weaving in and around both dialogue and image, simultaneously saluting the immigrant spirit and mourning a way of life already in the process of vanishing. Like the best film scoring, Rota's music conveys acres of information about the characters, if even on a subliminal level; when Michael visits his father in the hospital, thereby saving him from another assassination attempt, the minor-keyed "New Godfather" theme pushes through to the foreground for the first time, linking the two godfathers through the idea of dynastic succession.

The music heard throughout the film was not just the work of Rota but also that of Coppola's father, Carmine. In addition to composing the mood-setting incidental music heard at Connie's wedding reception, as well as the live music played at the gatherings set in Sicily, the senior Coppola even managed to tuck in a cameo as the piano-playing mobster glimpsed when the family "goes to the mattresses" at the start of the five-families war. Francis's championing of his father's music brought Carmine the recognition so long denied him and led to his work on the two subsequent *Godfather* sequels, an Academy Award shared with Nino Rota for part II, and the career-peak experience of composing his massive, majestic score for the restored version of Abel Gance's silent masterpiece *Napoléon*. In parts II and III, Carmine Coppola proved particularly skilled at underlining the near-operatic nature of the events through the repeated use of musical motifs; with their deliberate recurrence at crucial moments, his musical themes served as both reminders of past events and emotional cues commenting on Michael's inexorable decline. (Director Coppola's extraordinary attention to sound goes beyond his father's score to include such memorable touches as the crunching of pebbles underneath Michael's feet just before he has brother-in-law Carlo killed. Given the director's fidelity to the everyday rhythms of Italian-American life, one can only wish that he had added the sight and sound of one further essential feature of the characters' adherence to the Roman Catholic Church: the clicking of rosary beads.)

The contributions of Carmine Coppola, Gordon Willis, and Dean Tavoularis proved invaluable to the success of the film, but even without any of their high-level support, Marlon Brando's performance as Don Corleone would still have landed with extraordinary force. A mixture of familial warmth and quietly spoken murderous intent, Brando's portrayal deservedly won him the Academy Award for Best Actor. Never eschewing improvisation—the cat with whom he memorably plays in the film's opening scene simply happened to be wandering by on the set—the actor nonetheless prepared in meticulous fashion, his physical transformation guided by hours of time spent pondering the correct look and sound for an aging Mafia chief.

So spot on were Brando's initial instincts about Don Vito's physicality that the film's makeup man, Dick Smith, used Brando's original "audition" decisions as the basis for his final makeup. Combining old-age stipple (liquid latex compound), age spots, and dark brown dye for Brando's blond-gray hair, Smith and Brando succeeded in turning a forty-seven-year-old world-famous actor into an aging Italian immigrant. Conceiving the don's speech patterns as central to the mobster's personality, after listening to tapes of the Kefauver hearings provided by Coppola the actor further based part of his characterization on the gravel-voiced mob chieftain Frank Costello (who was, like Don Vito, known to disdain involvement in the distribution of drugs). Hoarse he may have been, but Brando deliberately decided to speak in a soft voice, reasoning simply and accurately: "Powerful people don't need to shout."

Brando felt simpatico with the character of Don Corleone, and his deliberately soft speaking voice dovetailed nicely with his decision to avoid all histrionics: "after I had read the book I decided that the part of Don Corleone lent itself perfectly to underplaying." In Brando's view, Don Corleone represented the typical immigrant's desire to survive in the strange new world of America: "I had a great deal of respect for Don Corleone; I saw him as a man of substance, tradition, dignity, refinement, a man of unerring instinct who just happened to live in a violent world and who had to protect himself and his family in this environment."

Finding himself in agreement with Coppola's conception of the Mafia as a metaphor for the rapacious world of American business, Brando became intrigued by the possibilities of delivering an indictment of American greed while entertaining a mass audience: "The story is about the corporate mind, because the Mafia is the best example of capitalists we have." Given Brando's outspoken political beliefs, it's not surprising that he further analyzed, "The key phrase in the story is . . . 'just business, nothing personal.' When I read that, McNamara, Johnson, and Rusk flashed before my eyes." The politically outspoken Brando found numerous, if unfortunate, parallels between the Mafia and the United States government: "At the time we made the film in the early 70s, there were not many things you could say about the Mafia that you couldn't say about other elements in the United States. Was there much difference between mob murders and Operation Phoenix, the CIA's assassination program in Vietnam?" Herein lies a view repeatedly echoed by Coppola himself, who baldly stated: "What's the difference between the United States' putting a guy like Trujillo in power so our companies can operate in the Dominican Republic, and the Mafia's handing the Boston territory to one of its capos?" So in sync did Brando feel with Don Corleone that at times he seemed to tacitly approve of the Mafia's methods: "I wonder what would happen if instead of having politicians swear on a Bible, we required politicians to promise to be honest at the price of having their feet encased in cement and dropped into the Potomac if they weren't. Political corruption would drop automatically."

Scrutinizing every one of Don Vito's words and motives, it was Brando who refused to speak the novel's most famous line—"A lawyer with his briefcase can steal more than a thousand men with guns." It's an extraordinarily cynical line, one in keeping with the tone of the novel, but, as Brando correctly reasoned, it seems more suited to the coldly murderous Michael than the calculating but paternalistic Don Vito. It was, instead, Brando's reading of "make him an offer he can't refuse," the memorable guttural inflection immediately ripe for parody, that became the punch line heard round the world.

Great as Brando is, however, it is Pacino's characterization of Michael that even more thoroughly dominates the film. Based on the finished film, it seems hard to credit now, but the Paramount brass were, in fact, greatly dissatisfied with the actor's work during the first week of shooting. (Peter Bart has written that Pacino was so certain that he'd be fired that during the early stages of filming the actor "was drinking heavily every night.") While the rumors that he was going to be fired have, over the years, grown out of all proportion to the actual front-office dissatisfaction, it did take the dailies of the pivotal scene in which Michael kills McCluskey and Sollozzo to convince executives of Pacino's abilities. In this one sequence (based on the 1931 Coney Island restaurant murder of Joe "The Boss" Masseria), all of the emotions underlying Michael's descent into the realm of murder are transmitted through Pacino's eyes, his character's silent decision to kill punctuated only by the rumbling sound of the subway train in the background. When Michael emerges from the men's room with the gun that had been hidden in the toilet tank but pauses before shooting his enemies, the audience is actually concerned that he won't have the courage to follow through on his decision to avenge his father's death. Pacino's performance is here so convincing in its silent power that the audience finds itself willing Michael down the path to murder. Michael wants revenge—and so too does the audience. (Such was the force of Pacino's transformation in this scene, the turning point in the evolution of Michael Corleone from college graduate/war hero to mobster/assassin, that when the idea of an intermission for the film was still being floated, this was to be the end of the film's first half.) Fortunately for all involved, the filming of this restaurant shootout occurred a mere eight days into shooting, and once executives saw the range of Pacino's performance in the sequence— uncertainty playing over his face right before he grimly draws the gun and shoots both men at point-blank range—his continued employment was assured.

None of the effort behind Pacino's meticulously conceived characterization ever shows. Beginning with an all-American, indeed almost shy, manner in his opening scenes, Pacino conveys Michael's rise to power not just through his eyes but also through a change in his posture and an increasingly cold demeanor. By the time Michael confronts Vegas rival Moe Greene regarding a casino buyout, he cuts directly through Greene's condescension with a casual display of supreme arrogance. Audiences responded to the dark truth behind Pacino's performance, particularly to the nonverbal elements of characterization that delineated a man at his most dangerous when fully silent. Indeed, part of the brilliance of Pacino's and Brando's performances—and brilliant they are—lies in their nonverbal ways of embodying iron-willed control; no matter the on-screen situation, father and son alike remain men of few words and even fewer displays of impulse. With impassive faces and a mere tilt of the head, they radiate an unquestioned power that ensures the fulfillment of their every wish.

It's interesting—and more than a little startling—to learn that Pacino based part of his characterization on Coppola himself: "Partly I did Francis, partly I modeled him from several people I know . . . [Francis] is a strange kind of man. He's a voyeur that way. I never saw the likes of him. He can detach like nobody I've ever seen. For a man that emotionally powerful to be able to detach the way he does . . . like Michael Corleone. That's why Francis understood that character." Whomever Pacino holds as his role model, his eyes grow progressively colder and more distant throughout, until finally and irrevocably they lie empty, devoid of any humanity. The fact that while filming progressed Pacino had to undergo a gradual yet complete shift of character entirely out of sequence makes his achievement all the more impressive. There is nary a false note in his beautifully shaded performance and none of the shouting and chewing of scenery that would come to mar portions of his later screen work. As it is, his Academy Award–winning performance in *Scent of a Woman* does not hold a candle to the subtle gradations on display in all three *Godfather* films.

As the date for the film's opening grew close, the advance buzz on Pacino's performance, as well as the hype regarding what many were calling Brando's "comeback," created enormous expectations for the film. Opening on March 15, 1972, *The Godfather* delivered beyond the filmmakers' highest expectations. Reviews proved to be overwhelmingly favorable, with Charles Champlin in *The Los Angeles Times* terming it "an instant classic" and the esteemed Pauline Kael delivering the kind of quotation producers dream of receiving: "If ever there was a great example of how the best popular movies come out of a merger of commerce and art, *The Godfather* is it."

Not all the critics praised the epic, however, with some calling it "overlong," and Stanley Kauffman of *The New Republic* turning vitriolic in his condemnation: "They have put pudding in Brando's cheeks and dirtied his teeth, he speaks hoarsely and moves stiffly and these combined mechanics are hailed as great acting. Like star, like film, the key note is inflation." In the end, such naysayers proved to be in a decided minority, and as the grosses continued to skyrocket, the film grew into a juggernaut. Box-office champion, critical favorite, and inspiration for would-be filmmakers and stand-up comedians alike, *The Godfather* had very quickly acquired status as a worldwide cultural phenomenon.

The Godfather may have helped define the zeitgeist of the early 1970s, but the film has stood the test of time because it works as both an epic multigenerational saga (*Time* magazine called it a film with the "dynastic sweep of an Italian-American *Gone With the Wind*") and as the story of one family. Filled with beautiful, mood-setting cinematography, haunting music, and the now-legendary performances of Pacino and Brando, the film delivers on all levels. If, as W. P. Ker's definition would have it, a heroic epic is "the defense of a narrow place against odds," then with *The Godfather* the gangster/crime film had been successfully recodified and updated as both heroic epic and family saga. Granting audiences the tools with which to reexamine themselves has always remained the province of first-rank artists like Coppola, and in his meditation on power, money, and the nature of America itself, he succeeded in creating a new film genre complete unto itself: sociology as rapid-fire entertainment.

The redefinitions resulting from *The Godfather* did not stop with the audience but extended to the nature of Hollywood itself. The blockbuster rollout and extraordinary worldwide nature of the film's success came to influence the very manner in which Hollywood henceforth conducted business. As pointed out by author Harlan Lebo, in the wake of *The Godfather* producers began "investing more money in script development, bestselling books and new technology, and using broad new marketing techniques, thus beginning a trend toward large-scale box-office successes beyond anything ever seen before in the industry."

New marketing techniques in place, *The Godfather* received an impressive ten nods when Academy Award nominations were announced on February 13, 1973 (eleven if one includes the subsequently disallowed Nino Rota score). Only one egregious oversight marred the announcements, the nominators having ignored the beautiful mood-setting cinematography of Gordon Willis. Perhaps even more important to Paramount executives and the board of Gulf&Western was the fact that, thanks to some canny deal making, the studio had retained an unusually high 84 percent of the profits; this figure proved doubly significant when the film's multiple Academy Award nominations drove the worldwide grosses to the then-unheard-of level of several hundred million dollars, most of which ended up in the Gulf&Western coffers.

On the night of the actual awards ceremonies, Bob Fosse's *Cabaret* took home the most Oscars—eight to *The Godfather's* three—and while Coppola lost the award for Best Director to Fosse, he did win a well-deserved Oscar for Best Screenplay with Puzo. Further sweet consolation ensued when *The Godfather* won the biggest prize of all—Best Picture. (Producer Ruddy, who received the Oscar for Best Picture, won a second Oscar thirty-plus years later for producing

Clint Eastwood's *Million Dollar Baby*). With the imprimatur of the Academy Awards forever branded onto *The Godfather*, the on-screen Mafia had now officially passed into the land of indestructible myth.

As for Brando, the acclaim that had immediately greeted his performance resulted in his receiving a second Academy Award as Best Actor. True to his idiosyncratic nature, he refused the Oscar, sending Native American Sacheen Littlefeather, a former "Miss Vampire of 1970," to read a statement explaining that he would not accept the award because of the film industry's depiction of Native Americans. (Ironically, Littlefeather's heritage was not exclusively Native American, consisting, as it did, of French, German, and Dutch ancestry on her mother's side, along with the Native American bloodline of her father.) Word of Brando's fifteen-page speech having leaked out ahead of time, the show's producer, Howard Koch, intercepted Littlefeather before the announcement of the award for Best Actor and informed her that the time allocated for her remarks would be limited to one minute. Ad-libbing a sixty-second version of Brando's polemic, she was greeted with a mixture of applause and boos.

Brando's love/hate relationship with acting continued through the decades, and it ultimately made a perfect kind of sense that he would eventually parody the role of Don Vito on-screen, doing so in the 1990 film *The Freshman*. In paying a return visit to the land of the Mafia, Brando, portraying mob boss Carmine Sabatini, essentially reprised the character of Vito Corleone, but this time to comic effect. The actor made further peace with the shadow of Don Vito when, toward the end of his life, he recorded voice tracks for the official licensed *Godfather* video game (a game that Coppola, interestingly enough, condemned: "The game has taken the work we all did on the film, and transferred it into a 'kill or be killed' slaughter session"). Even after his death, the allure of Brando's godfather persona continued unabated, and in 2005, one year after he died, his heavily annotated script from the film sold for a record $312,800. In the end, the best summation of his complicated feelings about *The Godfather* came in his autobiography, *Songs My Mother Taught Me*: "When I saw *The Godfather* the first time, it made me sick; all I could see were my mistakes and I hated it. But years later, when I saw it on television from a different perspective, I decided it was a pretty good film."

To say the least.

When the legend becomes fact, print the legend. *Photofest*

8   Frank Sinatra

Sinatra told the truth no matter what. He is probably the last fa-mous person who didn't give a damn what you thought. He would tell you what he was thinking. And nobody ever told Frank Sinatra what to say, except maybe his mother.

—BILL ZEHME, *NEWSWEEK*, MAY 25, 1998

FRANK SINATRA, THE MOST famous Italian-American of all, intersects with the myth of *The Godfather* in endless, variable permutations. Mountains of ink have been spilled over Sinatra's alleged associa-tion with the Mafia, the resulting articles building on whispers, innuendo, and veiled accusations in order to pose and suggestively answer the ever-churning questions: Was Sinatra in the mob? Did Puzo base the character of singer-turned-actor Johnny Fontane on Sinatra? Exactly how did Sinatra land his career-making comeback role in the film *From Here to Eternity*? Was a horse's head involved? Interesting questions all, but striking as the parallels between Sina-tra and Johnny Fontane may be, the real interest here lies in the sheer scope of Sinatra's life. It's his extraordinary six-decade run in the public eye, the very Italian-ness of his talent, persona, and cultural shadow that refract the questions raised by *The Godfather* into the boldest, most elemental issues inherent in matters of American cultural identity.

Frank Sinatra lived his life as a defiantly proud Italian-American, one whose ethnic heritage informed the most important aspects of his art. Yet even for Sinatra himself, especially in his early years, pride in heritage was occasionally tinged by a propensity for the minstrel-show characterizations of Italian-Americans found on the radio series *Life with Luigi*. That radio serial's cast, led by the non-Italian J. Carrol Naish, spoke with exaggerated dis-a dat-a accents, and in Sinatra's own words: "I would hate myself for laughing at the goddamned thing." It didn't take long for Sinatra to outgrow the cartoonish nature of *Life with Luigi,* however, and one of the many reasons why he was determined to parlay his life's work as a singer into a major film career lay in his desire to offer an alternative version of Italian-American life on-screen. In the early 1940s, when Sinatra's screen career began in earnest, public role models were few, with the A to C range of Italian-Americans on-screen featuring either an organ-grinder with monkey, a murderous gangster, or a simpleminded paesano happy to squeeze-a da melons in his grocery store. In none of the roles did the Italian-American male ever evince a genuine intellect.

Such one-dimensional characters constituted the stereotypes that Mario Puzo attempted to avoid with his own novels, not only in *The Godfather* but also in his earlier works, *The Dark Arena* and *The Fortunate Pilgrim.* Said Puzo: "I never heard an Italian singing. None of the grown-ups I knew were charming or loving or understanding. So later in life when I was exposed to all the clichés of lovable Italians, singing Italians, happy-go-lucky Italians I wondered where the hell the moviemakers and storywriters got all their ideas from."

As for Sinatra, after beginning his screen career in lighthearted

MGM musicals, he made a conscious decision to seek out tougher, dramatic roles, none of which found him portraying the lovable happy-go-lucky Italians to whom Puzo referred. Instead, he portrayed men of complexity and oftentimes torment, their Italian subtext consistently present even when the character's surname did not end in a vowel. Has there ever been a darker screen idol than Frank Sinatra? One never pictures him on sunny suburban lawns romping with children. Instead, he strides rain-slicked nighttime city streets, morose, angry, vulnerable, but always fully human. What's most startling about Sinatra's Italian-ness, overt or subtextual, is that even at the start of his career in the late 1930s, a time when ethnicity was still something to be hidden, he remained defiantly and proudly Italian. Hide his ethnicity? Sinatra did just the opposite, refusing to change his name and underlining his heritage at every possible juncture. Italian-Americans loved Sinatra for this proud self-assertion, and in the 1940s and 1950s, his picture could be found in Italian-American homes right alongside those of FDR and Jesus.

Pride in ethnicity underlay Sinatra's appeal not just to Italians but also to immigrants of all nationalities. If he offended establishment sensibilities in the process—audiences who enjoyed the singing but not the public persona—the answer from Sinatra was a resounding "a fangoul." Sinatra seemed to revel in misbehaving, and for all his occasional vulgarity, audiences thrilled to his bravado and urban Italian street smarts. "If only," they thought. "If only I too could do it my way." In Thomas Ferraro's apt analysis, "In his youth, Frankie Sinatra was *an* urban villager; as a professional singer, Frank Sinatra showed the world what it meant to be *the* urban villager." As the urban villager, such was the reach and scope of Sinatra's power that when the *Apollo* astronauts undertook their historic first trip to the moon, the music that accompanied them on their otherworldly journey was Frank Sinatra singing "Fly Me to the Moon." Whether on this planet or the next, Frank Sinatra succeeded in making sure that his music provided what Albert Murray so accurately termed the "soundtrack to which we choreograph our daily activities."

By the time of *The Godfather*'s publication in 1969, Sinatra had long since become the most successful Italian-American entertainer in the history of the United States. Already acclaimed as "the" vocalist of the twentieth century, he had parlayed his singing talent into an equally important second career as an Academy Award–winning actor, top-ten Hollywood box-office attraction, and legendary movie star. As such, he actually spoke to Francis Ford Coppola about playing the role of Don Vito Corleone in the film version of *The Godfather*. According to Puzo's *Godfather Papers,* Sinatra and Coppola ran into each other in a Los Angeles club, whereupon Sinatra embraced Coppola and stated: "Francis, I'd play the Godfather for you. I wouldn't do it for those guys at Paramount, but I'd do it for you." Given Sinatra's decree that he would proceed if he and Coppola could buy back the rights from Paramount, the idea of such casting never progressed any further.

With his wide range as actor, Sinatra certainly could have handled the role of Vito with ease, blunt statements and veiled remarks both coming easily to him. When asked by his friend Vic Damone for advice as to whether he should accept the role of Johnny Fontane, Sinatra offered the capable-of-many-interpretations statement, "It's up to you, pal . . . You've got to make up your own mind. I can't tell you what you should do." At the other end of the spectrum, at the height of ex-wife Mia Farrow's troubles with Woody Allen, Sinatra, in Farrow's words, "even offered to break Woody's legs." Would Sinatra have been willing to submerge his own look and persona into that of an aging Mafia chieftain? It's an unanswerable question; he was never one for extensive makeup on-screen (although makeup always hid the neck scars that had resulted from the use of forceps during his difficult birth), and aside from a disastrous attempt at playing a Spanish peasant in *The Pride and the Passion,* eschewed any change in his voice. On the other hand, he thoroughly understood the character of a man who, like Sinatra himself, wielded great influence and reveled in his own power; if Don Vito spoke calmly of having judges and politicians in his pocket, Sinatra too enjoyed his thoroughly personal, if legal, relationships with presidents ranging from John Kennedy to Richard Nixon and Ronald Reagan.

Would there have been too many distracting layers of association for an audience if Sinatra, with his long-rumored mob associations, had played a mob boss in a film that included a character based on Sinatra himself? Chances are that the audience would have been widely split in its reaction, but Puzo certainly understood the Sinatra persona, writing of the singer, circa 1972: "He's the secret idol of every guilt ridden American male. No other famous man has managed to divorce his wife yet retain control of her life and the lives of their children, guiding them all to happiness and success while jealously guarding his own personal freedom."

Sinatra's relationship with *The Godfather* was famously complicated by his decided antipathy toward Puzo's creation of the too-close-for-comfort Johnny Fontane. Even the most casual of readers immediately understood that the character of Italian-American singer-turned-actor Johnny Fontane followed the arc of Sinatra's life and career very closely; like Sinatra, Fontane leaves his first wife in order to marry a beautiful Hollywood star (read Ava Gardner). Falling on hard times, Fontane eyes a blockbuster Hollywood film (think *From Here to Eternity*) as the key to a life-altering comeback. With the help of a Mafia godfather and a severed horse's head, Fontane's comeback is assured, a novelistic invention that particularly infuriated Sinatra and ensured that generations of readers and moviegoers would draw the same—and erroneous—conclusion about Sinatra's own award-winning comeback in *From Here to Eternity*.

It is this incident of the horse's head that accounts for the most notorious overlay of the Sinatra legend with the mob, the supposed parallels suggesting, at their most pernicious, that even the supremely talented Sinatra proved a success only because of mob influence. No matter the walk of life, for many observers "Italian" still equaled "mobster." In the public's persistent belief in the myth that the mob engineered Sinatra's comeback would seem to lie the real-life embodiment of the famous line from the classic John Ford film *The Man Who Shot Liberty Valance*: "When the legend becomes fact, print the legend."

Johnny Fontane may have landed his comeback with the help of his godfather Don Vito, but the real-life story of how Sinatra won his role in *From Here to Eternity* is every bit as interesting as the fantasy of the horse's head. By the early 1950s, Sinatra had lost both his film and recording contracts, and with no viable career prospects in sight, became obsessed with playing the role of Maggio in *From Here to Eternity*. Convinced he was the only person who could properly play the character—"in it I saw myself as clearly as I see myself every morning when I shave. I was Maggio"—and understanding that the character's juicy dramatic possibilities could spell Academy Award, Sinatra bombarded director Fred Zinnemann and producer Buddy Adler with telegrams signed "Maggio." Jobless and hanging around the African set of wife Ava Gardner's movie *Mogambo*, Sinatra, by then a veteran of twenty films, humbled himself to audition, flying back to Hollywood on his own dime for a ten-minute test (Sinatra was broke and owed the IRS money, so the flight turned out to be on Ava's dime, which she learned only after the fact). Even after Sinatra's first-rate test, the filmmakers still preferred Eli Wallach for the role, but Wallach begged off, preferring a starring role on Broadway in the Tennessee Williams play *Camino Real*. With the executives at the Harry Cohn–led Columbia Pictures wavering, Ava Gardner approached Cohn's wife and then Cohn himself, barking: "You know who's right for the part of Maggio, don't you? That son of a bitch of a husband of mine." The part was Sinatra's.

There was never any talk of Sinatra himself playing Johnny Fontane, but the intersection of character and mob deepened even further when it came time to cast *The Godfather*. The role was first offered to singer and part-time actor Vic Damone, who turned down the part for reasons variously rumored to be not enough money, too small a part, a none-too-subtle hint from the mob that he should not play the role, and a godfather-like fear of provoking Sinatra. (Having survived his own offstage problems with the mob, Damone certainly could have brought real-life experience to the role; early in his career, the singer had a disagreement with his then-fiancée Franny D'Angelo, the daughter of upstate New York mob boss Johnny D'Angelo. Father Johnny's solution to the disagreement was to try and throw Damone out of a fourteenth-story window in midtown Manhattan's Edison Hotel. The singer was saved only by the arrival of a friend.) Ultimately, Johnny Fontane was played by singer Al Martino in all three *Godfather* films, a somewhat fitting turn of events, given that Martino's own career had, along with Sinatra's life story, served as a partial model for Fontane. Indeed, shortly after the novel's publication, singer Phyllis McGuire, the girlfriend of mobster Sam Giancana, said to her friend Martino: "I just read a book, *The Godfather*. Al, Johnny Fontane is you, and I know you can play it in the movie."

In a plotline straight out of *The Godfather*, Martino himself had suffered through problems with the mob arising out of his contract with a personal manager. According to Martino, the mob threatened his personal manager with bodily harm if the manager failed to sign over the contract for free. The singer subsequently fired the mobsters as his managers, and, after disobeying their edict that he never again accept work on the East Coast, was savagely beaten in a nightclub parking lot. After signing a promissory note for the $80,000 that the mob told him represented "future earnings, the money we could have made off of you," the singer departed immediately for Europe, staying overseas for eight years. As detailed in Lebo's *The Godfather Legacy,* "He came back when he felt 'the heat was off.'" That peace was achieved in 1958, when in Martino's own recollection, he "called Angelo Bruno, 'the Gentle Don,' to broker his return."

Convinced he was the perfect choice for the role of Fontane, Martino set about wooing the notably unimpressed Coppola with a $20,000 party. Coppola remained unconvinced, at which point, in Martino's recollection: "I had to step on some toes to get people to realize that I was in the effing movie. I went to my godfather, Russ Bufalino." Unaware that producer Ruddy had made an agreement with Martino to give him the role, Coppola had by this point picked Damone. When Damone backed out, the role finally fell to Martino. Not one to ignore any perceived slight, even years later Martino still chafed over the truncated nature of the part, claiming that he had been ostracized by Coppola on the set (a rebuff he states was joined in by everyone but Brando). Coppola himself offered a much simpler explanation for Martino's dismay: the role of Johnny Fontane was shortened in order to compensate for Martino's inexperience as an actor.

And what of the actual sequence with the severed horse's head? The short answer is that forty years on, in a film stuffed with iconic scenes, images, and dialogue, the horse's head may hold sway as the movie's single most memorable set piece. It's a scene of such visceral power that after the release of the film, Coppola received more complaints over the decapitation of this one horse than he did over the on-screen deaths of dozens of human beings.

The scene lands with extraordinary force because of how cannily Coppola and Puzo have set up Don Vito's retribution. When Hollywood studio head Woltz explodes in anger over Tom Hagen's request that help be granted Fontane—"Johnny Fontane will never get that movie! I don't care how many dago, guinea, wop, greaseball, goombahs come out of the woodwork"—the audience knows that Woltz has made a very serious mistake. It's only Woltz himself who doesn't understand the severity of the error made in underestimating Don Vito's reach and power, a state of affairs that heightens the audience's anticipation of the payback to come. That retribution comes in the early-morning hours of the next day, when Woltz slowly wakes up to the realization that the blood soaking his sheets is from the severed head of his prize stallion. Screaming in terror, tough guy Woltz is shattered, broken by men capable of far more brutality than he could ever imagine possible.

It all makes for a sequence that is gory, fascinating, disgusting, and, most of all, wildly effective, with the audience equal parts horrified and titillated: the horror results from the beheading of a beautiful animal (the head of the destined-for-the-slaughterhouse horse was shipped to the filmmakers in a crate of dry ice), while the titillation arises out of the unfathomable power of the godfather. Coppola and Puzo have constructed the scene in such highly effective fashion that, for all of the violence on display, the audience does not turn away from the godfather; no one sees the godfather himself killing the horse because he is layers removed from the deed. He has instructed Hagen, who in turn has hired henchmen the godfather undoubtedly will never meet. The audience's sympathy for the godfather remains intact.

Given the Sinatra/Fontane parallels, as well as Sinatra's own explosive temperament, it is less than surprising to learn that when an overly persistent friend of Mario Puzo insisted on introducing star and author in Chasen's restaurant, all hell broke loose. Said Al Ruddy, who had accompanied Puzo to the restaurant: "The next thing I know a fight almost broke out. Sinatra was yelling and shouting and my friends were holding Mario." According to the even more dramatic recollection of the then Paramount executive Peter Bart, who was also dining at Chasen's that night, it was Puzo himself who willingly approached Sinatra, waving away Bart's objections with the self-deluding, "But I owe Frank a greeting . . . I know he had feelings about the Johnny Fontane character." Sinatra's response when Puzo approached? "Get out of my fucking sight . . . I'll tear your fucking head off."

In another version of the contretemps, Sinatra shouted, "I ought to break your legs. Did the F.B.I. help you with your book?" And Puzo himself recalls Sinatra calling him "a pimp" and threatening to "beat the hell" out of the writer "if you weren't so old." Never missing a chance to spin a story, Puzo sardonically observed: "What hurt was that here he was a Northern Italian, threatening me, a Southern Italian, with physical violence. This was roughly equivalent to Einstein pulling a knife on Al Capone." It's a great line, but only partially true; Sinatra's fair-haired mother, Dolly, did indeed hail from northern Italy, but the Sinatra clan of father Martin hailed from Sicily. North or south, Italy or America, the Sinatras knew a thing or two about tempers . . .

When Sinatra finally did watch *The Godfather,* it was at a private screening requested by the guest of honor at Sinatra's own Palm Desert home: Vice President Spiro T. Agnew. The eclectic viewing audience included Sinatra's mother, Dolly; best pal, Jilly Rizzo; comedian Jack Benny; and publisher Bennett Cerf. As related by Agnew's press secretary Victor Gold (also present at the screening)

Sinatra remained silent throughout, "exploding" with disgust only once: to express disdain for the manner in which Clemenza showed Michael how to prepare tomato sauce. The fascinating capper to the evening came when Agnew, asked what he thought of the film, replied that it was "O.K." except for Brando's performance. In the words of Gold, Agnew then "pushed the envelope" by further telling Sinatra: "You would have been better for the part." To which Sinatra, not missing a beat, narrowed his eyelids and with mock guttural, Brando-like inflection, replied, "You're right."

Even after the public fight with Puzo, some twenty years later Sinatra still seriously considered playing the role of Don Altobello in *The Godfather: Part III*—after all, in the eyes of the unceasingly career-obsessed Sinatra, a great part was a great part . . . As it happened, his flirtation with the role ended because he was neither available for, nor interested in, the long location shoot in Sicily. (Ironically, the part was played by Sinatra's *From Here to Eternity* rival Eli Wallach.) The idea was quashed for good when his wife, Barbara, always sensitive to her husband's public image, allowed as how the idea of Frank playing a Mafia chieftain was far from wonderful in her eyes.

At his frequent best, Sinatra, like Don Vito, personified the warm-hearted Italian-American male, supremely proud of his achievements, family, and heritage. Of course, hand in hand with such benevolence came huge outbursts of temper leading to Sonny-like impulsive, destructive behavior, which fit everyone's worst stereotype of southern Italian thugs. Inexcusable temper tantrums (he once threw a plate of hot pasta in the face of his valet because it wasn't cooked properly) would be followed by acts of generosity to friends and strangers alike, and it is estimated that this one-man conglomerate raised a staggering one billion dollars for charities in his lifetime. Hypersensitive to mob rumors and slurs on his ethnicity, it may just be that Sinatra's herculean efforts at raising money for charity stemmed from a hunger for respectability, like that found in Michael Corleone's gift of one hundred million dollars to establish the Vito Corleone Foundation. Perhaps the Corleone-like dichotomy in Sinatra's temperament is best summed up in his unintentionally revealing comment to rat pack pal Shirley MacLaine: "Oh, I just wish someone would try to hurt you so that I could kill them for you."

A shrewd businessman, Sinatra kept his own counsel and played his cards close to the vest. Like Don Corleone himself, he was streetwise, distrusted the establishment, and demanded control over not just the product (himself as singer and actor) but also the manner in which it was distributed. In this desire for complete autonomy lies the reason why he founded his own film-production companies as well as the record label Reprise. (In a nicely judged piece of black humor playing to his disputes with Capitol Records—and seemingly by extension to the talk of alleged mob connections that so annoyed him—Sinatra once casually stated that the company was called Reprise—with a long E—but could be pronounced Reprise, with a long I. As in . . . Reprisal.)

Power. Honor. Control. Street credibility. These very same qualities that Don Vito possesses underlie the reasons why Sinatra is respected in the black musical community in ways that elude all other white entertainers. Having experienced prejudice as an Italian-American, Sinatra always insisted on first-class treatment for African-American artists, doing so at a time when hotels and casinos still practiced segregation. The streetwise edge that Sinatra carried also goes a long way to explaining why he (like *The Godfather* itself) continues to speak to younger audiences today, in ways that will always elude the legacy of fellow Italian Perry Como, or even Bing Crosby. Immensely talented and hugely popular though he was, Crosby, even with his keen sense of jazz, possessed little in the way of street cred.

Just as the Corleones built their family compound first on Long Island and later in Lake Tahoe, Sinatra constructed his own compound in the California desert, a multihouse complex where he presided as both innkeeper and godfather. Provider of food and friendship, Frank, like Don Vito himself, inspired equal parts fear and love. No one wanted to make Sinatra mad, and even close friends like Peter Lawford found themselves instantly ex-communicated after incurring his displeasure. Pope and godfather both, he succeeded in creating his own self-contained universe.

Test his fans' patience he did, but in the end it was Sinatra's extraordinary artistry that mattered. Through his music as well as his varying screen personas—from sailor-suited musical boy next door to seen-it-all urban cop—Sinatra, like Don Vito, provided consolation, the sense that we are not alone. Both men fulfilled the role of the all-powerful paterfamilias, yet both men acknowledged the limits of their powers. Just as Don Vito gently tells his dying consiglieri Genco Abbandando that he has no powers to stave off his imminent death, Sinatra too acknowledged both his limits and the depth of the human mystery: "'You like people, . . . and they die on you. I go to too many goddamned funerals these days. And women,' he said, exhaling, and chuckling again. 'I don't know what the hell to make of them . . . Maybe that's what it's all about . . . Maybe all that happens is, you get older and you know less.'"

If Sinatra occasionally felt like he knew less than ever, audiences certainly didn't buy into it. When he put forth his "King of the Hill" routine in front of ten thousand enraptured listeners, they weren't turned off by his ego—they reveled in it. He did it his way, spinning the tale as if he was challenging his fans to do the same, and audiences loved him for the dare. Most of Sinatra's listeners didn't follow suit of course, not possessing the temperament, talent, or overwhelming need to do so, but they worshipped him all the more for the invitation. On his own unquestionably

Italian-American terms, Frank Sinatra was the local boy made good. His life represented the Horatio Alger myth incarnate, but in his hands it proved to be the Alger myth as filtered through the persona of the paesano on the street corner.

Frank Sinatra showed the world what it meant to be an American in distinctly Italian terms. Far from sacrificing his ethnicity, he immersed himself in it. Sinatra didn't want to outrun his roots: instead, he brought them with him on the journey from Hoboken to New York and on to Vegas and Hollywood. By asserting his ethnic-based hypermasculinity yet remaining unafraid of his tender feelings, Sinatra moved his fan base from women to men, from "I'll Never Smile Again" to "My Way," and in the process explicated both his cockiness and self-doubts.

"My Way" in particular registered as a quintessential expression of übermasculine individuality, one that in lesser hands could and did easily morph into poses of self-martyrdom. Sinatra ditched the self-martyring, perhaps recognizing that singing the opening words "and now the end is near" could not mean a great deal to someone who began singing the song just as he turned a very healthy fifty. Instead, he latched on to both the doomed heroism of the song's narrator, as well as his standing up to oppressive social forces; it was the latter action, of course, that happened to form the core appeal of the gangster. Never mind that gangsters themselves caused oppression by virtue of their lawbreaking behavior. Instead, it was the heroic stance that others applauded, in the Corleones and Sinatra alike.

In the end, the Sinatra family's journey of assimilation mirrored that of the Corleones. Sinatra's Italian-born grandparents emigrated to the United States, but in his own analysis never really left the Old World behind. His parents, Dolly and Martin, grew up in New Jersey and settled into life as Italian-American hyphenates, while Sinatra himself, born in the United States in 1915, always viewed himself as a proud, flag-waving American: five separate recordings of the patriotic anthem "The House I Live In" attest to this self-image. Indeed, aside from one brief phonetically sung aria in his early film *It Happened in Brooklyn,* Sinatra never recorded songs in Italian. Why not? Because for all his pride in heritage, he conceived of himself as American, occasionally as Italian-American, but decidedly not as Italian. Like Don Vito Corleone, Sinatra was an American on his own terms, and his journey of assimilation from Hoboken to New York, from Hollywood to Vegas and finally to Palm Springs, put worlds of distance between his origins and final destination. Just as proved true with the Corleones, by the time of Frank's children and more particularly his grandchildren, all traces of *la via vecchia* and the ethnic Italian ghetto had vanished. L'America reigned supreme.

Connie Corleone's wedding reception—the family at its zenith. *Photofest*

9 *La Famiglia* (di Santopietro, Corleone, *e* Coppola)

[He] did the unthinkable Italian crime. He walked out on his family. They don't even have a name for this.

—NICK SHAY IN DON DELILLO'S *UNDERWORLD*

IRONICALLY AND INEVITABLY, THE education so prized by my grandparents ended up the very instrument that pulled the family apart. The scattering began in the late 1960s, as all of the grandchildren pursued higher education and lives started anew in Georgia, California, and New York City—everywhere but Waterbury. But from the late 1950s through the late 1960s, when everyone was still healthy and living in Connecticut—before Aunt Gertrude died from the lump in her breast that she ignored, before Uncle Andrew dropped dead from a heart attack at her funeral, before the strokes, cancer, and Alzheimer's took their unceasing toll and Aunt Emma's kitchen dwindled into silence—the family gatherings glow in a memory only slightly augmented by time.

With the entire family then still living within five miles of each other, life unfolded as if the original immigrant impulse to huddle together had simply been translated into English and updated to JFK-era Connecticut. In 1961, my parents built a new house on the same street as my recently relocated grandparents, and with Aunt Emma and Uncle Carmine already living next door to my grandparents, it all rather resembled a Corleone-style compound. Granted, there did exist a few minor differences between the Santopietro/ Albino clan and the Corleones: my grandfather sold olive oil without using it as the front for a criminal empire, and, far from battling the police, my uncle Carmine actually was a cop—and an honest one. And, when my aunt Julia finally married at age fifty—living at home with her parents until the day of her wedding—the wedding reception did not exactly unfold on the same scale as Connie Corleone's.

When my beautiful aunt happily announced that she was going to marry widower Franklin Boyd, a machinist and World War II veteran with a teenage daughter, her joy was undercut by the Sonny Corleone–like protectiveness of her oldest brother, Andrew. So convinced was my uncle that Frank wanted Julia's money that the roadblocks he erected seemed insurmountable. How sad for my aunt. Here was an older brother all but publicly proclaiming, "You're not loved for yourself, just for your money." Money? My aunt worked as a timekeeper at a brass manufacturing company. My grandparents ran a grocery store, not a bank, and although they earned a solid living, they lost a great deal of money simply by carrying customers who were unable to pay their bills, particularly during the Depression. Leafing through my grandfather's dog-eared ledger, which I now possess, I was struck anew by the months and sometimes years during which he kept supplying food to these same nonpaying customers. They all came from my grandfather's village of Pontelandolfo, and, like others of his generation, my grandfather considered it his obligation to help his paesanos, passing along the help he had been granted upon arrival in the United

States. By the time of my father's generation, the first with extensive schooling, the desire to assist manifested itself in a wider circle; my father's financial records are littered with the names of patients who could not pay for his services, yet he continued to treat them, often for years at a time. The difference between the two generations lay in the fact that not all of these patients hailed from Pontelandolfo. My father's charity extended beyond his own ethnic group, a tacit acknowledgment of all the United States had made possible for father and son alike.

When viewed in conjunction with my mother's extraordinary efforts in the community—the establishment of day care centers for lower-income families; the presidencies of the Red Cross, Junior League, and child guidance clinics; the setting up of fuel banks and soup kitchens—my father's record fills me with pride as well as knowledge of my own decidedly lacking efforts at such outreach. In my less fervent attempts at charity, as well as my lack of attachment to the community at large, lies the downside of the immigrant journey. We of the third generation are solidly upper-middle-class, fully assimilated, and, for all of our electronic devices, noticeably disconnected. As Robert D. Putnam put it so aptly in his seminal 1995 book, we are all now "Bowling Alone": "Television, two-career families, suburban sprawl, generational changes in values—these and other changes in American society have meant that fewer and fewer of us find that the League of Women Voters, or the United Way, or the Shriners, or the monthly bridge club, or even a Sunday picnic with friends fits the way we have come to live. Our growing social-capital deficit threatens educational performance, safe neighborhoods, equitable tax collection, democratic responsiveness, everyday honesty, and even our health and happiness." Sad, depressing, and undeniably true.

But in 1964, the year of my aunt's marriage, communities and families were still connected, and my uncle's displeasure over his sister's engagement left our weekly family gatherings changed, as if our center of gravity had slipped a gear. For the first time in family memory, a palpable sense of unease filled the air in my grandparents' home. My uncle Andrew was a good man at heart, loved his parents, and, without children of his own, always treated his niece and three nephews with generosity and affection. Much as he loved his youngest sister, however, his impulsive nature and quick-tempered protectiveness took a decidedly erroneous and short-sighted turn when it came to the subject of her marriage. It may also of course be true that yet another level of Italian family life entered into the calculus of his thinking: with Julia single and living at home, my aging grandparents would be cared for by a loving family member. What would happen if Julia no longer lived at home?

My own parents remained firmly supportive of my aunt, welcoming Frank into the family with understanding and affection, but the wedding proved to be a very low-key affair, and at the notably subdued reception, there was certainly no Connie Corleone–like money purse, no gavonelike reminder of cash vulgarity. Just a fifty-year-old woman happy to have met a nice man, one who never spoke ill of his wife's older brother. A tough Swede from Brooklyn, Frank instantly understood that for Italian-Americans, family trumped all, and he wisely kept his silence—and the peace. Ten years old at the time, I remained baffled that anyone paid attention to Uncle Andrew's ideas. Who cared what he thought? I had a lot to learn about the place of the oldest son in an Italian immigrant family.

Uneasy truce in place, year-round family dinners continued, and over time the atmosphere eventually thawed. Week in and week out, holiday or not, the entire family gathered for Sunday dinners. Never mind church attendance; Sundays were reserved for the true religion of southern Italians—*la famiglia*. The sharing of Sunday dinner actually resembled a religious rite, the meal itself under-scoring the sense of each individual belonging to a greater commu-nal good. Eating together represented stability, a retention of the old order in the rapidly changing world of the 1960s. If it seems a stretch to say that some sort of higher spirit seemed to move around that table, it's nonetheless true that the shared laughter did gener-ate a sense of peace and well-being. Here we found a corner of un-derstanding and connection amid the chaos of everyday life, the dining room table affording a last common territory before assimi-lation triumphed and we all went our separate ways.

Even as a six-year-old, some part of me realized that my grand-mother was never happier than when preparing a Sunday meal for the entire family. As she moved ceaselessly around the kitchen that constituted the center of her universe, she would happily tolerate my relentless banging of pots and pans on the floor, her severely arthritic knees somehow bothering her less when the entire family was in attendance. In the ritual of food preparation lay certainty for her daily life.

Come each Sunday, the Anglo and Italian sides of my life would fully intersect for the first and only time of the week. With my fa-ther not given to attending church, my mother would take my sister and me to the Episcopal church and Sunday school. We would then drive to my grandmother's house for a meatball sandwich, after which we would go home, only to return one hour later for a full seven-course dinner. Why the two-stop visits? I suppose paesano Tevye in *Fiddler on the Roof* had it right—tradition. My mother was undoubtedly relieved she didn't have to cook. My father was re-lieved he didn't have to go to church. I was relieved that homework could be delayed. Church of England and meatballs all in the space of a few short hours.

When we returned to my grandmother's for the complete Sun-day dinner, we were greeted by the bounteous dishes of basic peasant Italian cooking now all the rage in twenty-first-century Manhattan. (When I ate at Torrisi, the hottest Italian restaurant in New York City, I found the extraordinary cooking to be sublime— and almost as good as that of my grandmother. Maria Valletta Santopietro could make her fortune cooking her favorite dishes today, a concept she would find laughable and inconceivable in equal measure.) Antipasto; roasted chicken with sliced, quartered potatoes crisped in olive oil; pasta swimming in homemade tomato sauce; meatballs; sausage; fresh Italian bread; salads of field greens— dish after dish arrived, one course flowing into another until silverware ceased clinking and plates were cleared—just in time for dessert.

Great the food was, but it proved secondary to the concept of family togetherness. Multiple conversations at the same time proved the norm, with revelations of my father and his siblings as youngsters, glimpses into the past that I found simultaneously amusing and slightly disconcerting. Does any child really want to learn about his parents' youthful possibilities? What if my parents hadn't met? What if my father had married his girlfriend Vonda? What if, what if, what if?

Above all, laughter floated around the table, and I retain the sweet, silly memory of being seven and making the entire dining room laugh as I imitated President Kennedy's Boston accent. Banter about one another's foibles remained central to the conversation, and if the teasing of one another was allowed, indeed almost encouraged, just let an outsider try the same thing and a Corleonelike protectiveness instantly emerged. When my cousin Don first brought his Irish-American fiancée, Anne, to meet the entire family, she immediately remarked on the laughter and nonstop talking at the table: "The warmth of it all," she wistfully recalled years later. "Such happiness. If only we had known."

These weekly celebrations of food and family provided the opportunities so essential to the immigrant experience—the celebrating of one another's existence. Here. Now. Not in the future and forget about the past. Let others long for the old country and *la via vecchia*. For my grandparents, the Statue of Liberty—America— was all. I would, from time to time, ask my grandmother if she wanted to go back and visit Pontelandolfo; fixing me with a look that roughly translated as "my grandson has lost his mind," she would simply say: "No. Never. America is my home. America gave us a life." In George Panetta's phrase, "Italian eyes are all dark, with a lot of yesterdays in them," and in my grandmother's dark eyes the yesterdays of a tough farming life in the old country still lingered. But nostalgia never did enter her worldview. She lived for and in the present, which is another reason why her endless keening after my grandfather's death proved so difficult; my forward-looking grandmother was now stuck in the past, unable and even unwilling to leave.

Food and drink provide one of the cornerstones of Italian-American culture, representing, as they do, equal parts hospitality and personal connection. Note how many times in all three *God-father* films the camera lingers over food. Particularly in the first film, Coppola underscores the triangular nature of the Corleones' universe by constantly intercutting images of food, death, and religion. When Clemenza and Rocco Lampone kill the traitorous Paulie Gatto on the highway outside New York, it's ironic and startling that Coppola frames the sequence with the Statue of Liberty hovering in the distant background; what's even more memorable, however, is that once the execution is complete and the two assassins prepare to leave the scene, Clemenza (in a line improvised by the actor Richard Castellano) matter-of-factly barks at Rocco: "Leave the gun. Take the cannoli." Murder and dessert, all in the same sentence.

So essential is the ritual of food preparation to the daily rhythms

of existence that even when the Corleone family "goes to the mattresses" in their all-out war with the other crime families, Caporegieme Clemenza still takes time to provide Michael with a
cooking lesson on the proper way to make sauce. If, as theatrical
legend Stephen Sondheim has it, "god is in the details," Puzo's and
Coppola's attention to detail about food underscores how their
painstaking efforts created a genuine, multilayered depiction of
Italian-American life. In one prime example of this justified obses-
siveness, Coppola, who wrote in San Francisco, sent Puzo, who la-
bored in Los Angeles and New York, his original draft pages in
which Clemenza exactingly showed Michael how to make a proper
tomato sauce—"use olive oil, garlic, and brown some sausage."
Puzo sent back those script pages with one correction: crossing out
the words "brown some sausage," he wrote in the margins, "Gangsters don't brown, gangsters fry." In this smart, funny, yet pointed
rejoinder lies a glimpse of how all action in *The Godfather* arose
out of character. Clemenza would never tell Michael to brown the
sausage—he'd bark out "fry the sausage," just like the tough-
talking wiseguy he is.

When Michael kills McCluskey and Sollozzo in the restaurant,
he shoots the men in the face and throat, and it's not just their blood
that flies everywhere: it's the wine and the tomato sauce from the
meal as well, a trifecta of family, food, and violence found everywhere within the film. The murders of McCluskey and Sollozzo
are quickly followed by a montage featuring newspaper headlines
of actual mob murders, the sequence climaxing not with another
murder but, instead, with a heaping portion of sauce-covered pasta
being dumped with a thud into a garbage can. (Coppola later revealed that the footage of the newspaper headlines proclaiming
"Vito Corleone Shot" was filmed by his friend George Lucas.)

So central to *The Godfather* are the images of food that many a
blogger's page has explored the symbolic meaning of the oranges

that pop up throughout all three films: it's a fruit vendor's display of oranges that is upended in the street by Don Vito after he has been shot, just as there's an orange peel in his mouth at the time of his fatal heart attack in the garden. Oranges are present on Hollywood studio head Woltz's dining room table, and in *Godfather: Part II*, Michael is shown eating an orange while plotting against Hyman Roth. Even in Michael's own death scene at the end of part III, his drab brown pants and sweater are accented by an unpeeled orange rolling against his feet as he draws his last breath. For Coppola, the oranges connoted peasant food and were simply reminiscent of Sicily itself. For others, they represent symbolic nourishment that, in the hands of the mob, can ripen or rot with equal ease. The best explanation for the repeated presence of the fruit would actually appear to be that of production designer Dean Tavoularis, who said that the color orange simply provided a nice contrast to the muted palette employed by cinematographer Gordon Willis. Or, as the well-known mob chieftain Sigmund Freud once had it, sometimes a cigar is just a cigar.

And sometimes, oranges or not, cigars or not, our own family meals could turn decidedly dark. Embarrassing behavior was not unknown, the foremost example being the early 1970s Thanksgiving when my aunt Gertrude hoisted a few too many cocktails—actually a lot too many cocktails—and flirted with my college roommate who had joined us for the day. Flirted? She took it upon herself to inform my college roommate that she no longer had sex with my uncle. My roommate was stunned into silence. Happy Thanksgiving.

The air could also turn decidedly frosty when the talk turned to politics. I remember a particularly vociferous argument over Richard Nixon, circa 1968, a debate centering on my disbelief that my aunts and uncles supported him. "Nixon? Really?! You've got to be kidding" said I from my perch in prep school, fourteen years old and full of myself. Twelve years later, by the time of Reagan, my grandparents were dead, their house sold to strangers, yet I still carried on at my aunt's dining room table, the preppy paesano all but shouting "Mannagia L'America" at the prospect of the *Death Valley Days* host in the White House. After this outburst was greeted by a rather distinct silence from my Reagan-supporting aunts and uncles, the uneasy quiet was purposefully broken by my uncle Frank, who muttered in his best Brooklyn-inflected Swedish version of Italian dialect—"Maronne—this meat is tough." When my aunt shot back "Hey—you don't like it, buy it and cook it yourself," the entire table burst out laughing and then headed back to the safer territory of talking about life on Division Street.

If Francis Ford Coppola's camera had panned around my grandparents' dining room at that "Nixon" Christmas of 1969, the last when the entire family came together in celebration, he would not, contrary to popular stereotype, have found any overweight men or women, and certainly none of the gavonelike outfits at which non-Italians loved to sneer. Oh, how the Anglo mouth watered at the sight of those clothes that somehow resulted in a tackiness both laughable and fascinating. For any and all assimilated Italian-Americans, gavone clothing and actions can induce uneasiness even in thought, let alone actual experience. It's as if just one "ignorant" immigrant can, with a single ill-chosen outfit, reinforce every negative stereotype associated with Italians and in the process remind non-Italians just how foreign these immigrants remain.

The humiliation of the gavone resides at the heart of George Panetta's novel *Viva Madison Avenue!* Central to the story is an Italian clothes salesman who colors his hair red in order to pass as non-Italian. Fully cognizant of his own shaky status as "American," it is this same salesman who sells a gavonelike white suit to Joe, a sweet, gauche immigrant. For the redheaded salesman, the clearly inappropriate suit represents money in the form of a sales commission. To

Joe, the suit remains an object of beauty. In the eyes of the story's narrator, Joe's friend and a more assimilated Italian-American, the suit makes Joe look like a worker for the department of sanitation. Complete with long lapels and cuffs that come to a point, the white suit acquires a near-palpable power to frighten the narrator, making him "scared of what the Anglo-Saxons would say when they saw it on him, scared of what would happen to Joe's office if a Brooks Brothers suit came in and stood beside him." As proved the case with *Scarface*'s wildly patterned suits, in this one piece of clothing lies the symbol of the clueless Italian immigrant.

The narrator's fears prove fully justified, as the Anglos file by the office for a glimpse of the suit—and a laugh at Joe's expense. Joe's clothes mark him in their eyes as a ridiculous Italian; give him a monkey and he could pass for an organ-grinder, the ultimate Uncle Tom symbol for Italian-Americans. No wonder the narrator is afraid: this one suit possesses the power to destroy carefully constructed walls of assimilation, the edifice of his belonging reduced to rubble by Anglo laughter.

In the power of these outward symbols of belonging lies another reason underlying Don Corleone's appeal. No one laughs at Don Vito, not in his tuxedo on the day of his daughter's wedding, not in his indifferent suits and everyday work clothes, and not in the peasantlike, stained, comfortable clothes of his retirement. For every person in the worldwide audience who suffered from exclusion or felt the sting of a laughter aimed at their otherness, Don Vito provides consolation. Forty feet high on the silver screen. Feared. Respected. Honored. Who's laughing now?

With the power of Don Vito's persona in mind, Coppola took great pains to explain that he had not made a film about the Mafia but "a romance about a king with three sons. It is a film about power. It could have been the Kennedys. The whole idea of a family living in a compound—that was all based on Hyannisport." The

Corleone compound proved an inspired idea, functioning as a bricks-and-mortar representation of cultural insularity and the pre-eminence of *la famiglia*. Like the Kennedys, the Corleones chose to live in a compound so that family could form a buffer against the outside world. Flesh and blood trumped all, and for the first generations of Italian-Americans, the very notion of leaving family of one's own free will proved literally incomprehensible; in the words of Jerre Mangione, "you left only when it was impossible to earn a living near them, or when you died."

As it was, in at least one version of the stories about the film's compound, procurement of the location came with mob associations attached. The Staten Island house under consideration as the Corleone homestead had at first been refused to the production company; according to associate producer Gray Fredrickson, volatile actor Gianni Russo (Carlo Rizzi) "talked to a few people" and the compound suddenly became available. Russo himself insisted that it was mob chief Joseph Colombo who made it happen, with the proviso that Russo be granted the part of Carlo. After a wild screen test featuring the scene in which Carlo beats Connie—the part of Connie undertaken for purposes of the test by a genuinely terrified production assistant—Russo was granted the role. (In the recollection of producer Al Ruddy, Joseph Colombo did indeed help secure the location by subtly but firmly persuading a reluctant home owner to allow filming; the producer has not, however, spoken of Russo's screen test ever being a part of the deal.)

At the time of the film's production, Russo may simply have been inflating the drama surrounding his part in securing the compound. When the 1930s-era eight-bedroom, three-bathroom Tudor home was put up for sale in December 2010 for a cool $2.9 million (the house sat on a 24,000-square-foot lot), he offered a decidedly more low-key take on the tale, saying that as the time for filming approached, he simply remembered the house from growing up on

Staten Island and took producer Ruddy to see it. In Russo's recollection, "Ruddy fell in love with it," and the house was subsequently secured for the filming. In this revised version of the tale, Colombo did not figure in the negotiations, and the difficulties encountered in renting the house arose simply because owner Edward Norton displayed no interest in renting the house out. His wife did, however, and agreed to the rental in exchange for a new slate roof. Speaking of these negotiations from the vantage point of 2010, Russo continued: "I could have gotten them much more money . . . [Now] I'm thinking of investing in it myself . . . I got married to Don Corleone's daughter in that yard. There is just so much there."

Inside or outside the compound, the concept of *la famiglia* blankets *The Godfather*, and in the light of that thematic underpinning, it's unfortunate that one crucial scene set at the time of Michael's return from exile in Italy was originally included in the shooting script but not in the final cut of the film. In this extraordinary scene, Don Vito explains in straight-from-the-heart terms how it's family, not government or love of country, that fulfills and sustains. (In his emphasis on family, Don Corleone espouses a philosophy slightly at odds with that of the most famous real-life don of the late twentieth century, Gambino family boss John Gotti Sr.; speaking of his father in 2010, John Gotti Jr. baldly stated: "His wife and kids were second to the street. He didn't care about the money—he liked the action.") After imploring Michael to start a family and raise children, Don Vito asks his son what he believes in. When Michael does not answer, Don Vito urges: "Believe in family. Can you believe in your country? Those pezzonovante of the state who decide what we shall do with our lives? Who declare wars they wish us to fight in to protect what they own? Do you put your fate in the hands of men whose only talent is that they tricked a bloc of people to vote for them?" For a twenty-first-century populace terminally mistrustful of empty political promises, Don Vito's words ring ever more loudly with the sound of truth.

Perhaps that scene simply stated the core themes too bluntly, because at Coppola's request, a crucial scene between Vito and Michael was added late in the filming, one that addressed the one element Coppola found lacking in both screenplay and novel: a clear delineation of the transfer of power from father to son, a sequence wherein the love between the two men is evident, if unspoken. The ensuing scene of a generational passing of the torch, beautifully written by Robert Towne (*Chinatown*), provided a crucial reinforcement of the film's underlying concerns regarding dreams and regrets: admits Vito: "I never—I never wanted this for you . . . I refused to be a fool dancing on a string held by all those big shots . . . I thought that—that when it was your time, that—that you would be the one to hold the strings, Senator Corleone, Governor Corleone, somethin'."

In handing over the Corleone family businesses to Michael, Don Vito is in effect trading his Old World wisdom for America's youth, his personal warmth and sense of family for education and the cult of individual achievement. Don Corleone wanted Michael to live a life far removed from that of organized crime, one more American than Sicilian in nature, but the influences of family and a culture of violence ultimately prove far stronger on Michael than do those of education, his Anglo wife, or even the United States Marine Corps.

It's this talk between Michael and Vito that represents Don Vito's most sustained speech in the entire film. For much of the three-hour running time his power is expressed through sentences of few words, his approval or disapproval indicated through weighted silence and a nod of the head. In this garden scene, however, he is fully engaged by his own son. He knows that Michael is the right man to succeed him as head of the family, yet he is, like all fathers, worried about what will happen to his offspring. Proud of his son he remains, but, like many men on the verge of retirement, he appears more than a touch conflicted about giving up his own power.

It is now Michael's responsibility to uphold the honor of the family while maintaining his father's success. This affirmation of the bond between father and son constitutes, in the words of Alessandro Camon, "the ultimate value; profit and power are just means to an end." By subsequently inverting that equation and making profit and power ends unto themselves, Michael destroys his own family and makes his tragedy all the greater. He has convinced himself that his actions are always undertaken in order to protect the family from outsiders, but it is, in fact, these very actions that have caused the family to disintegrate from within. This intrafamily collapse is what ultimately proves fatal, because no matter how powerful, wealthy, and influential the Corleones become, it still, in Coppola's words, "comes down to huddling in close bond in pajamas and relaxed clothes."

Michael does not support his son Anthony's dream of a career in opera and instead follows a singleminded vision centering on the acquisition of ever-greater wealth and power, not for the sake of his children but to fulfill his own monomaniacal obsessions with revenge. By defying his father's wishes and pursuing his dream of a career in opera, Anthony is the first Corleone who not only gains what he needs—artistic fulfillment and self-expression—but also obtains exactly what he wants: the happiness that, according to the ancient Greek definition of the word, arises out of the full use of one's powers along lines of excellence. In the entire course of the three films, Anthony alone succeeds in defying Michael, and it's another of the saga's unending ironies that he does so only by reversing his grandfather's journey and returning to the old country.

Coppola may revel in the Italian-ness of the Corleones, but he grows increasingly critical of them throughout the course of *The*

Godfather. All of the family relationships on display—father/son, husband/wife, and brother/brother—slowly dissipate after the warmth displayed in the opening wedding reception. It is unsettling but perfectly logical that at film's end, just as Clemenza kisses Michael's hand in a display of respect for the new godfather, Michael shuts the door in the face of his own wife. It is only now that Kay finally and unequivocally understands that her husband has lied about the murder of his brother-in-law Carlo. With Kay's realization of her husband's amorality, the chasm between husband and wife widens to an unbridgeable distance.

Coppola wants to make sure the audience considers the other side of the family equation, that of Kay Adams Corleone. Kay's non-Italian New England upbringing and utterly different worldview had offered Michael a chance at redemption, but he has turned his back on her. Michael's coldly calculated insistence on denying all of his feelings has ultimately led to his having no feelings at all, and it is this lack of feelings for others that allows him to serve as godfather to Connie's son Michael even while ordering a hit on the baby's father.

Shutting the door in Kay's face constitutes an interesting and noticeably different ending from that found in both the novel and Coppola's first filmed version of the final scene (the latter is included with other deleted scenes on the remastered DVD). In that original conclusion, the recently converted-to-Catholicism Kay silently lights candles in church as she prays for Michael's soul. In Italian-American culture, it is the women, not men, who are the true believers in the teachings of the church, trying to protect their families through prayer, not violence. Instead of Michael ever having attempted to assimilate into Anglo society, it is the Waspy Kay who has assumed the traditions of Italian-American life. Mama Corleone, and now Kay, will never leave the church, just as their husbands will never leave the mob. Kay's lighting of candles reads as both true to Puzo's novel and to Italian-American life, but it was not the ending Paramount wanted.

Instead, production chief Robert Evans insisted that the film's conclusion find Michael shutting the door in Kay's face, thereby imposing total isolation on his wife. While both endings are powerful in their silences, Evans's conclusion registers as notably tougher and more damning. It is clear that Kay has forfeited her freedom, and in her now-shattered insistence on her husband's innocence, she has lost her own sense of morality as well. Kay is adrift, belonging nowhere, and to no one.

Coppola and Evans fought not just over this ending but also over Evans's subsequent claims of heavy involvement in the editing. This grab for glory served to infuriate Coppola and brought about a swift rejoinder from producer Al Ruddy: "The final cut was Francis's cut—frame for fucking frame." (Peter Bart seems to take an opposite view, depicting Evans, wracked with back pain, lying on a gurney working "eighteen hour days" on the editing of the film; in Bart's further recollection, "now and then Coppola would glimpse some scenes and give his comments.") Although Coppola, whose contract did not mandate his right to the final cut, was first required to submit a version of the film running no longer than two hours and twenty minutes, Evans did ultimately approve the full 175-minute running time that constitutes the final released film. In Evans's version of the editing controversy, he asked Coppola to add footage in order to enhance the film. Coppola, however, insists that the final 175-minute version simply restored the extra thirty minutes of film that Evans himself had ordered cut in the first place. Perhaps the contentious Coppola-Evans relationship is best summed up in Evans's own forthright assessment: "Francis and I had a perfect record; we didn't agree on anything—from editing to music and sound."

By the time of *The Godfather: Part II,* Michael's bottomless pack of fabrications has grown until he tells the biggest lie of all: "I've learned that I have the strength to change." (It's a lie rivaled in its audacity only by his claim to Kay in the first film that "In five years the Corleone family will be completely legitimate.") Faced with actions she finds incomprehensibly evil, Kay lashes out at Michael in the most hurtful way she knows, deliberately telling him that she had an abortion and terminated the life of their unborn son: "This all must end." In this direct stab at Michael's heart lies the first blow from within the family directed at his traditional role as paterfamilias.

The sanctity of *la famiglia* is further weakened by the forces of assimilation at work in the lives of family members. When non-Italian spouses are brought into the family, these newcomers are unable to fully understand the traditional customs and rituals, spoken and unspoken alike, which bolstered family closeness. In this light, while Kay can't quite effect a seamless fit with the Corleone insularity, far worse is Fredo's inability to control his blowsy drunk of a non-Italian wife. Fredo has failed in his role as a strong Italian-American male, a situation made even worse by his wife's shameful public behavior.

The harmful effects of the drift from familial roots can be seen most vividly of all in the character of Connie. After Michael orders the murder of her husband Carlo, Connie begins having affairs and pays little or no attention to her own children. The depths to which she has sunk are illustrated by her dalliance with the ill-suited, weak, white-bread Merle Johnson (played by Troy Donahue, whose birth name was "Merle Johnson"). If Michael has lost touch with his father's greatness, proving himself incapable of Don Vito's warmth and human understanding, it is Connie who has traveled an even greater distance from the maternal example set by Mama Corleone.

Connie's wedding reception symbolizes the overly insular yet family-sustaining lost world of the Corleones; by way of contrast, her nephew Anthony's First Communion celebration, which opens part II, is an even grander affair, but it's lacking in any heart. This weakening of cultural ties manifests itself in a seemingly light-hearted yet chilling moment that finds the orchestra at the Communion party unable to play a traditional Italian tarantella. A dance—well, one may ask, so what? As it turns out, however, that dance does in fact mean a great deal. The participatory gusto of the tarantella symbolizes the essence of Italian gregariousness, but the clueless orchestra at Anthony's party can summon no melody closer to the tarantella than the similar-sounding-but-worlds-apart "Pop Goes the Weasel." The Italian-centric world of the Corleones is vanishing bit by bit, and, with it, so too is the family. The cultural loss is here framed in distinctly Italian terms yet rings true for audiences across the board. The loss of the core ethnicity is the outcome of assimilation, and is in many ways the point of it all, but the effect is devastating nonetheless.

Having lost their own genuine cultural identity, the Corleones take the only step left on the Italian road to hell: they turn against one another. When Fredo is passed over as head of the family in favor of younger brother Michael, he helps rival mobsters Hyman Roth and Johnny Ola attempt to assassinate Michael. Family, it seems, means nothing now. What started as a battle between the five crime families has turned into a deadly intrafamily fight, shattering all behavioral and familial codes in the process.

By the end of part III, Michael's actions have ruined the family in the most horrific way possible: because of his life of crime, his daughter is killed in a storm of bullets intended for Michael himself. He may be the most tradition-minded of Vito's three sons, but Michael has failed at this most basic aspect of Italian life: he cannot protect his own daughter. Coppola's stated goal of destroying Michael Corleone has been achieved. No wonder he wanted to call *Godfather: Part III* "The Death of Michael Corleone."

Particularly in the earliest sections of the first film, Coppola has, in the guise of a gangster film, created what he calls the "biggest home movie in history," drawing on his own memories to simultaneously represent and idealize the notion of an Italian family. Conceptualizing all three *Godfather* movies as "films about a family made by a family," he drew on the talents of his entire extended family to help depict the rise and fall of *la famiglia* Corleone: by the end of the trilogy, he had not only used the skills of his father Carmine and sister Talia, but also employed his sons and wife as extras in the first film's baptism scene, placed his mother Italia as an extra in the McCluskey murder sequence, and featured daughter Sofia as Mary Corleone in part III. If, in *Mean Streets,* Martin Scorsese draws on his own childhood memories of Little Italy in order to fashion a notably tough Italian neighborhood, Coppola goes the opposite route, lovingly capturing the warmth of family life before pulling the rug out and eviscerating any sense of comfort that the audience has developed. In depicting the duality of the Corleone family as symbolic of the two sides of America, Coppola, like all truly great artists, has delineated a greater truth than that found in a strict adherence to fact.

It's an extraordinarily ruminative Coppola who speaks about *Godfather III* in a DVD voice-over commentary, his voice that of an older man thinking aloud about violence on film and its effect on young people. Given the haziness of lines between an auteur's work and the issues in his personal life, it is not surprising that when listening to Coppola's commentary it is often difficult to ascertain when he is speaking about himself and when he is talking about the film. In expounding on family, children, and the preservation of a "long-term marriage," Francis Ford Coppola is ostensibly talk-

ing about *The Godfather* films, but he is revealing himself, oftentimes to an extraordinary degree. Indeed, when speaking about
the Corleone siblings, Coppola opines that "Michael's relationship
with his sister Connie is as complicated as my relationship with my
sister Talia playing his sister. Oh—it's too much for me to think
about." In the on-screen depiction of Michael and Connie, in the
offscreen commentary of Francis about Talia, audience members
can recognize relationships with their own siblings. Those listening closely will likely be riveted and discomfited in equal measure.

It's Coppola's voice-over commentary on all three *Godfather* DVDs
that reveals just how much he relishes the role of paterfamilias,
both personally and professionally. Monumental as his ego is, his
fateful decision to try and restart the studio system with his own
American Zoetrope Films/Studios seemed less a monomaniacal
desire to control than a wistful desire to create a family at work to
coexist alongside the one at home. (Indeed, in a 1974 interview, Coppola referred to his employees as "the family.") As Coppola ages, his
self-admitted desire to work less frequently and on less difficult
projects seems to stem predominantly from a desire to spend more
time with his own family.

Having turned seventy, Coppola appears to be taking stock and
grappling with the issues of what truly matters in a man's life. (The
director felt that his father, who passed away from a stroke on
the night of the Academy Awards for part III, actually died from
the shock of not winning the Oscar for Best Song; it was a death
Coppola did not necessarily feel was a bad one, reasoning that his
father died the way he lived—concerned about music.) Decades
earlier, in the July 1975 *Playboy* interview that hit newsstands one
year after the release of *Godfather: Part II*, Coppola had registered as
remarkably upbeat, explicitly stating that while Michael Corleone
would never change and was "damned," America itself was not
doomed. By the time of his commentary for the DVD version of

the restored part III, however, his voice carries a notable tinge of sadness, a melancholic understanding of time's passage undoubtedly colored by the deaths of his parents and the tragic loss of his son Gio in a boating accident. Much like Don Vito near the end of his life, Coppola appears to be most concerned with those matters he terms "important beyond fame and wealth. These do not really fulfill. What does fulfill is a life of children and seeing the life of the family going on." Spoken like a true aging godfather.

Al Pacino as Michael Corleone. Absolute power corrupting absolutely. *Photofest*

10   *The Godfather: Part II*

I think the movie business is far more crooked than Vegas, and, I was going to say, than the Mafia.

—MARIO PUZO, 1999

GIVEN THE WORLDWIDE SUCCESS of *The Godfather,* the powers at Paramount Pictures quickly began to badger Coppola for a sequel. The director's immediate reaction to the idea? A decided lack of interest. How, he wondered, could he ever duplicate the success of the first film? More to the point, even at this early stage of his career, Coppola's body of work already ranged from the musical *Finian's Rainbow* to the moody drama *The Rain People,* and in his consistent pursuit of diverse projects, he evinced no notable interest in revisiting the same characters.

Still nursing his bruises from the first film, producer Al Ruddy declined any participation in the sequel, so Coppola grudgingly agreed to produce the film, with Martin Scorsese directing. Worn down by Paramount's pleading, Coppola finally agreed to undertake direction of the film on two conditions: that Robert Evans "would have zero to do with it" and that Paramount grant him complete control of the entire production, from casting and production schedule to shooting and editing. Said Coppola: "Charlie Bluhdorn talked me into doing it, by convincing me that it was a challenge to try to make a sequel to a very successful film, and pull it off. I'm basically a gambler, so the challenge of it appealed to me." Granted a lucrative deal of $250,000 to co-write the screenplay, $200,000 to direct, $50,000 to produce, and 13 percent of the film's adjusted gross earnings, Coppola signed on. Long gone were the days on *The Godfather* when he proved so short of funds that he lived in the maid's room at James Caan's house while editing the film.

Even with the extraordinary control granted him by the studio, Coppola felt rushed in writing the screenplay, having a mere three months to write the script before instantly beginning preproduction: "I was making a $13 million movie as if it were a Roger Corman picture." Beginning work on the screenplay at once, he began fleshing out his idea of continuing the story of Michael's financial success and moral decline, while flashing back to the story of young Vito's rise to power in early-twentieth-century Little Italy. Coppola invented the scenes of Michael's life in Lake Tahoe, as well as his trip to Cuba, but drew on material from Puzo's novel to tell the story of Vito's ascension. Devising all of the scenes in outline form, Coppola then began to write the actual screenplay in conjunction with Puzo (Coppola himself has stated that he wrote more of part II than he did the first film). Together, the two men crafted a story that not only matched the sweep and scope of the original film but actually proved more ambitious and novelistic in structure. In the process they delivered the rarest of all Hollywood species: a sequel informed by such passion and depth that it succeeded in equaling, and ofttimes surpassing, the original classic.

Granted a budget of $13 million (as opposed to *The Godfather*'s $6.5 million), Coppola began production with a planned shooting schedule of 104 days, nearly double the first film's extremely tight 62 days; in the end, the filming ran from October 1973 until June 1974. Relishing his freedom and control, Coppola had a much better time making *Godfather II* than he did the first film, and although part II proved a much more complicated film in terms of logistics, the more relaxed schedule freed Coppola creatively.

Al Pacino, who would appear on-screen in virtually every scene set in the 1950s, secured a deal for $600,000 plus 10 percent of the film's adjusted gross income—a rather nice increase from the $35,000 he received for the first film ("about $15,000 [of which]," said Pacino, "I owed in legal fees" stemming from the *Gang That Couldn't Shoot Straight* contractual wrangling). An agreement was also secured for the return of Robert Duvall as Tom Hagen, but at the last minute Brando's cameo appearance fell through. In Coppola's words, "the night before we were going to shoot the ending, Marlon pulled one of his stunts and said he would not show." Already annoyed with Paramount over the small salary he received for *The Godfather*, Brando was undoubtedly further smarting from his decision three years earlier to give back his percentage points for a "quick $100,000 in cash." Watching others grow rich from a film forever identified with his performance could only have exacerbated the situation for the perpetually worried-about-money Brando, and *Godfather: Part II* proceeded without his participation. (Contractual disagreements also prevented the return of Richard Castellano as Clemenza, with Coppola, understandably enough, refusing the actor's demand to write all of his own dialogue.)

With Castellano out of the picture, the character of Clemenza was, for all intents and purposes, simply replaced by the addition of a new Corleone associate, Frankie Pentangeli, played to an Oscar-nominated fare-thee-well by playwright and actor Michael V. Gazzo. The creation of Pentangeli was a particularly smart move on the part of Coppola and Puzo because in this one character the screenwriters managed to crystallize the entire losing battle waged by *la via vecchia* against America. An Old World soul who did not understand the changing ways of the modern crime world, Pentangeli not only disagreed with Michael's New World–style decisions but also committed the ultimate betrayal: he cooperated with the government as a friendly witness.

In a razor-sharp sequence that finds Pentangeli appearing before the government committee investigating organized crime, he unexpectedly and instantaneously recants his testimony as soon as his thoroughly Old World brother appears in the hearing room. A mere glance from this older brother, a look that conveys volumes of information about dishonoring the family name, induces an overwhelming sense of shame in Pentangeli, leading him to undertake the solution cryptically suggested by Tom Hagen: suicide. Pantangeli, a made man, has broken the code of *omertà*, in the process destroying what old-style mobsters valued above all: honor. If he commits suicide without testifying, his family will be taken care of financially and the honor of the family name restored. This Old World solution provides the one means by which Pentangeli's betrayal can be rectified. (In an interesting real-life reversal of the "made man for life" philosophy, John Gotti Jr. bluntly stated in a *60 Minutes* interview: "The movies say you can't get out. Guys on the street would let me out of the life. But not the federal government.")

Given what was sure to be a pile-driving performance by Pacino in the role of Michael, casting anyone less than a heavyweight in the role of young Vito would have severely unbalanced the two parallel stories, a situation that was avoided by the inspired casting of the young Robert DeNiro in the part. Not quite right for the role of Sonny in the first film, DeNiro here fit the role of the youthful Vito effortlessly, successfully conveying both the character's warmth and the sense of power held in reserve. (Ironic it is, then, that De-

Niro portrays Vito Corleone at his most Italian, yet Coppola characterized his own upbringing as "very Italian-American, not like DeNiro, who grew up American.") Faced with the extraordinarily difficult task of playing a younger version of a world-renowned actor in his most famous, Academy Award–winning role, DeNiro managed the neat trick of suggesting but never imitating Brando's bulldog pugnacity.

In his customary fashion, the non-Sicilian-speaking DeNiro immersed himself in exhaustive preparation for the role, one that was, aside from a few random words of English, to be played entirely in Sicilian. Studying at a Berlitz language school as well as privately with Romano Pianti, a linguist hired by Coppola as a script consultant, DeNiro then journeyed throughout Sicily in order to soak up local color and gain a sense of the people and their customs. Returning to America, DeNiro analyzed the Sicilian character in canny fashion: "Suspicion runs high. And although they are very cordial to you as a tourist, you are still aware of this. Sicilians have a way of watching without watching; they'll scrutinize you thoroughly and you won't even know it." The result of DeNiro's meticulous preparation was a detailed yet effortless performance, one so finely nuanced that its authenticity in speech, gesture, and action was assumed by the audience from the first frames onward.

Although most of the reviews at the time of *The Godfather's* original release had proved to be highly favorable, the violence on display had occasioned the single biggest criticism aimed at the film, namely that the on-screen violence existed only for the sake of its own sensationalism, glorifying killers and simultaneously deceiving and lulling the audience into submission. Perhaps in large part because of this consistent strain of criticism, Coppola set out in part II to "destroy" Michael Corleone, purposely aiming to eliminate any possible sympathy for such a cold-blooded killer. Nowhere is this ruthless undercutting of Michael's appeal more evident than in his relationship with his brother Fredo (the extraordinary John Cazale). In a subtle, beautifully played scene that Pacino termed his favorite of the first two films, Fredo and Michael visit a sleazy Cuban nightclub, in which Fredo inadvertently tells Michael, "Johnny always used to take me here." Given Johnny Ola's standing as close friend of Hyman Roth, Michael realizes that Fredo has betrayed him, and reacting with fierce dismay, kisses his brother while whispering "I know it was you Fredo. You broke my heart." At first claiming to forgive Fredo, Michael embraces his brother to the accompaniment of an emotional swell of music on the soundtrack, but Pacino's gestures and glances convey Michael's true meaning: Fredo will die. In the words of one of the film's most famous lines: "Keep your friends close but your enemies closer."

Pacino's performance in part II may well be the finest of his entire storied career. It's not only that he effortlessly conveys Michael's descent into hell; it's that he must do so in the most subtle of fashions, because Michael essentially acts like the same man from beginning to end, his journey into amorality one of infinitesimal yet cumulatively overpowering steps. There are no explosive blowouts filled with shouting and breast beating but, rather, a largely silent yet extraordinarily detailed and understated depiction of self-delusion morphing into unfettered evil. Having started out in the first film telling Kay, "That's my family, not me," Michael, thanks to Pacino's skill, has become, in the words of Coppola, "not only the mirror image of what he'd come from but worse . . . the greatest evil on earth is done by sane human beings who are miserable in themselves."

Convinced of his own godlike powers, Michael proves to be a man of such harshness that he sanctions his brother's existence only so long as their mother lives. The bitter, rock-hard dialogue with which Puzo and Coppola supply Michael limns the essence of a soul sliding into hell, yet Pacino never stoops to obvious theatrics, no matter how tempting the chance to do so. He delivers Michael's climactic lines to brother Fredo in quietly chilling tones that prove all the more devastating precisely because of the emotion withheld: "Fredo—you're nothing to me now. You're not a brother, you're not a friend. I don't want to know you or what you do." Upon the death of Mama Corleone, Michael stands in the compound's waterfront window, watching impassively as, under chilly, darkening skies, Fredo is assassinated in a fishing boat. This is very dark material for a major Hollywood film—for any film—and every last bit of it is presented by Pacino and Coppola in unflinching fashion.

Above and beyond the work of the actors and writers, the overall effectiveness of this epic was further enhanced by the look, style, and feel of the film, the cumulative affect arising out of the award-winning work of production designer Dean Tavoularis, cinematographer Gordon Willis, and costume designer Theadora Van Runkle. The mania for detail displayed by all three artists resulted in work so thoroughly nuanced that the essential Italian-American feel of the film enveloped the audience right from the mood-setting opening of young Anthony's First Communion party.

Tavoularis's painstaking methods had certainly succeeded on all levels in *The Godfather,* but in part II, his extraordinarily detailed work delivered an even greater payoff. Using dark textures for both the interior and exterior settings, he successfully conveyed the pervading atmosphere of evil through the heaviness of the bleak-looking buildings found in the Lake Tahoe compound. In Tavoularis's design, the physical settings reflected the isolated nature of the compound, the buildings therein literally and figuratively keeping Michael's family prisoners. So doom-laden do the settings read throughout that, in the aftermath of the attempted assassination of Michael and Kay in their bedroom, the stark atmosphere conjured by the overpoweringly harsh floodlights cutting through the darkness of the compound's perimeter remind one of nothing so much as the towers and lights of a Nazi death camp.

Even more noteworthy is Tavoularis's work on the turn-of-the-century sequences set in New York City. For the scenes of immigrants arriving on Ellis Island, the Trieste, Italy, fish market was transformed into the Immigration Arrival Center circa 1901. It's a bravura piece of production and costume design featuring some eight hundred extras, including American servicemen then stationed overseas who portrayed the government and health officials processing the immigrants. Here was an example of period re-creation that, far from appearing to be overly reverential, seemed to come alive with the clamor of teeming hordes, their expressions conveying the mixture of fear and hope with which the newly arrived immigrants greeted America. Based on this extraordinary work, one can only imagine the verisimilitude Tavoularis could have brought to the terrific-sounding sequences that were never filmed, chief among them those depicting the building of the New York City subway system.

The designer's crowning achievement, however, lay in his re-creation of Little Italy itself. Having spent weeks transforming New York City's East Sixth Street between Avenues A and B into Little Italy circa 1912, Tavoularis provided the ideal visual accompaniment for Coppola's bravura storytelling. As the director's camera glides through the crowds packing the dirt streets, children running by as mothers peruse the open-air stalls selling fruits and vegetables, the viewer is enveloped in a bygone world, and the distance inherent in viewing a film completely vanishes. An intense perfectionist for whom no single item proved too small, Tavoularis explained the methods behind his obsessions: "In a period film, every detail is important. You can't, for example, just put a can of soup on a shelf—it has to be the right can of soup . . . I like the idea of layers. I always want to put a door in the wall, and see the wall of the next room, and maybe put a window in it . . . and add a light in the neighborhood house."

Even in the modern (1950s) sequences, the changed world of the Corleones is made instantly apparent simply by virtue of the film's look; gone are the burnished browns and golds of the first film, replaced instead by the cold blues and grays of the churning water slapping against the fortresslike structure of the family compound. Even the film-opening First Communion party is, for all its surface gaiety, similarly chilly. A grimly professional dancing couple has replaced the first film's images of family and friends happily dancing the tarantella. All warmth has left the world of the Corleones, and when Michael attempts to expand his empire into Cuba, the scenes are brightly lit but garish, the brittle surface appeal of Battista's Cuba about to split wide open.

Great production design and superb acting the film has in abundance, but the lasting appeal of *Godfather: Part II* remains firmly grounded in the decision to tell the parallel stories of the young Vito and the adult Michael. Part II depicts a Vito on his way up, thereby supplying audiences who eagerly anticipate his "success" with a definite, rooting interest. By way of contrast, in the modern sequences, Michael may have succeeded by material measures, having gathered wealth far beyond even Don Vito's imaginings, but it is made clear that he has failed as both father and husband. By Coppola's estimation, Michael and Kay's union "may seem like a long time, but actually they're together only six or seven years," and along with Kay's demand for a divorce, Michael's children remain a distant presence in his life. Money and business overrule family in the world of Michael Corleone, a state of affairs that Don Vito would never have allowed. In "winning," Michael has lost everything that truly matters.

Coppola's cutting between the two stories enhanced flow and sense of contrast, yet the director smartly realized that the plethora of flashbacks in his first cut diluted the dramatic impact of events. As a result, he trimmed the number of interstory cuts from twenty to twelve, a move that greatly increased the film's effectiveness. Relying heavily on editor Barry Malkin, he did in fact re-edit the first two films into strictly chronological order for broadcast on NBC television in November of 1977, in the process adding back scenes cut at the time of original release. The broadcast was deemed a success, but Coppola came to feel—correctly—that the cutting back and forth across time, generations, and stories actually enhanced the narrative, adding a richness missing in the more straightforward chronological format.

Well received, if not ecstatically so, at the time of its original release, *The Godfather: Part II* has, over the years, evolved into an acknowledged masterpiece. Although a big hit, it did not surpass the original film's gross, for the same reasons that made it an even better film: it's darker and more tough-minded than the first, both richer and deeper, and as such is harder for audiences to accept. It's a film that lingers in the mind more than the heart, disturbing and fascinating in equal measure. Nominated for eleven Oscars (although cinematographer Willis was once again inexplicably overlooked), the film won six, including Best Supporting Actor (DeNiro), Art Direction (Tavoularis), Score (Carmine Coppola and Nino Rota), Screenplay (Francis Ford Coppola and Puzo), Director, and, most fittingly, Best Picture.

In 2010, while appearing on Broadway in *The Merchant of Venice,* Al Pacino was asked if he still watched *The Godfather* films. Although answering in the negative, Pacino did add that he had recently come across part II on television and was surprised at how well the film held up. He may just be the only viewer who is surprised; so enduring is the legacy of the first two films that a 2007 survey of American Film Institute voting members ranked *The Godfather* third on the list of the hundred greatest movies ever made in the United States, while a 2002 survey of "the greatest movies of all time" in the British film magazine *Sight and Sound* placed the first two *Godfather* movies in fourth place, topped only by *Citizen Kane, Vertigo,* and *Rules of the Game.* Not bad for a couple of gangster flicks.

Top: Patriarchy Italian-style, 1924. My grandparents, Orazio and Maria, with, left to right, daughters Julia and Emma, niece Katherine, sons Andrew and my seven-year-old father, Olindo. *Family photo*

Bottom: Patriarchy in the WASP manner, 1929. My mother, Nancy, age five, sitting on the couch, ribbon in her hair, with her beloved grandfather Edgar G. Norton. Left to right, cousins Barbara, Anne, Ginny. *Family photo*

11   Patriarchy

Women and children can afford to be careless. Men cannot.

—Don Vito Corleone

Both *The Godfather* and *Godfather: Part II* portray an Old World patriarchy in which women remain at home and carve out their sphere of influence on the smaller stage of family life. Such stratification may actually represent the single biggest reason why men remain greater fans of the saga than do women; women certainly appreciate *The Godfather* films for their sweeping story line and the sheer excellence of the acting and production, but they much less frequently respond to it with the overwhelming passion and reverence with which men react. Ironic and amusing it remains, then, to learn that Puzo based his conception of Don Corleone on his own mother, drawing on her strength and love of family as the defining characteristics of the godfather himself: "She wielded power like the Godfather did. She could be ruthless, yet she inspired a great deal of affection." (Although Puzo never specified any role models beyond his mother, many felt that Vito also represented a blend of reported Mafia chieftains, Vito Genovese and Joe Profaci. Other observers cite Carlo Gambino [New York] and Angelo Bruno [Philadelphia], further positing that with the deaths of Gambino [1976] and Bruno [1980], the era of Don Vito Corleone had ended forever.)

The dichotomy between the übermale world of Don Vito and Puzo's use of his mother as role model for the character can actually be traced in large part to the differences found in family structure between Italy and the United States. If the dominant relationship in Italian-American families is that between father and son, in Italy the culture continues to center on the dynamic between mother and son. This mothercentric conception of family life has continued into the twenty-first century, with a startling number of Italian men still living at home well into their thirties. Currently, eight out of ten Italians under the age of thirty live at home; men account for 67 percent of those staying put, a phenomenon defined with the sarcastic phrase "mammoni" or "Big Mommy's boys" (the average age for moving out of the parental abode is a surprisingly old thirty-six). As documented in a 2001 *60 Minutes* report on the *mammoni* phenomenon, more than one young man interviewed was heard to remark: "My mother cooks and cleans for me. She takes care of me. Why should I move out?" The response of the then Italian finance minister Tomasso Padoa-Schioppa: "Let's get these big babies out of the house."

American fathers, on the other hand, urge their sons to strike out on their own—in effect stating "Go West, Young Man." (If in Italy young men were taught to respect their father and follow his path, in the United States it was understood that sons should aspire to surpass their fathers.) No worse fate can await an American male than to be perceived as being tied to Mommy's apron strings or acting feminine; in expressing displeasure with his godson Johnny Fontane, Don Vito slaps him in the face and yells, "What's the matter with you?! Is this how you turned out? A Hollywood finocchio that cries like a woman?" By way of contrast, mothers in Italy proudly protect their sons, coddling them well into their adult years. It may well be a result of this maternal influence that for all of their macho behavior, Italian men, unlike their American counterparts, have never had a problem admitting the presence of their feminine side. Italian males hug one another and kiss one another on both cheeks without any loss of masculine credibility, but in America such behavior is still regarded as highly suspect. Suspect equals gay, unless, of course, the men in question are mafiosi, for whom such kissing constitutes a form of respect—and one usually learned from watching *The Godfather*.

It's a measure of *The Godfather*'s all-encompassing power that audiences of the early 1970s accepted the sight of men kissing on both cheeks without a murmur of objection. "Well," they seemed to rationalize, "no one is more manly than a gangster. He kills people to make his point. He's not gay." (Which is why series creator David Chase's—born De Cesare—purposeful tweaking of the conventions with the chubby gay mobster in *The Sopranos* registers as both funny and subversive.) Rationalization in place, audiences were ready to acknowledge that, while Sonny Corleone possesses the most macho of temperaments, the real power lies in Don Vito's much gentler, more nearly feminine "walk softly and carry a big stick" approach.

The Godfather poses incessant questions regarding filial loyalty, centering, as it does, on Michael's relationship with his father. Mama Corleone, on the other hand, has no real identity beyond that of mother. What is her first name anyway? Turns out it's Carmella, but no one ever calls her that. She is known to one and all as "Mama," which is exactly what all offspring and in-laws called my grandmother Santopietro. In the universe of *The Godfather*, women like Mama Corleone exist for mothering, and their mission lies in teaching their sons how to love, not how to fight. In light of Mama Corleone's identity and role, it is particularly noteworthy that in *Godfather: Part III*, when Michael attempts to atone for the murder of his brother Fredo, his confession is framed not with the words "I killed my brother" but with the statement "I have killed my mother's son." Even in death, Fredo remains Mama Corleone's son rather than Michael's brother.

As newly arrived immigrants like Don Vito (and my grandfather) began to traverse the new territory of their workplace, immigrant women faced a different set of problems. Stranded on the homefront, these women had to directly confront the reality that cultural traditions were being lost in the rush to Americanize; in his beautiful—and best—novel, *The Fortunate Pilgrim*, which centers on the mother/son dynamic as surely as *The Godfather* does that of father/son, Mario Puzo writes of mothers "filled with hope, with a vigor never sounded in their homeland . . . they spoke with guilty loyalty of customs they had themselves trampled into dust."

It was the very trampling of these customs that allowed children raised in America to become, in Puzo's words, "members of a different race." As a result, mothers feared these new ways at the same time that they embraced them, inculcating in their children a burning desire for a new life, yet one that always rebounded to the glory of the family. In the words of Francis Ford Coppola: "If you were raised as I was, everything you do is to make your family proud of you. It relates to the immigrant thing. Get an education, have a good reputation, have your picture in the paper in a suit, and have lots of money and security." Wanting the best for their children, the immigrant mothers seized on the new opportunities available in L'America, yet by guiding their children along these new paths, they ensured that their children moved further away, literally and figuratively, from the center of traditional Italian culture: the mother holding the family together.

Early in the twentieth century, immigrant Italian women stayed at home, perhaps working as seamstresses while mixing almost exclusively with fellow immigrants. Forced to observe and listen, information became their currency. Seldom venturing beyond the confines of their immediate neighborhood, these women were much more likely than male immigrants to lack any true fluency in the speaking, let alone reading or writing, of English. When these women did in fact travel out of the Italian ghetto, they were faced with constant reminders, both verbal and visual, that their social values, clothes, and gregarious manner of speech were considered inferior to those of the refined ruling class descended from English stock. Outsider status proved the order of the day for the women just as surely as it did the men.

Some, like my aunt Emma, chose this world of home and hearth by and for themselves. Born in Waterbury in 1912, and the first of my grandparents' four children to marry, my aunt Emma proved the most traditional of all in her roles: she did not work, she stayed home tending to her two boys and house, and she never learned to drive. (She did in fact take driving lessons as an adult, and we all applauded this step toward independence, but my then-seventy-year-old aunt's career as a student driver ended rather abruptly one summer afternoon. "What happened?" I asked, whereupon she explained that her instructor had asked her to take the next left, and so she did—into the neighbor's driveway. Aunt Emma's matter-of-fact explanation: "That made him really mad.") So slowly did the Old World customs fade from her world that, as late as the 1970s, both my aunt and uncle referred to pregnancy as "being in the family way."

Used to a life without bosses, Aunt Emma moved at her own pace. Upon returning from a trip to Europe with Emma, her brother-in-law Frank, by then married to Emma's younger, feistier sister Julia, remarked: "Emma has two speeds. Slow—and stop." A woman of exceptional kindness, she delighted in the triumphs of her entire extended family and remained a sensational cook, making chocolate cakes, pastas with homemade tomato sauce, and, best of all, succulent roasted potatoes slightly crisped and topped with just the right amount of salt. Such recipes were never written down. Like her mother, she cooked from a lifetime of knowledge, measuring by hand while relying on a near-infallible intuition. Forty years later I can still smell the kitchen where I spent so many hours, hear the two-step hitch in the opening of the refrigerator door, and feel the grooves in the worn linoleum floor. The kitchen cupboards would open, and there in mint condition lay a dazzling collection of Depression-era glassware, painstakingly collected through visits to dish-night giveaway at Loew's Poli Theatre during the Depression. If a life of limited choice lay within those kitchen walls, so too did a life of security.

Emma's husband Carmine took care of the driving, yard work, and all home repairs. Aunt Emma reigned over her interior domain, remaining oblivious of such undertakings as the filling of the underground oil tank that supplied heat to the house. When Uncle Carmine became too aged to take care of such tasks, it would not be uncommon for Aunt Emma to casually remark of a day, "I can't get any heat in the house. What do you suppose that's about?" Close as Emma and her sister Julia were, Julia's response to such a statement would be a snort of disdain: "That's my sister. She thinks the tank fills itself hocus-pocus." For her part, Julia remained fiercely independent, learning to drive at the youngest possible age, working in a factory, and taking no guff from anyone, including her bosses. Having worked for years without a raise, she spoke up about the inequality of the men receiving raises before the women and was rewarded with a visit from the floor supervisor, who informed her that she'd receive a three-cents-per-hour raise. Her clipped response was a disgusted "Three cents? After all these years? Keep it, you big cheapskate."

When my father was first hit by the devastating series of illnesses that threatened his life shortly after turning seventy, he was cursed more than blessed by his medical knowledge, remaining more attuned to the pros and cons of his treatment than were the attending physicians with whom he had worked for so many decades. Forced good cheer proved utterly pointless, and he could not/would not eat anything. But Aunt Emma persevered, and her chicken soup with tiny cutup carrots and pastini, her small bowls of homemade tapioca, became the first items my father would eat. When she visited my father in the hospital, a three-week stay that found him dealing in quick succession with a heart attack, a stroke, and the amputation of a leg, Julia fiercely admonished her sister: "Don't you dare cry. Don't you dare look downhearted in front of your brother. You are there to help him, not to show how sorry you are." Aunt Emma performed like a trouper and saved her tears for home. It was a small world that she inhabited, but it suited her. Secure in her domain, she developed a will of iron that enabled her to exert her own quiet influence.

Like Vito Corleone, Emma's husband Carmine Albini had his name changed upon arrival at Ellis Island in 1921 at age seventeen, when, with the stroke of a pen, an immigration official switched his surname to Albino. Bringing his Old World work ethic with him to America, Uncle Carmine remained a workhorse who did not and could not stop his physical labor until nearing the age of ninety. A handsome man, he late in life told me that in the 1920s, he had been approached about appearing in a Hollywood screen test as a Rudolph Valentino–like figure. He stated this almost shyly, a seven-decades-later musing about what might have been. It was not a lengthy discussion, nor did he evince any particular sadness, but in his brief story he seemed to be explaining—to himself as much as to me—that seventy years earlier, as a recent immigrant who spoke limited English, the idea of moving to California and appearing on-screen had proved well beyond the limits of his worldview.

Instead, Uncle Carmine became a policeman, and in my early 1960s childhood, when the notion of downtown still existed and policemen directed traffic while wearing white gloves, my sister and I would glimpse him from the window of my mother's station wagon as we inched along during rush-hour traffic. With his whistle blowing and hands gesturing powerfully, he would spare a fleeting smile and nod in our direction, the dichotomy between the policeman on display and the Uncle Carmine I'd see working in his vegetable garden one hour later proving both odd and oddly comforting.

It was at a family dinner at Carmine and Emma's in the early 1970s that I was pulled aside by my uncle Andrew, who even then remained the family's impulsive rapid-fire Sonny Corleone to my father's more deliberate, understated Michael (that is, if one can compare a dentist and a doctor to members of the Corleone family . . .). It was time, Andrew explained, that he tell me the story behind Carmine's lack of promotion on the force. Decades earlier, when Andrew, as the eldest son, strode into City Hall to inquire as to why Carmine had not received his promotion while less-deserving junior officers leapfrogged ahead, the answer he received from the officer in charge was the silent opening of a drawer, followed by a nod to the cash-filled lockbox located therein. Not a word was exchanged. Refusing to pay, Uncle Andrew stood up and left, and Uncle Carmine never received his promotion. He remained on traffic duty, where, in November of 1962, he was crushed by a runaway car as he prepared to report back to the police station in order to check out at 11 P.M. As he was about to open the door to his car, he was hit by a woman from New York City visiting her brother in

Waterbury. The driver in question was drunk, carried a suspended license, and had taken her brother's car without his permission. Driving straight into my uncle's right hip, she pinned him against his car and continued to drive, dragging him down the street until she hit another car and was forced to stop. My uncle suffered a dislocated hip, multiple bruises, kidney damage, and a forced retirement because of a now-permanent limp. True to form, Uncle Carmine did not rail against the fates, instead pointing out that he would have suffered even worse injuries if he had not been wearing the layers of clothing he had donned against the frigid November nighttime weather. The driver's punishment for my uncle's injuries and forced retirement? A ninety-day suspended sentence and a $100 fine.

Between his giant-sized work ethic and fervent desire to save, Uncle Carmine qualified as the quintessential paesano. In his spare time, he would moonlight as a housepainter, and on his retirement from the police force, he took on two new jobs, delivering cars for the local Ford dealership and working as a jack-of-all-trades bartender, barrista, and handyman at the Pontelandolfo Social Club. Like Don Vito himself, Uncle Carmine happily tended an enormous vegetable garden in the back of his home, and in the decade of the 1970s, after working in the garden, he would walk next door in order to bring his severely arthritis-ridden mother-in-law to his own home for dinner. Calling out "Mama" as he walked into her house, Carmine would scoop my grandmother up in his arms and carry her into the kitchen of his house so that she could eat dinner with her daughter and son-in-law. Meal finished, he would carry her back home and make sure she was settled in for the evening.

When their son Donald moved with his wife and two sons to Atlanta, Uncle Carmine and Aunt Emma would pack up for months-long visits. Carmine's suitcases often held multiple Italian delicacies because, in his view, such great foods could never be available in a backwater southern town like Atlanta . . . On one memorable occasion he packed a suitcase so heavy that it could not be lifted. Literally. When queried by Donald as to what he possibly could have packed that necessitated the use of a dolly just to move the bag, Uncle Carmine replied: "Tools. You might not have them, and you'll need them for home repairs." Donald's reply was a rather laconic, "I thought I went through graduate school just so that I wouldn't have to be a laborer all my life."

As proved to be the case with so many early-twentieth-century immigrants, unstinting physical labor gave my uncle's life purpose and meaning. His unbounded strength and energy remained a reassuring presence for everyone in the family, which is why his decline seemed more jarring than inevitable. Checking on him one summer afternoon, I found him slumped against the back wall of his house, wanting to garden and move boulders but confused as to where he was and what he was doing. At age eighty-four, time had finally caught up with him. For several minutes I couldn't move beyond a childish feeling that this happened to other people, but not to Uncle Carmine, when, in a last gasp of total self-absorption, I realized that mixed in with his shockingly sudden decline lay the final sundered chords of my own childhood, as well as the last tangible family connection to the old country.

While I never heard Aunt Emma herself express an interest in entering the workplace, part of her stay-at-home life arose out of Carmine's desire that his wife not work. He was, like all of us, a mass of contradictions, and at the same time that he wanted his wife to stay home, it was also not lost on him that my grandmother's devotion to family existed right alongside her work in the grocery store with my grandfather. In my grandmother, Uncle Carmine recognized and admired a work ethic as fierce as his own, understanding that she worked both in order to save the salary that would have been required by a nonfamily member employee, as well as to keep an eye on her nearby children. As for my grandmother herself, I think she enjoyed being with my grandfather in the workplace, but the concept of expressing herself through her work would have remained incomprehensible to her. She worked because it was right for the family—end of story. Born in 1888, she was a traditional Italian woman of her time and unquestioningly accepted the centuries-old roles assigned to both men and women.

I hold a distinct memory of my grandmother fiercely telling me out of the blue one day: "Tommy—you're the last one with the name of Santopietro. You must continue the name. That's the most important thing of all." I couldn't have been more than ten, but remember being slightly puzzled, thinking to myself: "I thought education was the most important thing. This too? And why is my name more important than my cousins'? They're her grandsons too. What's the difference?" The idea of my sister not taking her husband's name would never have entered my grandmother's thinking; she simply assumed that my sister would marry, begin using her husband's name, and have children. At the time I didn't spend long trying to figure it all out. But—the Old World cultural assumption struck a jarring note, one to be puzzled out at a later date.

There was, however, nothing puzzling about the look my grandmother shot me on one of the rare occasions I sarcastically talked back to my father. I was, on the whole, an almost abnormally polite young boy: such were the lessons of respect taught in an Italian household, and, even more notably, the lessons learned from my mother. Those WASP table manners were drilled into my head, as were a "please" and "thank you" before and after each request. Adults were accorded deference, and the very concept of calling one of my parents' friends by his or her first name remained unimaginable. (As a young boy, when I heard a friend and contemporary refer to our neighbor Mrs. Poindexter as Brenda, I felt as if I had just heard him speak Swahili.) Polite I was, but, entering adolescence, I acquired the habit of sarcasm endemic to those years, and at one family gathering shot back a snide, obnoxious answer to a question posed by my father. My grandmother turned around before I even finished speaking, fixing me with a look that filled me with shame. Being a teenager, I was, I realize in retrospect, both ashamed and resentful, but I shut up. Fast.

My grandmother's displeasure with me was entirely nonverbal, but the unspoken message was clear: "You don't disrespect your father. Ever. He is the head of the family." In her view, his position as head of the family remained preeminent and unchallenged. When my grandfather died on Christmas Day, 1970, I was sixteen years old. Even in the midst of my adolescent self-absorption, I was aware enough to realize that the entire family had turned to my father in a collective, unspoken question of, What now? Uncle Andrew was older, and my cousin Robert a practicing attorney, but my father was the doctor, and as such he was accorded unspoken deference. Dealing with his own sorrow, my father nonetheless consoled his mother, began plans for the funeral service, and spoke to his sisters about the emotional and physical difficulties that lay ahead for my grandmother. I was immensely proud of my father. I didn't yet have the tools with which to express such admiration, but when I overheard my mother talking to my father later that night, I began to understand, perhaps for the first time, how marriage could work. I heard the love and support, the sorrow and comfort, the give and take. Whatever the stresses, their bond endured. If, as one grows older, one learns that life is rarely black and white, unfolding, instead, as an endless array of grays, the pride I felt, arising as it did out of my grandfather's death, may have been the first tangible sign that I had begun to understand the grays that dominate all of our lives. Sorry-Grateful I was and remain.

My grandmother's Mama Corleone–like outlook on the role of women was defined not only by her Old World Italian point of view but, perhaps even more so, by her generational viewpoint. It was the same outlook I heard espoused by my grandmother Parker in a mid-1970s discussion about Ella Grasso running for governor of Connecticut. As a fellow graduate of Mount Holyoke College, my mother remained a fervent supporter of Ella. Waxing enthusiastic about the candidate—and my mother was a woman of great enthusiasm and optimism—she was nonetheless startled into silence when my grandmother looked up from her needlepoint and stated: "I'm not voting for her. I don't think politics is suitable for women." My sister burst out laughing and said, "Nana—that's completely ridiculous." My mother smiled. I had the sense to keep quiet.

It would never have occurred to my grandmother Santopietro to question the fact that at the end of the work day, it was still she who cooked dinner for her husband and four children, a task she undertook with flair and, above all, economy. Along the way she managed to turn all four of her children into excellent cooks, and my mother always acknowledged that after she married my father in July of 1950, it was he who taught her how to cook. So sick had my grandmother Parker been while my mother was growing up that a housekeeper/cook had been hired to help prepare the meals. After several years of living more or less comfortably with this jerry-rigged solution, my mother and her parents awoke one day to find that the cook had run off with a married man, never to darken the streets of Watertown, Connecticut, again.

To the end of her life, my mother cooked more out of necessity than from any great love of the process, any enjoyment she received pressed out of her by fifteen years of cooking two separate meals every night: one for her two young children, and another after my father came home late from making housecalls. She fixed lunches for my sister and me to take to school and grew into a more than proficient cook, hosting dinner parties for the social set in which she and my father moved, but had, I think, other things on her mind. Cooking was a means to an end, not an end in and of itself.

It was an attitude toward cooking markedly different from that displayed by my father's sisters. Julia worked until she married at age fifty and reveled in the fact that after marriage she could quit her job and spend her time cooking. And cook she did, in heaping quantities out of all proportion to necessity. Preparing meals just for herself and her husband Frank, she would still shop at Costco and come home with three dozen eggs—because they were on sale. A true child of the Depression, and inculcated by my grand-parents' fear of *la miseria* returning, my aunt delighted in sniffing out a bargain. Sherlock Holmes had nothing on a first-generation Italian-American when it came to sleuthing out the best deals in town, and when I happened to ask my aunt exactly what she intended to do with those three dozen eggs, she instantly replied, "Make cheesecakes." For whom she was going to make a dozen cheesecakes I never could figure out, but the act of cooking proved pleasurable for her in and of itself.

If *The Godfather* is purposefully filled with intermingled images of family and food, so too are my memories of holidays through the decades, from the Eisenhower era housefuls of boisterous, joy-filled relatives to the quiet late 1990s. With our numbers painfully diminished, the last-ever Christmas Eve at Julia's proved particu-larly difficult, the memory nagging me still, some fifteen years later. Having prepared the customary Italian feast of the seven fishes, the problem my aunt could not solve, that none of us could overcome,

was that the family had shrunk irrevocably, and those who remained lived scattered between Georgia, California, and Florida.
The neighbors who used to drop in had grown old, moved away, or
died, yet even with only seven of us in attendance, platters for
thirty still overflowed the holiday table. I ate three times what I
wanted, as if such overeating could justify my aunt's efforts and
somehow hold back the forces of time. We all gamely attempted to
keep up the holiday mood, but it proved an uphill battle, and the
previously nonstop talk dwindled into silence as we thought of
something—anything—to break the oppressive quiet, our shared
terra firma shrinking before our eyes.

Over the years, three of my four grandparents had died in Christmas week, and I think those memories, combined with our diminished numbers, tinged those latter-day family Christmases with an
undercurrent of sadness. Not unexpectedly, it is at Christmas that
Aunt Julia, ninety-seven years old as of this writing, most often
plaintively asks: "Is my mother alive?"

Thanksgiving, Christmas Eve, Fourth of July—cooking helped
anchor Aunt Julia's place in the world, and I'm still not quite sure
which she liked more: preparing the feast or finding the grocery
store bargain that helped infuse her cooking with joy. And it
wasn't just Aunt Julia for whom bargain hunting ruled. Her sister,
Emma, could and did raise thriftiness to an art form, especially
where clothes were concerned. The owner of a beautiful winter
coat purchased by her two sons, Emma kept the coat tucked away
in the closet because it was "meant only for special occasions." Year
in, year out, the coat hung in a protective garment bag, until it finally saw the light of day at the end of the Vietnam war. Having
survived the constant worry of having her eldest son serve in Vietnam, she decided that the special church service to celebrate peace
deserved the "new" coat. As I watched her carefully button the coat
against the chill, I remembered thinking, "I should take pictures of

this for her sons." I don't think the coat ever made another guest appearance.

With hindsight, I realize that my aunts, and especially my father, never completely outgrew their Depression-era beginnings. My father established a highly successful medical practice but worried about money. He followed the stock market obsessively and, generous as he was with all of us, shared an attitude common with many paesanos who survived the Depression: it could all happen again. Especially after he became ill at the end of his life, money grew into an enormous concern. Even with the horrendous health care bills he faced, he always had more than enough money, but the worry persisted.

With his ever-diminishing physical mastery of anything in his life, cutting coupons and saving dollars at the grocery store became matters of great import, such bargain hunting helping him reestablish a sense of order and control while simultaneously decreasing mine. Having left New York to move home and help my mother care for him, on bad days I just wanted my life back. I was exhausted, and not happy about driving across town to save $13 in discounts at the Stop and Shop. Clutching the coupons my father had clipped, I wheeled the cart around the too-big-by-half store, all the while wondering where my grandfather's comforting, small-scaled, and most of all personal neighborhood store was when I needed it. It may have been mid-July, but in the frigid, overly air-conditioned environs of the barn-sized "Super" Stop and Shop, it felt like February. The constant search for the products on sale took me over thirty minutes, until I finally ended the arctic trek in a long checkout line manned by a surly cashier. Briefly giving me the drop-dead look, she proceeded to hurl my items down the conveyor belt while I threw down the coupons and yelled, "Remember to deduct these damn things!" It was not a happy time—for my father, me, or the cashier.

When I arrived home with the groceries, my father carefully scrutinized the bill, the savings marked in red raising a fleeting smile. In a dark time filled with very few smiles. I softened and understood. Raised to save money, to use every scrap of food, my father had retightened the financial restraints that had grown slack over fifty years of marriage and prosperity. If I now finally understood the phrase "child is father to the man," it was not a comprehension that granted me much comfort in the midst of my father's sadness.

Raised in a household where his mother worked in a family store attached to the front of the house, and faced with the example of his sister Emma rarely leaving her house, I think my father was unprepared for my mother's force of will on the subject of staying at home. My mother loved making a home, and one of the great documents from their fifty-year marriage is the scrapbook full of the ideas they collected for the home they eventually built in 1961. But—my mother was not going to stay home all day. Ever. When clearing out the family home after both of my parents had died, I came across papers that made it clear that my mother had, in those long-gone days of limited workplace options for women, made it understood that she would involve herself in the community, putting her masters degree in social work to use. Her volunteer work became, in effect, a full-time job, and she served as president of seventeen different community organizations, in the process receiving myriad awards from the Chamber of Commerce, Junior League, and local hospital. I think that in the early 1950s, while saddled with a toddler, a very ill mother, and the horrific, successive deaths of her beloved father and grandfather during the same month in which I was born, my mother was saved by her community involvement. So often was she out at meetings that one night my father baked her a cake and wrote "Welcome Home" in icing. Familiar only with the model of his mother and two sisters, my father was surprised by my mother's iron will on the subject, but they worked at an understanding, and I love the sardonic humor of the cake. Besides, he always was a good cook.

My mother's life and interests could not have been further removed from the lives of the Mama Corleones populating my father's Division Street childhood. Her upbringing and Mount Holyoke education were, of course, part of the attraction for my father, and at the same time, a cause of bafflement. As a successful physician possessed of an extraordinary grasp of finance and international affairs, he was worldly in the extreme, yet at the same time proved notably parochial as a result of his upbringing. In the 1920s and 1930s, Italian neighborhoods were not just close-knit— they limited one's worldview. As he grew older, my father understood the limitations of this outlook, and as the complacent 1950s changed into the tumultuous 1960s and free-for-all 1970s, he encouraged my mother to reenter the workplace. Having met her when he was completing his medical residency and she was beginning her career as a medical social worker, my father liked both the idea of my mother returning to social work and the thought of a second income. My mother was not interested. A volunteer she would remain.

A part of my father yearned for the traditional Italian-American home life, patriarchal position intact, yet he had to have known in advance that my mother would never, could never, follow that model. Indeed, it was a model rejected in part even by his own sister Julia. Musing one time about her late-in-life marriage, she bluntly stated: "I never wanted to be anyone. I learned to drive and I always worked. I wasn't ever under anybody's thumb." Such words may constitute an everyday, understandable outlook in the twenty-first century, but for an Italian-American girl born in 1914, they remain remarkable.

What did my grandparents make of a daughter-in-law who,

even in the conformist 1950s, followed her own path? I know that they loved my mother with a fierceness that brought her into their hearts. They understood her extraordinary gentleness, and took pleasure in her wholehearted love for them. Unlike me, my mother would never have felt any discomfort with their Italian ways so different from her own, and she loved hearing my grandfather call her Nunziata. She may be the only person I have known who accepted everyone on their own terms, embracing the quirks others might reject. This was, I think, her greatest gift, and why, when she died, three separate ministers, in churches of three different denominations, eulogized her life and achievements.

I like to think that if and when my grandparents discussed their daughter-in-law's different ways, they'd smile and say, "Eh—what are ya gonna do?"—but this time with a smile of acceptance, not a shrug of resignation. Her polite but firm rejection of the traditional Italian family model was, I suspect, harder on my father than on anyone else in his family. Like Vito and Mama Corleone, my grandparents, aunts, and uncles would not want to interfere in another family member's marriage. My mother's life was remarkably different from that of my aunts in all ways, but my father's sisters loved her without reservation, as she did them. When my mother was dying, Aunt Julia would have us to dinner every single night, a trip to her house giving my mother a shred of contact with the outside world she had always inhabited with such zest; my mother's idea of hell, after all, had always been that of camping in the wilderness with no one else around. When my mother died, Aunt Julia hugged me with all the strength she carried on her five-foot-two-inch frame, and simply said, "She was my sister. Nancy was my sister, and I loved her more than you can possibly know."

In many ways, *The Godfather* itself functions as a look at the vanishing traditional Italian patriarchy with which my father grew up. Both the novel (1969) and the film (1972) were created in the rising shadow of feminism, during a time when the figure of the unquestioned patriarchal head of the family was fast disappearing from the scene. Part of the appeal of *The Godfather* lies in one's reaction to these seismic societal changes; the world of Don Vito's study—the dark and golden hues, the silences filled by the murmurs of powerful men—granted viewers the sense of a vanishing world of male certainty, a kingdom poised on the age of extinction. In the politically correct twenty-first century, when the concept of the strong, silent, virile man is under attack, routinely ridiculed in academia as well as popular culture as an unwanted symbol of chauvinism, the appeal of the aggressive and macho Italian-American male still persists.

And yet. Taking the construct one step further, the appeal of such a figure may actually represent another manifestation of lingering prejudice against Italians. Positing the question in 1994, author Gay Talese wondered: "Could it be that . . . the Italian-American actor is the only type that can satisfy some filmgoers' fondness for 'men who are men'—crude, aggressive, macho—while not indicting male society as a whole, because Italian Americans are marginal people?" Perhaps the fully formed response lies in accepting the truth of Talese's query while still acknowledging that the appeal of such retro, overtly masculine behavior also extends beyond the boundaries of Italian-American life. It is, after all, just such anachronistic behavior that lies at the heart of the public's fascination with the boozing, handsome, womanizing Don Draper of the hit television series *Mad Men*. As it is, in matters both business and sexual, Don Draper plays like nothing so much as an early 1960s Anglo version of the traditional Italian-American male.

Don Draper or Don Corleone, WASP or Italian, the changes in the roles for such men are more than matched by the evolution in roles assumed by Italian-American women during the past half century. The very actions of Italian-American women in general, and mob wives in particular, have changed in ways unthinkable to Mama Corleone. When, in *The Godfather*, Lucy Mancini becomes pregnant by the married Sonny Corleone, the pregnancy is considered to be her fault, not Sonny's. In the widely held Old World view, she simply should have said no, realizing, in the words of the classic James Brown song, "It's a Man's, Man's World." Jilted by Sonny, she assumes the only role available to her: outcast. By way of marked contrast, in *The Sopranos*, for all of Tony Soprano's bulk and bravado (his boat, the scene of several murders, is named *Stugots*, which translates as "balls"), he is ofttimes emasculated in his role as paterfamilias by both wife Carmella and daughter Meadow. Carmella yells at Tony and throws him out of his own house, and Meadow (one can only imagine Don Vito's reaction to the name) feels free to openly and loudly disagree with her father. Analyzed in traditional Italian-American terms, in his need to talk about his life and anxieties, Tony is acting like a woman. He recognizes the distance between his murderous, hypermasculine actions and his "feminine" feelings (in the world of Tony Soprano—and the Corleones—an examined life is the province of females), but in the end, regular sessions with his female psychiatrist or not, he is at a loss as to how he can reconcile the two.

The changing role of women is a key reason why, in the overly maligned *Godfather III*, the most interesting character of all turns out to be the still-evolving Connie Corleone. Beautifully played throughout all three films by Talia Shire, the Connie of the first film is presented as a spoiled Italian-American princess, traditional and submissive in her roles, a woman infantilized by the physical and emotional abuse she suffers at the hands of her husband Carlo. In Shire's own words, the Connie presented in the first film is "a spoiled, pain-in-the-ass whiny person." (Given the traditional sanctity of male and female roles within the Italian-American family, it's entirely consistent that when Sonny first wants to avenge his sister's mistreatment by Carlo, both Don Vito and Mama Corleone advise, in effect: "Don't interfere. That's between a husband and wife.") In *Godfather: Part II*, Connie swoops in for the opening Communion party, all flashy bracelets and affected air, resembling nothing so much as an upscale gavone. Vulgar in a nouveau riche kind of way, she is determined to lash out at her brother Michael for ordering the murder of her husband. By film's end, the metamorphosis back to her roots complete, she gently touches her brother, and in Shire's beautifully calibrated reading, speaks volumes by quietly stating: "Michael, I'd like to come home now."

By the time of *Godfather III*, Connie is the fiercest family warrior of all, the champion of Sonny's illegitimate son, Vincent Mancini (a first-rate Academy Award–nominated Andy Garcia). It is Connie who counsels revenge against rival Joey Zasa, and she actually steps over the vascillating Michael in order to push through Vincent's murderous, albeit misplaced, plan for vengeance. In a wonderfully staged bit of business, Coppola films Connie fiercely urging a murderous revenge—"Do it," she insists—after which she kneels to pray in the hospital chapel. Through the course of three films, Connie Corleone has evolved from simpering bride to tough mafiosa. Michael may no longer fully care about "the game" and its attendant turf, but Connie does. She's the new caporegieme in town.

Connie's dramatic arc through the three films is a measure of how far a distance Puzo and Coppola purposefully traveled in their depiction of Italian-American culture. Beginning with the strictly defined Old World masculinity of Don Vito, the coauthors eventually travel to a land of female empowerment undreamt of by the original immigrants. Indeed, one reason why part III was not as popular with audiences as were the first two films lies in the fact that it dispensed altogether with the sense of lost white male privilege that suffused those two films, or more precisely, that audiences read into the films. *The Godfather* and *Godfather: Part II* both presented a notably homogeneous world, a virtual fantasy land inhabited only by Italian-American males who still adhered to *la via vecchia* in all matters business, sexual, and familial. One needn't spend too long looking for any signs of African-American or Hispanic life in those worlds—there weren't any to be found.

At the end of *The Godfather*, as Michael receives homage from those who kiss his hand, he reigns supreme as a last vestige of the white American male in full power mode. Here lies the highpoint of Michael's life, and as his world steadily unravels throughout parts II and III, one realizes that with the cunning and stealth of trained assassins, the screenwriters have laid waste to the cultural assumptions that attracted their audience in the first place. Like the greatest of artists, Puzo and Coppola have remained fearless throughout.

Loro cianne i coglioni.

The Godfather, Part III: mobsters dressed as priests rub out the opposition.
Photofest

12 Religion, Death, and Grief

Religion blushing, veils her sacred fires,
And unawares Morality expires.

—ALEXANDER POPE

PART OF ANY AUDIENCE'S fascination with *The Godfather* lies in the fact that the mobsters in question spend their waking moments in violent, criminal activities, yet they also take part in all the sacred rituals of the Catholic church, from weddings and baptisms to wakes and funerals. Fully participating in religious life without any seeming wink of irony, these mafiosi exemplify that most universal of human conditions, self-contradiction. Killing rival family men without a qualm, the mobsters nonetheless remain devoted to their own families, indeed to the very idea of family itself. The tenets of the Catholic church hold that their activities condemn them to an eternity of hell, so off to church they march, souls seeking balm. Then, with church attendance completed, back to killing they go.

Given both the overt and subtextual references to religion

throughout the first film, one wonders if Coppola and Puzo were having fun at the expense of the Catholic church when Michael and girlfriend Kay are shown exiting Radio City Music Hall after having just watched *The Bells of St. Mary's*, starring Bing Crosby and Ingrid Bergman as priest and nun. It certainly seems likely—and the mere fact of Kay cheekily asking Michael if he'd prefer her as a nun underscores a knowing, ironic stance toward the church. Perhaps the seeds for part III's scathing condemnation of the church's obsession with money were sown here, because if an old-style Hollywood film like *The Bells of St. Mary's* tells its audience that God is in his heaven and all's right with the world, *The Godfather* succeeds in proving just the opposite.

The contradiction between murderous Italian gangsters and religious fealty clearly fascinates Puzo and Coppola, and religious festivals figure prominently in all three films. Serving as cornerstones for the movies, these rituals, most famously symbolized by the simultaneous baptism and murders found at the end of *The Godfather*, are further echoed by young Don Vito's killing of Fanucci during the Festa of San Rocco in part II. When, in part III, the shooting of the traitorous, preening Joey Zasa takes place during the Feast of San Gennaro, it is clear that Puzo and Coppola have succeeded in fully carrying out their mission: the setting up of a call-and-response religious house of mirrors throughout all three films.

Call-and-response rhetorical flourishes are a key part of African-American religious services, and while *The Godfather* did enjoy great popularity in the African-American community, it is a mark of the film's remarkable complexity that Puzo and Coppola never allow the audience to completely forget the casual racism displayed by the characters. Black audiences who cheered the Corleones' murderous rampages were brought up noticeably short by the mob's nonchalant, racist Old World approach to drug dealing: "Leave

that to the coloreds. They're animals anyway." Even with such purposefully racist dialogue, black audiences still responded highly
favorably to the film, perhaps glimpsing echoes of their own expe-
riences with organized religion in the interplay of the Catholic
church and Italian-American life. For both African-Americans and
Italian-Americans, outsiders continually searching for justice, church
functions as simultaneous instrument of liberation—eternal salvation awaits you—and repression—damnation ensues unless the
teachings of the church are strictly followed. Banishment of primal
urges, church members are told, can and will produce rewards in
the afterlife, but only for true believers.

Blood, wine, and Catholic imagery are intermingled throughout all three *Godfather* films, the murders on-screen ofttimes
enveloped in a near-ritual reminiscent of the Catholic catechism.
The duality of the traditional roles of the Italian-American male,
seeped as it is in the traditions of the Catholic church, is reflected in
Michael Corleone's own actions: on the one hand lies procreation—
the birth and baptism of a child—and on the other rests the need
to protect—even by means of murder if necessary.

The role of the church lies everywhere in Coppola's vision, a
thematic underpinning that lends another layer to his bravura film-
ending montage of murder and Catholic ritual. In a scene invented
by Coppola for the *Godfather* movie, the murders of Michael's fiercest
enemies are carried out at the exact same time that he is in church
personally renouncing Satan in his role as godfather to namesake
nephew Michael Rizzi (in the novel the murders occur after the
baptism). In a five-minute-long sequence that contains some sixty-
seven shots, nine of Michael's enemies are dispatched one after another with machine-calibrated precision: Clemenza murders three
men in an elevator, Vegas foe Moe Greene is shot dead through
the eye, Cuneo is killed as he tries to escape from a locked revolv-
ing door, Rocco Lampone shoots the hated Tattaglia, and, finally,

Michael's bodyguard Al Neri dispatches Tattaglia's bodyguard/ chauffeur on the steps of a federal court building. As Coppola's camera closes in on the bloody corpses, each shot is intercut with that of a priest intoning the Latin words of the ancient christening ritual: "In Nomine Patris . . . et Filii . . . Spiritus Sancti," the increasingly shortened shots increasing the dizzying pace of events. Baby Michael is baptized into the life of Christ at precisely the same moment that his godfather is successfully baptized into power through a succession of murderous acts, with the entire sequence capped by the priest stating, "Go in peace and may the Lord be with you. Amen." Filmmaking, not to mention irony, doesn't come any better than this.

In its dichotomy of killing and religion, murder and the saving of souls, this nearly wordless montage stunningly depicts the full extent of Michael's hypocrisy. So fluid is the presentation that when caught up in the excitement and flashy editing, viewers will likely find themselves divided in loyalty: rooting for Michael's revenge yet fully aware of Coppola's condemnation of the events at hand. Here, in a nutshell, lies the source of the film's appeal. When, shortly after these killings, Michael shuts the door on his own wife, audiences realize that they have just spent three hours cheering for the success of a murderous mobster whose actions they abhor. If irony underlies all great literature, so too does it here buttress the best filmmaking.

With each succeeding film in the saga, the religious underpinnings loom in terms both larger and darker—Puzo and Coppola have much more on their minds than a simple iteration of "the more things change, the more they stay the same." By the time of part III, the changing mores and attendant decline of the Corleones are successfully laid out simply by means of the religious setting for the murder of Joey Zasa. Disguised as a policeman on horseback, Vincent Mancini shoots Zasa in the midst of a crowded religious street festival, in the process endangering women and children. He is breaking an ironclad edict of his grandfather Don Vito, who, although willingly choosing a life of danger, spent a great amount of time defending the sanctity of family and community. Part II's assassination attempt on Michael in his own home may have broken a centuries-old mob rule by placing his wife Kay in danger, but here in part III, Vincent's wild attack during a religious procession endangers not just one but dozens of innocent women and children. The concept of honor among thieves has been irrevocably shattered, and just to make sure we don't miss the point, Coppola films a statue of the Madonna hitting the street in the aftermath of the shooting.

Coppola ups the religious duality throughout *The Godfather: Part III*, with Michael returning to Italy as the possessor of a major stake in Immobiliare, the Vatican's real estate holding company. Immobiliare itself exercises control over millions of Italian citizens because of its land ownership, which means that by virtue of his holdings in the company, Michael has now perverted the original intent of the Mafia, namely the protection of powerless citizens against the draconian measures of an indifferent government. He is now in effect the enemy of his peasant ancestors, ensnared no matter how high he climbs. In his own words: "The higher I go, the crookeder it becomes."

What's most noteworthy about the epic's intermingling of religion and death is that it turns the popular conception of Italian grief on its head. After decades of pop culture depictions featuring larger-than-life, heavily emoting Italians responding to death with body-wrenching sobs and the shaking of fists at heaven, *The Godfather* undercuts the stereotypes. Note how stoically Mama Corleone reacts when informed that Vito has been shot. She simply moves as if to gather her belongings for a trip to the hospital. When Sonny is killed, tears gather in the corner of Don Vito's eyes, but that is all. He feels the loss in his core, but control over his emotions remains of paramount importance, even in the face of family tragedy.

It is only when Michael sees his daughter Mary shot to death on the opera-house stairs that animalistic rage is expressed. Even here, however, Coppola and editor Barry Malkin at first let Michael's grief play out silently, his face contorted, mouth open but no sound emanating. Coppola cuts between the faces of Kay, Connie, and Vincent, until finally Michael's scream is heard, an unearthly sound that overwhelms the music on the soundtrack. Here at last, near the very end of the third film, is the display of guilt and gut-level grief so lacking in Michael since he entered the land of murderers by shooting Sollozzo and McCluskey. What grants this scene an additional resonance is the realization that the filmmakers are here inverting the depiction of that first murder; the decision to kill Sollozzo and McCluskey played out silently across Michael's face, the screeching of the subway train in the background supplying the one audio element (until the shots ring out). Two films and thirty years later, Michael's grief at realizing that his murderous ways have caused the death of his daughter is first expressed silently, until he explodes in agony, his primal screams providing the only sound heard.

Michael's grief is bone-deep and unrelenting, and in its overwhelming intensity immediately reminded me, in uncomfortable but unavoidable fashion, of my grandmother Santopietro's reaction when her husband of over fifty years died in the early hours of Christmas Day, 1970. For weeks afterward, she would rock back and forth, crying as she endlessly repeated "campagnio mio"—my companion. I sat with her for hours, family providing her with consolation yet also reinforcing her overwhelming sense of loss. My cousin Donald, her second oldest grandchild, received forty-eight hours' leave from the navy to travel home for the funeral, and her face lit up when he arrived, only to crumple with a convulsive sob moments later as the sense of loss washed all over her again. Aunt Julia made my grandmother the black dress of mourning that she insisted on wearing for years after, taking comfort in putting on this tangible sign of mourning and respect for her soul mate.

Faced with the death of a loved one for the first time, I reacted to the grief on display with both a renewed sense of family closeness and more than a bit of discomfort. Passion and feeling this elemental, this Italian and peasantlike, was new to me. It was all light-years away from my heavily Anglo prep school in Connecticut, and I surrendered to the pull of family while still holding myself at a slight but definite remove.

My grandmother's mourning continued month after month, her zest for life permanently deflated. Holidays proved the most difficult times of all, and I clearly remember seeing *The Godfather* for the first time on an Easter Sunday some sixteen months after my grandfather had died. After hours of my grandmother's tears and listlessness, the film provided a welcome escape. What also sticks in my mind is that my father and I, mutual devotees of the novel, loved the film, both of us wrapped up in the story, the look, and the sheer excitement of experiencing the newly released film then dominating cultural, religious, and political talk in the United States. My mother, who shied away from violence in films, disliked the movie in the extreme, constantly leaning over in the dark to ask, "How much longer?" Years later, her antipathy toward the film turned into a family joke, but at the time I was only annoyed, insisting, "Stop asking. There's a good part coming—Michael's going to kill Sollozzo and McCluskey." The scene in question came and went. It was not my mother's idea of a good part.

My warm, loving grandmother, so different from my equally loving but more austere grandfather, had begun to disappear in the wake of his death, yet even in my obtuse teenage state I was learning from her reaction. Her raw emotion made me uncomfortable, but it was real, and, in an odd way, a welcome contrast to the already-changing mores of the American public, which dictated that death should be spoken of euphemistically, if at all. All of a sudden, people stopped using the two words "he died." Instead, men and women alike began to whisper "he passed" or, even worse, "he passed over." Huh? Passed over? Where to? To the "Heaviside Layer" made so famous by those endlessly singing and dancing cats in Andrew Lloyd Webber's musical? "Passed" is a cloying term rivaled only by the much-overused "closure." News flash: there's no such thing. If you love someone, you always miss them. And that's not a bad thing. It's part of who and what we are. With time, the hurt moves to a different, easier place, and we all go on with our lives. The sense of tidiness implied by the word "closure," as if speaking those two syllables magically provides the proverbial balm in Gilead, does everyone a disservice. (My dislike of the word does, however, pale in comparison to the thoughts of Gambino family mob boss John Gotti Sr. on the subject: "Closure is a word for over-educated, under-intelligent motherfuckers. It's a new 90s word I don't like." Oh.) It has all begun to seem endlessly juvenile, with perpetually adolescent Americans viewing heaven as the all-white never-never land found in the MGM musical *Till the Clouds Roll By*. Whatever and wherever heaven is, it is most decidedly not likely to feature that film's tableau of a white-suited Frank Sinatra standing on a pillar while crooning "Ol' Man River" in front of an all-white orchestra.

I prefer the peasant Italian mode of dealing with death: confront it head-on. The original immigrants possessed a peasant-bred awareness of how unexpectedly death can rear its unwelcome head, and while these immigrants may have feared death, once a loved one had "passed over," visits to the cemetery became a part of family life and ceased to repel. Indeed, many an Italian-American comedian has made hay discussing family visits to cemeteries, where, after tending to the family plot, a picnic proved the order of the day.

Especially in the first half of the twentieth century, it was left to the skilled Italian-immigrant stonemasons to build the monuments and ornate sarcophagi with which Americans marked the final resting place of family members. With my grandfather having purchased a family plot in advance, my grandmother already knew that a suitable, fully engraved headstone would mark his place—it was the act of choosing a proper coffin that became a matter of surpassing importance to her. She fretted over the proper choice until the sturdiest and most airtight model of all could be found, and she mentioned her choice over and over, the utterance of the words representing a mantra that granted her a measure of peace. My grandmother lived for five more years after my grandfather died, and while she finally acceded to the family's collective wish that she cease wearing black, life never again held the same joy for her. As the end of her life approached, her greatest comfort lay in knowing that she would, in the end, rest side by side with her companion.

It wasn't just the carving of headstones and larger-than-life mausoleums that marked the Italian approach to death. Irish have their wakes, and Jews sit shiva, but for Italians funerals and calling hours constitute a form of theater. One almost expects the funeral director to knock on the coffin and, in theatrical parlance, tell the deceased: "Five minutes to places, Mr. Corleone."

Italian communities are always at their best in times of extreme joy or sadness: weddings or funerals, the gathering of the clan continues the celebration of one another's existence. My grandmother's sister, Aunt Angeline, all four foot nine inches of her, used the funeral-home calling hours as a chance to socialize. She may have mourned the deceased, but in the midst of her sorrow, the fact of the death almost mattered more, as if she were continually awaiting the arrival of new and noteworthy tragedy. Here was true performance art: calling hours as entertainment. Aunt Angeline would perch on one of the chairs in the viewing room, her feet never reaching the ground as she swung her legs back and forth, loudly proclaiming her own entertaining Italian-American version of who's who. Her prime topics of interest: when she had last encountered the deceased, how both she and the deceased knew the mourners who had already appeared for the calling hours, and how big a crowd was expected for the funeral. This running commentary was conducted in a compelling if ofttimes incomprehensible mixture of broken English and thick Italian dialect, and always at a volume that would have caused Ethel Merman to step back in admiration.

My father's cousins, Raymond, Salvatore, and Mario Albini, ran the leading Italian funeral home in the city, all three of them smart, savvy, theatrical characters of such stature that, even when young, I was fascinated by their ritualistic presentation of both the calling hours and the subsequent trip from church to cemetery. List in hand, homburg perched on his head, Mario would read out the list of mourners and their assigned place in the procession to the cemetery. Ts were detonated, and Rs were rolled—it wasn't "Mr. Mario Ratrenelli," but, rather, "Mr. Marrrrrio RRRatrrrrenlli." Here was a stage manager calling cues.

Having unexpectedly started to cry by my grandfather's casket, I remember the relief I felt at hearing those rolled Rs—there was something surreal about the moment that stopped my tears. The surreal then morphed into the outright comic when one of the cars in the funeral procession broke down in the middle of the entrance to the cemetery. With the road blocked, the lineup of stalled cars stretched for hundreds of yards. The culprit whose ancient car had broken down for good? A distant in-law who had permanently held the position of not-to-be-trusted outsider. It didn't matter that by this time he had been married to his wife for twenty years—he was still an outsider. My sorrow at my grandfather's death was instantly, albeit momentarily, quashed as I observed Mario leap out of his car to find out "what the hell is going on." That interest turned into outright fascination as I heard curses tumbling out, followed by the loud proclamation: "Marron—I told that gavone not to drive that piece of shit car to the funeral. If he had half a brain he might be dangerous." On Mario strode to the car in question, loud oaths following in his wake. It wasn't just me—I noticed car windows everywhere in the vicinity rolling down, all eyes and ears eager for the denouement. This was theater.

Good as it was, this theater was more than equaled by the extraordinary activities of my father's cousin Victoria, sister of the funeral home directors. Victoria held down two jobs: prison matron and beautician in charge of the hair and makeup for the corpses. She was heavy-set and loud and used language that would make a sailor pass out as soon as blush. She was also possessed of a genuinely beautiful face and soulful eyes that radiated kindness. In her job as prison matron, she would of necessity interact with the prostitutes picked up for solicitation, and after they had been released from jail, she'd invite them home for a home-cooked meal of pasta. No judgment—just an acknowledgment that they needed a little help. I didn't see Victoria often, but when I did I knew I was in for a good time. If she spotted one of the women once again plying her trade on a street corner, she'd drive her car up to the curb, all the while yelling, "You're under arrest!" The prostitute would curse her out, and both would burst into gales of laughter. Life was never dull around Victoria.

Everyone loved Victoria, yet she did once run afoul of my grandfather (her uncle), a gentle soul who never used profanity. At one family gathering, as Victoria embellished her very funny story with a wildly inventive string of profanity, my grandfather simply said, "Victoria—please do not use that language in this house." So chastened was Victoria, so respectful of her uncle, that she murmured, "Su Orazio—I'm very sorry"—and no further curses were heard. Until the next day.

Victoria's two daughters, Diana and Debbie, were cut from a different cloth than their mother, but were very close to her all the same. When my own mother lay dying in the hospital from cancer, Diana, a registered nurse, would consistently check in on her, regardless of the fact that her own station was on a different floor. She was a gentle, loving presence in a terrible time, and it is only in retrospect that I fully understand the surreal, quintessentially Italian care she took: as my mother slipped into an irreversible coma, there was a constant flood of visitors into her room, family, friends, and even hospital workers wanting one last chance to say goodbye. Debbie arranged for food and coffee to be brought into the room, arrayed on a table near the foot of my mother's bed. It makes for a decidedly odd picture to be sure, not just the idea of the food in a hospital room, but also an Italian repast for my dying Anglo mother. A strange scenario, yes, but also strangely comforting, and one that actually made a curious kind of sense; my mother had always treasured the compliment of a friend who had commented on her fierce devotion to my sister and me by exclaiming: "Nancy— you're a cross between an Italian mama and a Jewish mother!" My mother revered family, moved her own mother into our house to take care of her when she became ill, and expressed affection clearly and without reservation. She was, I think, Italian in another life.

C-55-1

"Just when I thought I was out . . . they pull me back in." *Photofest*

13   *The Godfather: Part III*

Many men would take the death-sentence without a whimper, to escape the life-sentence which fate carries in her other hand.

—T. E. Lawrence

The desires of the heart are as crooked as corkscrews
Not to be born is the best for man.

—W. H. Auden, "Death's Echo"

The whole point of learning about the human race presumably is to give it mercy.

—Reynolds Price

After the worldwide success of both *The Godfather* and *The Godfather: Part II,* Paramount began a steady, years-long campaign aimed at persuading Coppola that a third visit to the land of the Corleones was not only desired but necessary. The director remained unconvinced, and as a result, between 1974 and 1989, Paramount spent almost $800,000 on writers who churned out treatments and a dozen ultimately unacceptable scripts for the proposed *Godfather: Part III.*

Coppola was not the only key player to remain uninterested. Puzo himself evinced little enthusiasm for part III until Paramount offered him $250,000 for a fifty-page treatment (plus 6 percent of the gross for any film subsequently produced therefrom). Puzo actually handed in a treatment in 1978, but the result was deemed top-heavy with plot and weak on characterization, and the prospects for a part III dimmed noticeably when a second treatment he handed in generated even less excitement.

Finally, after years of Paramount's insistent pleadings, Coppola agreed to undertake *Godfather: Part III.* Faced with huge overhead from Zoetrope Studios, as well as the Napa Valley winery that he had purchased in 1975, and sensing a chance to wipe out the film industry's memory of the checkered box-office reception afforded his most recent films (*The Cotton Club, Tucker*), Coppola acquiesced after obtaining the total creative control he demanded. Six million dollars to write and direct, plus a percentage of the profits, had a remarkable way of making his doubts vanish.

Working once again with Puzo as his co-screenwriter, Coppola used *King Lear* as the inspiration for the film's story, with Michael as Lear and Sonny's illegitimate son Vincent in the role of Edmund. Deciding that Coppola would write the first half of the screenplay and Puzo the second, the co-screenwriters set the action of the new film in 1979, weaving together Michael's attempts at family reconciliation with the overarching issues of succession and redemption. In the eyes of the scripters, if, in the course of the first two films, Michael, like America itself, had won untold power and riches but lost his very soul, then the conclusion of his personal journey would inevitably have to include a quest for redemption. Here lay the peg on which they planned to hang the film.

Budgeted at $44 million, the film called for nine weeks of location shooting in Sicily (the better to keep Paramount executives at a distance in Coppola's view), with interior sequences to be filmed at Rome's Cinecitta Studios. The script fashioned by Coppola and Puzo called for the return of leading players Pacino, Keaton, and Duvall, but casting problems soon arose because of Paramount studio executive Frank Mancuso's intransigence over money matters: Mancuso agreed to Pacino's $5 million price tag, as well as Diane Keaton's salary of $1.7 million, but Duvall, angered over an offer only one-quarter as large as Pacino's, could not come to terms with the studio. With Mancuso refusing to budge, Coppola undertook a fast rewrite of the script and replaced Duvall's Tom Hagen with the new character of B. J. Harrison (played by George Hamilton), a polished establishment lawyer and trusted Corleone adviser.

Coppola and Puzo's original script for part III focused less on Michael than on Vincent Mancini, the cousin with whom Michael's daughter, Mary, falls in love. When Coppola subsequently decided that the focus should remain on Michael, the key problem became that of creating an adversary strong enough to challenge Michael's supremacy. With Michael's wealth and power surpassing that of any other Mafia chieftain, who or what would prove a worthy adversary? The answer, as outlined by Peter Bart, lay in the tangled strands of a front-page story.

It was Bart who was the first to go public with a story of financial maneuvers worthy of the Corleones themselves, namely the fact that a large investment in Paramount had been made by Sicilian financier Michele Sindona, a man long rumored to be the investment counselor for the Gambino crime family. According to Bart, Gulf&Western chairman Charles Bluhdorn helped Sindona acquire a 20 percent stake in the Vatican-held Società General Immobiliare, which in turn then purchased a "significant interest" in Paramount. The net result lay in the rather startling fact that at this one point in time, Paramount Pictures was largely owned by the Vatican Bank. In the words of Jon Lewis's essay "If History Has Taught Us Anything," "According to Bart, in an effort to convince

Coppola to make a third *Godfather* film in the early eighties, Bluh-dorn told Coppola what he knew about Sindona, about his deal with the Vatican and how the mysterious death of the so-called Smiling Pope, John Paul I, perhaps stemmed from it." Upon hearing Bluhdorn's words, Coppola knew that he had found his third film. (Subsequently convicted on sixty-five counts of fraud and perjury in 1980, Sindona was extradited to Italy four years later, where in 1986 he was found guilty of ordering the murder of Giorgio Ambrosoli, an attorney who had been hired in 1974 to sort through Sindona's financial records. In 1986, Sindona died in a Milan jail "under mysterious circumstances," having taken—or likely been forced to swallow—cyanide, the Mafia's favored means for eliminating stool pigeons.)

Set in 1979, the dawn of the "greed is good" ethos prevalent in the 1980–88 years of Reaganomics, part III dovetails nicely with that era's evolution of business practices. Just as American corporations were then beginning to merge into giant conglomerates, placing ever-greater power into the hands of fewer individuals, the business at the heart of part III is less about the individual, honor-based world of Don Vito and more about the oligarchical interests of the church, most particularly those of Immobiliare. If, at the end of part II, Michael Corleone cynically states, "If history has taught us anything, it is that you can kill anybody," the darkest iteration regarding the bloated corporate failure of the American political and financial systems can be found here in part III, in Don Lucchesi's blunt statement to Vincent Mancini: "Finance is guns. Politics is knowing when to pull the trigger." By the end of part III, Puzo and Coppola have pulled the trigger—with a vengeance—on the myth of the American dream. In the light of the financial crisis of the twenty-first century and the attendant lack of accountability for Wall Street tycoons, Coppola's own description of the film seems downright prescient: "[It is a] story of . . . what the real Mafia is:

people in the world who run everything and have absolute power without having to account to anyone about it."

The grim tone found throughout part III begins with the very opening images, the deserted Lake Tahoe compound submerged in chilly winter waters that convey the dark state of the family. (It is only when the characters return to the old country that any lightness appears on-screen, the Italy on display painted as a country of wealth, glorious operas, bountiful food, and endless sunshine.) Once again using public celebrations to illuminate private behavior, Coppola begins the film with a church ceremony honoring Michael for his $100 million charitable contribution to establish the Vito Corleone Foundation. The secular rituals of the Corleones now coexist side by side with the religious rituals of the church; the Catholic church has obtained a new foundation thanks to Michael's lifetime of crime, and in return godfather Michael is rewarded with legitimacy in the form of the Papal Order of Saint Benedict.

If the First Communion party in part II was not as warm or enveloping as part I's wedding reception, then part III's opening public celebration, a scaled-down party after Michael's investiture, possesses even less in the way of genuine emotion. Everything is more than a little off, the dancing light-years removed from that of the happy couples glimpsed at Connie's wedding reception. Here, it is Connie herself who gamely attempts to lead the guests in an Italian sing-along, but in her near-manic determination to force enthusiasm, it is clear that she is fighting a losing battle: the Old World has vanished forever.

Deliberate echoes of the first two films abound in part III. A family photograph is taken to mark the occasion of Michael's investiture, and just as Don Vito insisted that Connie's wedding photograph be halted until Michael arrived, here the actual snapping of the photo is delayed until Vincent can pose with the rest of the family. Unlike Michael at the start of *The Godfather,* however, there is nothing the least bit innocent about Vincent. He's a tough, cocky hood with a chip on his shoulder, and if Don Vito represented the Old World mobster living in the New World and Michael a blend of the old and new, then Vincent registers as the complete embodiment of the new. The demolition of *la via vecchia* at the hands of L'America is complete.

In *Godfather: Part III,* Michael Corleone possesses a genuine problem of self-identity. He wants to restore honor to the Corleone name, and even sells off his gambling interests before making the $100 million gift he hopes will represent the starting point of his salvation. The problem, and ultimate irony, lies in the fact that Michael is attempting to atone for his transgressions while making a donation of blood money to a church itself rife with fraud, lies, and, eventually, murder. Inevitably, he is sucked back into the world of violence from which he wants to escape and realizes that he has simply traded one form of prison for another.

Endlessly re-sorting his past, anxiously searching for ways to atone, Michael has finally come to understand that the most devastating personal conflicts are those internal in nature. He is desperate to recapture his sense of self that existed before; in Pacino's word, he "bit" into the lifestyle. In the actor's view, the Michael of those earliest days actually held a certain disdain for gangsters; aware of his own Ivy League schooling, he possessed an educational snobbery that allowed him to dissemble and compartmentalize the various aspects of his existence. The life Michael lived as a child and young man in college—content, striving for independence yet comforted by the knowledge that his family provided unconditional love—has turned out to be the most successful part of his life. It is this self-knowledge that motivates the older Michael of part III to try and regain his family, and, with it, his peace of mind. His drive for legitimacy in business is inextricably intertwined with this desire to reconnect with his family, and as he attempts to effect a reconciliation with his children, he is simultaneously forging an uneasy truce with former wife Kay.

The Michael Corleone of part III has actually developed a conscience. Aware of his own encroaching mortality, he is in pain, and the compartmentalization necessary to hold his life together can no longer succeed. He has let in his self-doubts, and the past, far from providing consolation, now haunts him. Wherever he journeys, death follows; the more he reaches for salvation, the further it recedes from his grasp, until, inevitably, the full import of his deeds crashes down on him at the film's climax.

The last third of *Godfather III* appears to aim for the sense of tragedy and attendant hope for salvation that permeates so much of grand opera. The music of Pietro Mascagni's *Cavalleria rusticana,* the opera that Michael's son Anthony is performing in Rome on the night of Mary's murder, continually weaves in and out of the action, the violence found in the opera anticipating the bloodshed that soon explodes outside of the theater. Although most prominently on display in part III, *Cavalleria rusticana*'s mix of insult, revenge, and Old World peasant mentality would seem to run throughout all three of the *Godfather* films; indeed, in critic Pauline Kael's review of *The Godfather: Part II,* she pointed out that "Coppola is the inheritor of the traditions of the novel, the theatre, and—especially—opera and movies."

In operatic terms, the plotline of *Godfather III* even more closely resembles that found in Verdi's *Rigoletto,* which culminates in the murder of daughter Gilda through the mistakes of her father, Rigoletto. In her entertaining article "Family Ceremonies," Naomi Greene cites the argument made in Catherine Clement's book *Opera; or, The Undoing of Women* that "opera is always about transgressions committed against patriarchy, authority, power. Operatic characters die 'for transgression—for transgression of familial rules, political rules, the things at stake in sexual and authoritarian power.'" In other words, they die as a result of the very same transgressions that lie at the heart of *The Godfather* saga.

For all intents and purposes, music functions as an additional character in *The Godfather: Part III*, the hyperemotional melodies and attendant textured chorale passages of *Cavalleria rusticana* highlighting the sense of doom that increases minute by minute, frame by frame. The stylized ritual of opera on-stage is vividly contrasted with the murderous actions of Michael's would-be assassins prowling the opera house, and the music from *Cavalleria rusticana*, as well as that composed by Carmine Coppola for the film, conveys a sense of events careening out of control. Violence is about to destroy both the Corleone family and the "holy ritual" of opera, and by cutting between the on-stage production, the fevered attempts to assassinate Michael, the unexpected death of the new pope, and the poisoning of Don Altobello, Coppola continually ratchets up the excitement to a Hitchcockian level particularly reminiscent of the Albert Hall "Storm Warning Cantata"/assassination attempt at the climax of 1956's *The Man Who Knew Too Much*. So skillfully shot and edited is the entire, lengthy opera house sequence that, like Hitchcock, Coppola even manages to throw a nicely judged piece of black humor into the setup. As Connie avidly watches Don Altobello gorge himself on the poison-laced cannoli she has brought him, her impatience at having to wait for his death leading her to all but shout "Die already, old man!," the audience actually laughs, relieved to be afforded a moment's respite before Coppola plunges them once again into the attempt on Michael's life. It's emblematic of the saga's continued hold on audiences that even here they root for the murderous Michael to escape assassination.

With such finely honed sequences buttressing Pacino's extraordinary multilayered characterization of Michael, why then did *Godfather III* fail to fulfill audience expectations? Answer number 1:

George Hamilton. The film suffers from Duvall's absence, not because Hamilton is actually bad, but because he can bring no sense of history to the table and lacks Duvall's gravitas as an actor. Answer number 2: Sofia Coppola. When, after shooting began in November of 1989, actress Winona Ryder dropped out of her role as Michael's daughter Mary (citing exhaustion), Coppola made the fateful decision to replace her with his daughter Sofia. An untrained actress essaying a high-profile, complex role in the glare of worldwide scrutiny, Sofia proved unable to fully express the character's appropriate emotions either physically or vocally. Her tentative take on Mary's strong-willed personality undercut the essence of a conflicted charcter in love with her own cousin, robbing the film of crucial passion; even with the stunning tableau of Mary's death on the opera house steps, the ending lacks the true weight and grandeur necessary to achieve director Coppola's hoped-for tragedy of classical proportion.

Coppola himself hesitantly lays Sofia's problems at the feet of her vocal patterns, but a comment about her California-speak is the only criticism he can bring himself to utter; proud father that he is, he goes on to say that she is "full" on-screen—"She's there—it's all there in her eyes." In reality, just as Frank Sinatra Jr. always seems more comfortable conducting, rather than singing, so too does Sofia Coppola seem most comfortable behind the camera rather than in front of it.

Not surprisingly, even the ever-confident Coppola crumbled when faced with the devastating barbs aimed at Sofia, criticism that only reinforced, however unintentionally, many of the reasons why he made *Godfather III* in the first place. Referring to a scathing *Vanity Fair* article on the subject of Sofia's performance, a strikingly vulnerable Coppola speaks in aggrieved yet wounded tones: "They shot bullets at Sofia—like at Mary—but they were really pointed at me. 'He's vulnerable here. Kill him here.' There's no worse way to pay for your sins than to have your children included in the punishment. That's what the film is really about."

Over the course of the two-plus decades since the film's release, it has become clear that the casting of Sofia Coppola has cast an unfair shadow over the film's reputation; the shelf life of the controversy has lasted well past its expiration date precisely because Sofia is the director's daughter. In an interesting analysis of the controversy, Sofia's aunt, Talia Shire, mused that the entire film might have collapsed if Sofia had not undertaken the role on only several hours' notice: "My gut feeling was, had Francis wasted even one week, the whole damn thing could have just come undone. Sofia was kind of heroic, and somebody ought to remember that."

Casting controversies aside, a third reason for the film's relative lack of acceptance lay in the complicated financial plotline that occupied a sizable portion of the running time. So byzantine were the on-screen financial maneuvers driving the plot that, in trying to work all of them into the complicated screenplay, Coppola and Puzo actually muddied the waters, never fully clarifying the motives of the financial power players. In many ways the screenwriters' work is first-rate, but criticism of the confusion resulting from the characters' financial machinations remains justified.

The actual physical appearance of Michael Corleone in *The Godfather: Part III* supplied one final hurdle in the way of total audience acceptance, and hindered the film in tangible, if hard to quantify, fashion. Audiences for part III entered the theater carrying the image of Michael from parts I and II in their minds. Confronted with a twenty-years-older Michael who is diabetic and rapidly aging, viewers seemed to feel uneasy in the face of such physical and moral degeneration.

Focusing on Michael's soulless character may have fulfilled Coppola's stated intention of killing him off, but such a bleak outlook resulted in the audience lacking a rooting interest. This now-anemic-acting version of Michael, too physically and spiritually bankrupt to marshal his interior resources, no longer seemed to care. Audiences remained baffled: was this washed-out man shown vacillating between inaction and despair really Michael Corleone? This wasn't the sacred monster they had followed over the course of two films and several decades, and his very passivity underscored the reason why audiences responded to Vincent's brash, gavonelike demeanor with something approaching relief. Vincent is a thug, but he's vital and will fight for the Corleone name. He's a man of action and as such finally supplies the audience with a character to cheer.

When Michael is faced with an attempted assassination, the spectral presence of blinding lights, whirling blades, and helicopter-mounted machine guns seems to render him incapable of movement, and he is saved only by Vincent's quick thinking. Coppola is underlining Michael's decline through his lack of action; the aging don is no longer in total control, and the torch has been passed to the new generation. The Michael Corleone on display here is old before his time, concerned, in Coppola's words, with "matters of heart and soul" rather than revenge. More interested in making up for past mistakes than in expanding his future powers, he is vulnerable precisely because his concerns remain personal and not those of business.

So overwhelmed with guilt is Michael that he even attempts to repent, confessing his sins to the soon-to-be pontiff, Cardinal Lamberto (a figure clearly based on Pope John Paul I, and nicely etched by Raf Vallone). "What," Michael wonders aloud, "is the point of confessing if I don't repent?" The idea of the pontiff of crime confessing to the pope-in-waiting is a terrific stroke of invention, yet so extreme are Michael's sins that the cardinal is unable to grant him absolution. Attempting a confession to a cardinal who shortly thereafter is murdered himself, Michael finds himself standing at the abyss, and there's no sign of heaven in sight.

Failing in his confession to Cardinal Lamberto, Michael renews his efforts at emotional intimacy with Kay, and once again attempts to justify his actions to her: "I loved my father. I swore I would never be a man like him, but I loved him. But he was in danger— what could I do? Then later you were in danger, our children were in danger. You were all I loved and valued most in the world. And now you're gone. And it was all for nothing. You have to understand I had a whole different destiny planned." This tentative reconciliation, beautifully underplayed by both Pacino and Keaton, is an affecting scene, but when all was said and done, audiences didn't much care for this new Michael Corleone, a self-aware man who, far from emerging triumphant, admits to a misspent life. Audiences wanted the old Michael back, the Michael who bestrode the world of crime like a colossus. Coming to theaters in anticipation that part III would provide more of what they found so thrilling in parts I and II, viewers found the emotional payoff lacking. It's a tribute to the underlying power of Coppola's vision that the audience still cared at all about a man capable of murdering his own brother, but the bottom line remained: a murderous thug they could accept, but a more passive, albeit infinitely more self-aware, godfather they did not.

It may just be that Michael's obsession with past mistakes and his contemplation of roads not taken all hit a little too close to home for the audience, because genuine Hollywood blockbusters rarely deliver truth in such unvarnished fashion. In *The Godfather*, Coppola and Puzo's ruthless message was softened by a somewhat rose-colored view of mobsters past, the harsh metaphor equating the Mafia with American business cloaked by the warmth of the family saga. Such layering of tough truths inside an appealing package utterly vanished in part III and, along with it, so too did the first film's extraordinary appeal at the box office. As actor Joe Mantegna smartly phrased it: "There are no good guys here. There are only bad bad guys and good bad guys. The violence cancels out the warmth."

Throughout three films and three generations, the world of the Corleones expanded from a small village in Sicily to the confines of New York City's Little Italy, from a Long Island compound to Las Vegas and the wide-open spaces of Lake Tahoe. The tragedy of Michael Corleone is that with his education and opportunities, his horizons might have remained limitless, yet, in the end, he has circled back to where Don Vito started: he returns to New York City and, ultimately, Sicily, buried by his Old World adherence to notions of revenge, violence, and the role of paterfamilias.

Michael has failed in his attempt to fulfill the traditional Italian male roles of procreation and protection, and if the Italian male has failed his family, he has nothing—he is no longer a man. It's a concept of failure that hovers throughout Italian-American literature, most bluntly and concisely laid out in Don DeLillo's *Underworld*: "[He] did the unthinkable Italian crime. He walked out on his family. They don't even have a name for this." In effect, Michael long ago walked out on his family because, even when physically present, he remained emotionally absent, landing at a self-inflicted and unbridgeable distance from the role of paterfamilias so expertly enacted by his own father.

In achieving all—money, power, success—Michael Corleone has ruined his life. He is filled with remorse for what he has done and regret for all that is left undone. His soul shriveling over the years (Coppola called him a "living corpse" at the end of part II), he dies in every sense but the physical once his daughter Mary is shot to death. It is Mary's death that kills off the last remaining shred of decency in Michael; he has caused first the splitting apart and finally the destruction of his family, forfeiting his soul in the process and ultimately embodying the living proof of Mario Puzo's statement in *The Godfather Papers* that "the most successful Italian man I know admits that, though the one human act he never could understand was suicide, he understood it when he became a success." In the film's penultimate moments, the viewer is transported back in time through a montage of Michael dancing with the women in his life—Kay, first wife Apollonia, and Mary—but music and movement have now vanished from his life forever. If, in dealing with grief, memory is first a curse and eventually a balm, Michael will forever be denied the comfort found when memories outlast the pain. In his tortured self-awareness that his criminality caused his own daughter's death lies his enemies' ultimate revenge. When he dies at the very end of the film, he is utterly alone in the garden of his Sicilian villa, attended only by a rather indifferent-looking dog. It's a chilling final image, Coppola's deliberate long shot emphasizing the isolated nature of the death.

Endlessly compared with its two predecessors, *Godfather: Part III* possesses its own poignant quality that deepens with each viewing. In the lingering controversy over the casting, audiences and commentators alike have forgotten that the two-hundred-minute epic actually garnered seven Academy Award nominations, most notably Best Supporting Actor (Andy Garcia), Best Director, and Best Picture. The shortsightedness of critics and audiences endlessly comparing the film with its award-winning predecessors, and thereby depriving themselves of the substantial pleasures to be found in part III on its own, is best summed up in the review of *Rolling Stone* critic Peter Travers: "So when it sinks in that this nearly three hour sequel is not up to the level of its predecessors, the disappointment runs deep. Is part III worth your time? Of course. It's still *The Godfather* and some of it is deeply affecting."

Godfather: Part III holds its own notable rewards, and the sense of absolute doom that hangs over Michael permeates the film, darkening the texture while hooking an audience with an unflinching gaze at evil. An amoral man has met his utterly desolate end, his wasted life and lonely death presented in images that linger and disturb. While Michael's demise seems inevitable, it nonetheless rivets. How many of their own bad decisions do audiences see in Michael's? Are viewers reminded of missed opportunities with their own families? When all is said and done, and notwithstanding its unevenness, this concluding chapter of the Corleone saga still registers with force: thought provoking, darkly pleasurable, and, most of all, haunting.

HBO's brilliant series *The Sopranos*. Tony Soprano (James Gandolfini) flanked by his capos Sylvio (Steven Van Zandt) and Paulie Walnuts (Tony Sirico) *Photofest*

14   The Shadow of *The Godfather*

The Godfather *is the Italian* Star Wars.

ACTOR JOE MANTEGNA

IN THE WAKE OF *The Godfather* trilogy, the Mafia acquired the one element it had never before possessed: glamour. Danger, excitement, thrills, violence—all of these elements had always figured into any discussion of the mob, but with Marlon Brando and Al Pacino emoting on-screen in all their larger-than-life charisma, the Mafia suddenly became hip. Mobsters and showbiz had met, and both liked what they saw.

Real-life mobsters now had their fifteen minutes of fame, and they were not about to relinquish it, dressing for the spotlight that seemed to perpetually follow in their wake. The media telegenic John Gotti, the "Dapper Don" of two-thousand-dollar custom-tailored suits and hand-painted ties, seemed to revel in his own publicity, a man who cut "la bella figura" just as smartly as did his on-screen counterpart, Joey Zasa. On-screen and in real life alike, the lure of the

Corleones had permeated the American imagination, the shadow of the saga lengthening rather than diminishing with the passing of the decades.

The more publicity the Mafia received and the more glamorous the coverage, the less threatening it seemed to become, at least in the mind of the general public. With John Gotti flourishing in the headlines of the *New York Post* and his offspring later starring in the reality television show *Growing Up Gotti,* the mystery and danger associated with the mob inevitably decreased. The mob may or may not have been less dangerous, but it was perceived as such, and in the show-business-hungry America of the late twentieth century, image mattered more than ever.

At the same time that this emphasis on image increased, so too did the number of criminals willing to turn state's evidence, and as a result the actual reach of the mob decreased. The original intent of the Mafia had been completely subverted, or in the words of the essay collection *From Wiseguys to Wise Men,* "'This focus on image, on the way they are perceived by others, especially those not involved directly with crime, is a far cry from the origins of Mafioso behavior, and it helped contribute to the eventual downfall of the gangster."

The widespread power of the mob may have decreased, but onscreen and in print the influence and spell of *The Godfather* continued to spawn endless spin-offs, sincere and comedic alike. Besides the two *Godfather* film sequels, Puzo himself continued his exploration of the mob in the novels *Omerta, The Sicilian,* and *The Last Don.* The American public—and Puzo's publishers—wouldn't let go, and even his death in 2004 couldn't stop the juggernaut, leading to Random House's 2004 publication of *The Godfather Returns,* by Mark Winegardner, as well as the same author's 2006 novel *The Godfather's Revenge.* Winegardner's books may not have registered with the force of Puzo's original novel, but they were solidly entertaining, and in combination with the commercials, cartoons, and even rap videos paying tribute to the Corleones, the tidal wave rolled on with no end in sight. June 2012 will see the publication of *The Family Corleone,* a Puzo-estate-authorized prequel to the events of the original novel, adapted by author Ed Falco from one of Puzo's unproduced screenplays. In the very smart words of actor Joe Mantegna, *The Godfather* remains "the Italian *Star Wars.*"

Although even the decidedly non-Italian but award-winning John Huston joined the mob rollout by directing the gangster-centric *Prizzi's Honor,* the most notable of all such releases in the post-Godfather years was Italian-American director Martin Scorsese's trio of mob films: *Mean Streets, Goodfellas,* and *Casino.* If, in Italian-American music, Sinatra, Tony Bennett, and Dean Martin exist as the holy trinity, in Italian-American film, the same exalted positions are held by the three Coppola *Godfather* films and Scorsese's own trilogy. Scorsese's films constitute the most well-known films to have arisen from the shadow of *The Godfather,* but his trilogy is also notably grittier than the *Godfather* triptych, all traces of romance erased in a down-and-dirty take on gangster life and culture.

While Coppola's films depict a patriarchal society and the relationship of fathers to sons, Scorsese's films center on sons attempting to break away from their neighborhoods and, just as important, from the maternal influence. *Mean Streets* famously opens with the soundtrack blasting the Ronettes' "Be My Baby," a song underscoring the actions of neighborhood goombas trying to act like men, rather than babies still under the influence of a woman/mother. It's not just that in most Scorsese films the women seem both frightened and frightening. It's that these tough guys in *Mean Streets* still act like adolescents, constantly fighting and pulling teenage pranks like throwing firecrackers down mailboxes. Charlie (Harvey Keitel) aspires to a position of power within the mob, yet his mother still lays out freshly laundered shirts for him, complete with a note. So lacking in any sense of true adult responsibility is Charlie that he deserts girlfriend Teresa (Amy Robinson) while she is having an epileptic seizure in order to chase the near-psychotic Johnny Boy (Robert DeNiro) down the street. In typical ignorant adolescent fashion, such characters treat Teresa's epilepsy as a mental defect: she is perceived as half crazy—damaged goods.

In the twenty-first-century's most noteworthy twist on the Italian-American male/female relationship, David Chase, the creator of *The Sopranos,* placed the mother/son bond at the forefront of the series' plot; Tony Soprano may be following in his father's footsteps by becoming a gangster, but it is mother Livia who controls him, at one point even trying to arrange a hit on him. Livia may very well stand as the most unpleasant, whiny, grasping—and fascinating—mother yet glimpsed in a television series, a woman so sour that her response to her teenage grandson's search for the meaning of life is a disgusted, "It's all a big nothing. What makes you think you're so special?"

Lying and stealing may result in a state of disgrace by the lights of polite society, but in Scorsese films such actions ensure that the perpetrators are perceived in their neighborhoods as men of the world. Writes Franco La Cecla, "because the state of grace is perceived as feminine . . . this state of disgrace must be achieved alongside and in front of other men." At its most extreme, and Scorsese films are all about extremes, this involves earning status as a made man, the killing of others functioning as a rite of passage into a crime family that may itself replace one's own biological family.

Scorsese's films are masterful, but in their studied lack of romance achieve a less-universal iconic status than do the *Godfather* films. Just as Sinatra towers over all other Italian singers, overshadowing the Vic Damones, Al Martinos, and Jerry Vales of the world, so too do the *Godfather* movies overshadow all other mob films. What *The Godfather* saga has achieved proves possible only with the greatest popular art: when taken together, the films explain America to itself. *The Godfather* hasn't just Italianized America—it has held up a national mirror to the American public and told the truth.

And yet. If America sees itself in the *Godfather* mirror, what then to make of the latter-day on-screen characterizations of Italian-American men and women, portrayals that a 1981 study of prime-time television found to be more "denigrating" than positive by a margin of two to one: "Most Italian-American characters held low-status jobs, only one in seven being shown working as an executive, manager or professional, and the majority spoke improper English, which made them the butt of jokes."

Disingenuous at best, and cynically uncaring at worst, the perpetrators of such mass media portrayals choose to ignore the effects on the image of Italian-Americans; a report released in 2009 by the Italic Institute of America cited a set of statistics compiled by the FBI that indicated only 0.00782% of Italian-Americans possessed any criminal associations, yet a national Zogby poll found a staggering 74 percent of the American public believed that Italian-Americans have ties to the mob.

Is it Italian-Americans themselves who embrace these stereotypes most readily, who chuckle knowingly at the movie mama serving heaping plates of pasta? Think Marie Barone, the bossy, smothering mother on television's *Everybody Loves Raymond*, simultaneously deploying love and control through heaping trays of lasagna. Does the plethora of two-dimensional characters on-screen create a ragged, confusing self-image among Italian-Americans, causing them to embrace their own version of a minstrel show? The question of self-image among Italian-Americans flooded with images of mobsters had actually been raised at the time of *The*

Godfather's filming by the decidedly non-Italian, but liberal, New York City politician Paul O'Dwyer, who stated: "The Italians are damned well burnt up and I think they're right. There are millions of Italians in the United States and just a dozen or two dozen or a hundred hoods, and yet these hoods have become symbolic of Italian Americans. This kind of thing affects their children."

Perhaps it's even Italian-Americans who watch a hopelessly sad, imbecilic reality show like *Jersey Shore*, wherein the lead characters, who spend their time tanning and working out, refer to themselves as guidos and guidettes. Sad to say, the most well-known image of Italian-Americans in the country right now may be that of Nicole "Snooki" Polizzi of *Jersey Shore* fame, who, name notwithstanding, is not even Italian. Chilean by birth and adopted by an Italian-American family, this twenty-something Jersey girl (from Upstate New York) with the memorably Italian surname is the most visible cast member of the show that constitutes the most overtly Italian show on all of television. Polizzi, who "authored" a book while admitting that she had only read two books in her entire life, remains famous for a hedonistic life consisting of equal parts tanning, booze, and the primping of her voluminous poof-styled hairdo. Immersed in her own version of Italian-American culture, Polizzi, a self-described guidette, seemingly laughs at the stereotype before anyone else, oblivious and calculating in equal measure. (Her response to the show's vociferous critics among leaders of Italian-American civil rights organizations? A ladylike "Fuck you! If you don't want to watch, don't watch . . . I'm serious. Fuck you!")

Such was the measure of Snooki's renown in fame-obsessed twenty-first-century America that she received a payment of $32,000 for a pair of one-hour question-and-answer sessions with students at Rutgers University, precisely $2,000 more than the same university paid to Nobel Prize–winning author Toni Morrison for her commencement address . . . Asked about her inspiration in life, the diva responded: "Being tan. When you're tan, you feel better about yourself." Her advice to the students? "Study hard, but party harder."

When the cast of *Jersey Shore* landed in Italy for the filming of its fourth season, the caricatured appearances and actions displayed by the cast were not viewed as those of Italian-Americans but, rather, as those of buffoonish Americans. Labeled by the Italian press on day one as "supercafoni" ("super boors"), the cast members proceeded to get into a car accident with police while displaying a total lack of interest in the artistic and cultural traditions of Florence. The nadir of this supposed "return to roots," however, may well have been reached with the appearance of cast member JWoww on Italian television with interviewer Simona Ventura. When asked by Ventura to look into a wishing well and describe her future, the Jerseyite (from New York) looked into the decorative wishing well, frowned, and responded: "I don't see nothing. What do you mean?"

Which leads to the key question: is this how the journey from urban ghetto to suburbia ends—in a caricature just as garish as those on display one hundred years ago? Who are these people we now see on-screen? If Mario Puzo famously declared that in his youth he never met even one of the singing, happy-go-lucky Italians so beloved of Hollywood, then it is equally certain that *Jersey Shore*'s young men and women, obsessed as they are with tanning and flat abs, are equally unrepresentative of the country's millions of Italian-Americans. Are all twenty-something Americans like this, or are Italian-Americans specifically picked for their larger-than-life actions and speaking voices? Is it the New Joisey accents that people find laughable, and hence worthy of a reality show at which to condescendingly chuckle? Is this, God forbid, what it means to be an Italian-American in the twenty-first century? Then again, it may just be a matter of what makes for compelling television. In the assessment of commentator Bill Tonelli, "There are many more

Italian-American CPAs than hit men, not that I want to watch a cable TV series about accountants."

Is the record any stronger when it comes to feature films? In the post-*Godfather* years, has there actually been an evolution in the depiction of Italian-American men and women on-screen? Hit films featuring Italians abound, but are the characters in, say, the Oscar-winning *Moonstruck* (1987) really so far removed from stereotype? Ronny Cammareri (played by the Italian-American relative of Coppola, Nicolas Cage), the baker/boyfriend of Cher's Loretta Castorini, is a hot-tempered, opera-loving male sweating it out by the bakery ovens; with little discernible effort, he could easily be transposed to a studio film from the 1940s. The *Moonstruck* universe is Italian-centric, but there still remains an essential "otherness" about the characters on display, as if they inhabit a separate universe located in that exotic metropolitan burg known as Brooklyn.

The Academy Award–winning *Rocky* presents the lovable Italian lug with a never-say-die spirit, part buffoon but warmly human. Scorsese's *Raging Bull* does *Rocky* one better—or several better—in its depiction of a real-life Italian-American boxer. In the darkly accomplished hands of Scorsese and Robert DeNiro, Jake La Motta comes alive in dozens of minute, instantly understandable ways: by turns strong, mealymouthed, contemptible, and oddly sympathetic, *Raging Bull*'s La Motta may not be admirable, but he is fully, recognizably human, which in the last analysis counts for much more. (La Motta also earned a memorable put-down at the hands of Frank Sinatra and cronies in one of their late-night discussions regarding "worst living American." Said Sinatra: "He dumped the fight to Billy Fox and never told his father, who bet his life savings on Jake . . . Lower than whale shit." Proudly Italian though he was, Sinatra proved as merciless analyzing his paesanos as he did everyone else.)

Perhaps *Saturday Night Fever* (1977) encapsulates the best and worst of Italian-American characters in its tale of Brooklynite Tony Manero (John Travolta), paint-store clerk by day and king of the disco dance floor at night. For all its flaws, the film nonetheless manages to rather movingly portray a bright but inarticulate young Italian-American who dreams of a better life and an escape from Brooklyn. Along the way to self-discovery and the not-so-incidental acknowledgment that women should be treated as more than sex objects, Tony both revels in his Italian roots (posters of Al Pacino as Serpico and Sylvester Stallone as Rocky hang on his walls) and embodies the worst clichés of clueless goombahs; image is everything for Tony, and after spending hours on the all-important look of his hair, he explodes at his father for hitting him: "Would you just watch the hair? I work a long time on my hair and you hit it!"

Tony is caught in the midst of a loving but wildly dysfunctional family, one filled with near caricatures of inarticulate Italians. Witness the dialogue when an absent Tony finally returns home and is confronted by his parents:

MOTHER: Where you been?

[*no answer*]

FATHER: Your mother wants to know where you been. Where you been?

MOTHER: Your father's askin ya—where ya been?

Proust it isn't, but in the film's nonromanticized coming-of-age story and exploration of pointed socioeconomic themes, it achieves a certain, if shaky, gravitas. The famous disco dancing may appear hilariously dated (and just try stacking up Travolta's supposedly great moves against those found in any Gene Kelly or Fred Astaire musical), but there is an odd kind of wisdom to snatches of the dialogue, an acknowledgment that the inchoate longings of these Italian goombahs, obscene as they may be, constitute sentiments well worth exploring:

TONY: "Oh fuck the future!"
FUSCO: "No, Tony! You can't fuck the future. The future fucks you! It catches up with you and it fucks you if you ain't planned for it."

The problem remains, however, that for every *Saturday Night Fever* or genuinely first-rate movie like *Serpico* (1973) or *Donnie Brasco* (1997), Hollywood has continued to roll out a dozen comedies that treat Italian-Americans as buffoonish caricatures. It's worth noting that of the most notable mob parody/comedies that followed in the wake of *The Godfather*, namely *My Blue Heaven* (1990), *Analyze This* (1999), and *Analyze That* (2002), not one was created by Italian-Americans. In *The Kid Stays in the Picture*, the 2004 documentary on the life and career of Robert Evans, Evans muses that before *The Godfather*, films about the mob had inevitably failed because they were written or directed by Jews, not Italians, the most notable such failure being Paramount's own 1969 release *The Brotherhood*, starring Kirk Douglas. It was this very paucity of Italian-Americans behind the camera that led to Evans's insistence that only an Italian-American could successfully direct *The Godfather*. Forty years after the initial release of *The Godfather*, the more things have changed, the more they've stayed the same.

Not all Italian-Americans are criminals, but you wouldn't know it from the movies Hollywood continues to routinely churn out; Italians on-screen still come in only two colors: buffoon or murderer. Why do all the men speak-a with accents like-a this? Why did the Italian women on-screen seem to like nothing better than to cook tomato sauce all day? Intermittently amusing though an

Analyze This could be, such films feature cartoon characters written for the screen by men and women for whom Italian-Americans inherently represent figures of fun. This stereotypical portrayal of Italian-Americans has even carried over into cartoons, as when, in the 2004 DreamWorks release *Shark Tale,* Robert DeNiro himself voiced the character of the most feared shark in the water: Don Lino.

It's worth noting that DeNiro himself directed 1993's *A Bronx Tale,* which explores the Italian-American push/pull between life lived on the poor but straight and narrow and the monied allure of the flashy gangster. Adapted by Chazz Palminteri from his semi-autobiographical play of the same title, the film, set in the Bronx of the 1960s, follows young Calogero "C" Anello as he navigates the path between his bus-driving, law-abiding father, Lorenzo (De-Niro), and the all-powerful neighborhood mobster Sonny LoSpecchio (Palminteri) to whom he has taken a shine. After witnessing Sonny murder a rival in broad daylight, the six-year-old Calogero protects the mobster by lying to the police; his silence ensures his family's survival, with Lorenzo telling his son: "You just did a good thing for a bad man."

The dramatic center of the film stems from the tension that arises between Sonny and Lorenzo over Calogero's future, yet for all of the gangland flash and occasional violence, here's the rare Italian-American film filled with well-rounded characters. Lorenzo is aware of his own shortcomings and resents Sonny's easy money. For his part, Sonny is not all bad and actually tries to deter "C" from entering a life of crime. Thanks to the first-rate writing and acting of Palminteri and the remarkably assured direction of De-Niro, the film subtly explores both sides of the gangland equation. Lorenzo has spent ten years battling Sonny's influence over his son, but even at the movie's end, after Sonny has been killed, Lorenzo simply tells Calogero: "I never hated Sonny. I just didn't like him making you grow up so fast." As proved the case with the Corleones, here are Italian-Americans depicted not in black and white, but instead, numerous, recognizable shades of gray.

There is even the occasional film in which Italian-American characters start out as stereotypes yet end up as men and women who, for all of their quirks, triumph with brains, not brawn. In the very popular *My Cousin Vinnie,* the title character, one Vinny Gambini, is, in the form of Joe Pesci's portrayal, a fast-talking Noo Yawk personal injury lawyer who has never won a case, a consistently loud, crass buffoon incapable of pronouncing the word "youth." He may represent a boorish cartoon character come to life, but he also evolves into a genuinely funny, street-smart attorney who, with the help of his flamboyant girlfriend Mona Lisa Vito (the Academy Award–winning Marisa Tomei), wins a murder trial without any previous experience. That delightful, if ridiculous fantasy helped the film to rate number 3 in the August 2008 *American Bar Association Journal* cover story on the twenty-five greatest legal movies ever made—right after *To Kill a Mockingbird* and *Twelve Angry Men* . . .

Yet for the most part, virtually nothing authentically Italian shows up on the screen. In *Married to the Mob,* a film entirely inhabited by comic gangsters and big-haired guidettes, the one character without a name along the lines of Cucumber Frank, or Vinnie the Slug, and certainly the only character who speaks quietly without waving his arms incessantly, is, no surprise, the Waspy FBI agent, Mike Downey, played by Matthew Modine. The similarly popular *My Blue Heaven* features Steve Martin's portrayal of Vincent "Vinnie" Antonelli, a character raggedly sketched by the decidedly non-Italian Nora Ephron, a characterization that may rank as the least believable Italian-American heard or seen since J. Carrol Naish's portrayal of the title character on *Life with Luigi.* Martin's depiction of an Italian-American mobster registers as nothing so much as another of his distanced, knowingly ironic portrayals, and while it's a safe bet that Ephron and director Herbert Ross would never have undertaken a comic film trading in such stereotypical portrayals of African-American life, they seemingly held no such qualms about Italian-Americans.

In the end, it has been left to cable television to portray Italian-Americans as three-dimensional human beings, the corrective ironically arriving in the form of another gangster saga, the brilliant and wildly popular television series *The Sopranos*. In this smart, funny, cynical HBO series featuring a uniformly excellent cast led by James Gandolfini, Edie Falco, and Dominic Chianese, viewers came face-to-face with the ultimate twenty-first-century manifestation of Italian mobsters as the suburban men next door. Created by David Chase, an Italian-American whose knowledge of the culture manifested itself in countless details glimpsed throughout the series' six-year run, *The Sopranos* possessed a textural richness lacking in virtually all films about Italian-Americans except those of Coppola and Scorsese. The attention to food, family rituals, and changing generational values lent the show an undeniable feeling of authenticity, the characterizations growing out of genuine, recognizably complex emotions. For all the volatility of the characters, Chase inherently understood the holes in each of their psyches, the gaps of self-knowledge underpinning the wildest actions on display.

Having *The Sopranos* live in the land of well-heeled suburbia sent one clear message: whether gained honestly or through crime, money trumps all in America. Coppola's idea of the mob as metaphor for American business has here been brilliantly updated for the twenty-first century; Tony's life as a "waste management consultant" revolves around the god of money, and in the season two episode entitled "From Where to Eternity," the series writers provided him with a brilliant speech that explicitly underlined all of the reasons why: "Men like the Rockefellers needed us to build their cities and dig their subways and make them richer . . . But some of us didn't want to swarm around their hive and lose who we were. We wanted to stay Italian and preserve the things that mean something to us: honor and family and loyalty . . . And some of us wanted a piece of the action."

Tony attempts to solve problems of guilt and rage with conspicuous consumption of food, sex, and money. In the process, he remains noticeably, identifiably Italian, confined by the prism of otherness through which he is always viewed, yet living in a sprawling suburban McMansion while grappling with many of the same psychic problems that affect his bland, white-collar neighbors: wayward children, recalcitrant co-workers, upsetting dreams, and a wide-ranging, free-floating anxiety disorder. If audiences saw an unpleasant but undeniable reflection of the American business ethos in the Corleone family, the sight of the family's isolated compounds still allowed those same viewers to hold themselves at a remove, reasoning that their own living situation bore no resemblance to such fortress-like conditions. In *The Sopranos,* however, Tony is presented as the everyday bathrobe-clad next door neighbor padding out to pick up his morning newspaper. Given his on-screen persona as a harried (albeit murderous) suburban husband/father dealing with problems caused by his wife and children, no such remove can here exist. Not all Americans may wear velour tracksuits, but all seem to recognize a bit of themselves in the personal problems that beset Tony Soprano.

The shadow of *The Godfather* lies everywhere in *The Sopranos,* which plays out as a less noble, less Italian, more fully American version of Puzo's epic. In the world of *The Sopranos,* reverence for *The Godfather* actually reveals character. Tony's fellow mobsters, Big Pussy and Paulie Walnuts, may argue about the exact provenance of classic *Godfather* lines, but nephew Christopher, younger and often at odds with Paulie, doesn't really care about the three *Godfather* films, constantly mixing up his film facts, much to the disgust of the older men. Nothing delineates the generational clash in *The Sopranos* more than the fact that for Christopher, it's the 1983 remake of *Scarface*, complete with a coked-out-of-his-mind, Cuban Tony Montana (Al Pacino) that speaks to him most clearly. Christopher represents a younger generation that, far from caring about the film's critical drubbing at the time of its release, has turned the remake into a certified cult classic, one whose style and ethos have influenced hip-hop style to this day. Actually, even Don Corleone himself, not to mention any victim of the present-day mortgage disaster caused by Wall Street speculators, would recognize Tony Montana's barebones philosophy of capitalism: "You know what capitalism is? 'Fuck You'!"

In Tony Soprano's mind, *The Godfather* presents a rather noble picture of past mob life to which he pays tribute in the very name of his own strip club/headquarters: the Bada Bing! (Says the amused Sonny Corleone in his dismissal of brother Michael's offer to avenge the shooting of their father: "What do you think this is, the army, where you shoot 'em a mile away? You gotta get up close, like this— bada bing! You blow their brains all over your nice Ivy League suit.") So thorough is Tony's identification with, or rather longing for, the world of *The Godfather*, that the director deliberately shows Tony buying orange juice right before the attempt on his life, just as Don Vito himself was perusing oranges when cut down in a storm of bullets.

Series creator David Chase even cheekily—and successfully— mirrors *The Godfather*'s famed film-ending baptism/murder dichotomy, but this time with his own less-murderous juxtapositioning of the church and sex. Instead of showing multiple murders of revenge taking place at the same time as a family baptism, Chase positions Carmella Soprano on the floor of her den in front of the television as she confesses her shortcomings to parish priest Father Phil. In a scene shot through with erotic tension, Carmella admits that she has chosen the path of deliberate ignorance when it comes to the issue of how Tony acquires the money that supports the upwardly mobile lifestyle she so craves. Following this confession, Carmella and Father Phil fall asleep, and when they wake up, it is with a kiss.

Born in 1960, Tony Soprano feels at sea, yearning for a past he never personally experienced. He only knows that long-gone world from *The Godfather,* a fact that makes his nostalgic worldview doubly ironic, given that Don Vito's own embrace of the Sicilian codes of silence and honor reads as nostalgic, rooted as those codes were in Old World customs. The lure of days gone by suffuses Tony's dissatisfaction with his own life, and he responds to *The Godfather* as received truth, seduced by the power of its sustained reverie about the past. For Tony, the past is not just another country, it is one more worthy of respect, where even the problems of mob business seemed more glamorous; when trouble came for the Corleone family, it involved testimony before a United States Senate committee. Tony's problems come in the much more prosaic form of the FBI's New Jersey branch.

Tony may have acquired enough distance from the mind-set of Little Italy to know that he should move on from the past and solve his problems with brainpower, not violence, but he can't quite complete the journey. Stuck between the old and the new in every area of his life, his Sonny Corleone–like temper defeats him time after time. He lives in a multicultural world and is utterly confused by it, asking himself—and others—how to make sense of this not-so-brave new world.

Fruitlessly searching for authenticity, Tony's quest resembles nothing so much as that of the Italian-Americans who make pilgrimages to a Little Italy so different from their own suburban lives. Viewing *The Godfather* as guide, touchstone, and blessing, he does not comprehend that the inevitable destruction of the Corleone family was built into its very DNA. For the Tony Sopranos of the world, *The Godfather* proves just as much curse as blessing. It's not just that the best is over—it's that the past they so desire never existed at all.

Coppola's scenario would place Don Vito's illegitimate grandson, Vincent Mancini (Andy Garcia), front and center as the final Don. *Photofest*

15   *Godfather: Part IV?*

I want to keep rocking the boat. Taking chances is what makes you strong, makes you wise.

—Francis Ford Coppola

I've learned how to spend money, and Francis has learned how to make it.

—George Lucas, referring to Coppola's second career as vintner and entrepreneur

The real Godfather *for me is the experience I had making it.*

—Francis Ford Coppola to actor Rob Lowe

The inevitable question remains: will a fourth *Godfather* film ever see the light of day? Twenty-plus years may have passed since the release of *Godfather III*, but Coppola has yet to completely rule out the possibility. In a tantalizing piece of information included on the DVD commentary track to "The Coppola Collection—*The Godfather: Part III*," the director actually muses aloud about a possible fourth film, explicating what sounds like a surefire narrative structure.

In Coppola's vision, *Godfather IV*, like part II, would alternate between two different stories and time periods: the first would follow Vito Corleone from the end of his story in part II up to the post–World War II time period depicted in the first film. By covering Vito from his midtwenties to his late fifties, the decades in which he consolidated power and established his dominance, the film would afford audiences the chance to experience, in effect, "Vito Corleone: The Unknown Years." At the same time, Coppola would explore the character of Sonny Corleone, with Sonny's life as a young man juxtapositioned alongside a second, more modern story centering on his illegitimate son, Vincent Mancini. In that modern story, Vincent, the head of the Corleone empire in the wake of Michael's death, will have drawn the family into the cocaine wars, the high-octane hunting of a drug lord in Colombia contrasted on-screen with the original pre–World War II rise of the family.

Having learned the limits of his audience with part III, Coppola has here come up with a scenario that allows filmmaker and audience alike the chance to have it both ways: a wallow in the more romantic family-centric past, and a harsh modern update of the family's final destruction and descent into hell. It would prove interesting to see how twenty-first-century audiences would react to the saga; raised on a steady diet of ever-increasing violence that makes most of *The Godfather* seem tame, younger audiences would certainly accept the Colombia drug sequences, but at the same time might yet succumb to a loving re-creation of pre–World War II mob life. By the same token, older audiences, inherently drawn to the nostalgia-bathed early scenes, would more than likely accept the harsh implosion of the family under Vinnie's leadership as the logical, justified end of the Corleones.

Given Coppola's formidable skills, *Godfather IV* might indeed scale the heights of greatness, but after listening to the director's DVD commentary on "The Coppola Restoration," one wonders whether he possesses the desire for one more major-league turn at bat. Having won every award and honor known to the film industry, he would have to think long and hard before signing on; does he really want to listen to the know-nothing executives of the new Hollywood pick apart his screenplay and question his directorial decisions? Is he happier working on idiosyncratic low-budget films like *Tetro* and *Youth without Youth*? Would Coppola, like Don Corleone, simply prefer to take it easy, his own highly regarded winery now functioning as a (much) larger version of Vito's vegetable garden? Is the chance to sit back with family and friends, playing the role of paterfamilias, more rewarding than suiting up for one last major battle?

One hopes that Coppola ultimately responds to the challenge, because as the years pass, and there are no longer any immigrants alive to recount firsthand stories of life in early-twentieth-century Little Italy, the actual fabric of that immigrant life has become nearly extinct. Through his films, it is Coppola who has picked up the baton, re-creating a century's worth of American life by continuing the recital of family lore that first began around kitchen tables. In the process, he has supplied not just an Italian-American book of memories but a penetrating look into the twentieth-century experience for all Americans.

"Ah," one thinks, "just one more meeting with the Corleones." A final opportunity to see Vito in his prime. The sobering sight of his grandson presiding over the final dissolution of the family. A chance to muse about our own ancestors and their journey through the American century, until inevitably, on-screen and off, we all circle back to one final shot of young Vito Andolini singing softly to himself as he stares at the Statue of Liberty . . .

16 March 3, 1902

America thou half-brother of the world!
With something good and bad of every land
—PHILIP JAMES BAILEY, *FESTUS*, SCENE 10

WHY IS IT THAT forty years after *The Godfather*'s initial release it still seems a living, breathing organism, a touchstone for Americans of all sorts? How have Coppola and Puzo managed the extraordinary feat of making Don Vito and Michael seem to have arrived from a very distant past, yet at the same time appear nearly contemporary?

Well, to paraphrase the film's own mantra, it's personal, not just business. We all see aspects of our very American lives up there on the screen, a mirror to our private and national identities. Coppola may have started out filming a well-known novel, intending to make an entertaining crime movie while using the mob family as metaphor for out-of-control American capitalism, but he ended up with something far greater: a genre-bending seminal work of pop culture that has continued to reverberate over the course of four decades and still shows no signs of abating. In creating the world of the Corleones over the course of three films, Coppola and Puzo not only recast the image of Italian-Americans but also succeeded in redefining how Americans of all stripes perceived their own heritage and place in the U.S. For good and occasionally bad, in a manner comedic, serious, and oftentimes highly profound, *The Godfather* did nothing less than help Italianize the United States.

In *The Godfather*, Francis Ford Coppola has managed the rather extraordinary feat of humanizing the idea of the Statue of Liberty, personalizing that first sight of L'America glimpsed by those long-ago immigrants, a symbol towering over all of the Vito Andolinis and Orazio Santopietros of the world. My young grandfather viewed the Statue of Liberty as the physical embodiment of the American dream, and if the promise was broken as often as kept, a promise it remained nonetheless, one speaking to the very idea of human possibility.

I think—actually I know—that my grandfather had moments of Mannagia L'America—of damning a country that values free speech above all yet thinks nothing of sending the FBI for a friendly chat about newspaper subscriptions. But my grandfather still cherished the dream, fully appreciating what America offered. When all is said and done, naming one's first daughter after the poet whose words anchor the Statue of Liberty remains the act of a true believer.

True believer he was, but I feel certain that my grandfather would still recognize every cynical motive on display in *The Godfather*, shaking his head in smiling recognition before launching into a scholarly discourse on economic conditions in nineteenth-century southern Italy. This time I'd listen. And in knowing that I'd listen, I wonder anew at his journey and what he would make of America in the twenty-first century. What would my grandfather actually say to me today? Would he approve of how I've spent my time? Would any pride in accomplishments be outweighed by disappointment that the family name ends with me? I like to think not, but it's a pipe dream to transform his Old World attitudes into a twenty-first-century acceptance of a single life lived at an emotional and physical remove from *la famiglia* of fifty years past.

I like to visit Ellis Island from time to time. I hop on the number 1 subway train and arrive at the southern tip of Manhattan in no more than forty-five minutes. A quick ten-minute ferry ride later, and I'm standing in the refurbished, tourist-friendly great hall. It's all a far cry from my grandfather's weeks-long voyage on the cramped, dirty steamship *Trave,* uncertainty, a brand-new language, and most of all hope awaiting him on land. For some reason I instinctively gravitate toward Ellis Island on days of light rain, the mist on the harbor partially obscuring the sights as I wander alone. I check out the exhibits, make sure yet again that our family's contribution is noted, but most of all do precisely what I don't usually do in noisy, oppressive, yet exhilarating Manhattan: I let my mind wander.

It is, of course, the lure of the past that haunts me—the thought of Lieutenant Thomas Parker, killed in World War I, running alongside the dream of my newly married grandmother's voyage to America on the *Oceania.* When I really let go, empty my mind of everything but the vivid imaginings of my grandparents on the ship—their clothes, the food they ate, the mix of uneasiness and hope—it always remains just a little scary. It all seems so near, yet a tantalizing inch or two out of reach. Do I want it to remain slightly beyond my comprehension? Perhaps Michael Corleone's channeling of Robert Browning was right after all: "A man's reach should exceed his grasp / Or what's a heaven for?"

More than anything, of course, these visits remain my own secular prayer of thanks, an acknowledgment of all I never took the time to say while my grandparents were alive. On every visit I wait for the one absolutely quiet moment that catches me off guard. It doesn't matter if I'm alone or surrounded by others because I see him—I see young Vito Andolini staring at the Statue of Liberty, softly singing of the old country as he contemplates his new world. Gently swinging his legs back and forth, he is every Italian immigrant who passed through Ellis Island in search of a better life, but most of all, he is my impossibly young grandfather, thirteen-year-old Orazio Santopietro on March 3, 1902, a boy on the verge of wonder, twenty lira in his pocket and touching American soil for the very first time. He whispers to me, and wrapped in some bittersweet mist from the old country, I seem to be borne back into the past. I know it's my grandfather because the cadence of his speech is the same, the accented vowels and noticeable breathing exactly as I remember them from childhood. On a good visit the words travel right through me, but I don't always catch them, a sharp noise breaking my reverie or a screaming baby bringing me back to present-day Manhattan.

Patriotic as I am, I don't believe in America in the same way as did my grandfather. I can't. I'm too assimilated and my worldview too ironic. It is only after turning forty that I fully appreciated just how on-target Puzo was: it is money that trumps all in L'America—trumps common sense, justice, and humanity. More than occasionally I despair over the country's bone-deep, reflexive cynicism and its attendant whining demand for instant gratification. But—believe I do nonetheless. If I sit quietly staring at the Statue of Liberty, always the promise of America flickers anew for me. In all my trips to the tip of Manhattan, that sense of renewal has never failed to appear, yet I remain afraid that it won't, that unconditional despair will wash over me.

As I hurtle down the path toward my sixtieth birthday it gives me a certain pleasure that my closest friends have begun to call me

Tommy all over again. I had jettisoned the nickname at age four-teen upon entering grade nine at that Connecticut prep school light years removed from my grandparents' village of Pontelan-dolfo, preferring the more grown-up Tom. When I came to New York twelve years later, my friends called me Saint Pete, a friendly reference to my most Italian of surnames. But now it's Tommy again, and I like not only the youthful playfulness of it all but, more to the point, the affection lying behind the diminutive. It is also, I realize, the only name by which my grandfather addressed me. It was never Tom or Thomas, but always Tommy, and when I hear Tommy, I hear my grandfather.

I hear him once more in the very first words of *The Godfather*: "I believe in America." And then he's gone.

Acknowledgments

I am particularly indebted to Jerre Mangione and Ben Morreale for their invaluable *La Storia: Five Centuries of the Italian American Experience,* the best overview of Italians in America that I have yet read. I also owe thanks to Harlan Lebo for his encyclopedic and entertaining study of *The Godfather* on film, *The Godfather Legacy.* Although the focus of both books is different from mine, each proved invaluable in supplying fascinating background information, which I hope I have adequately noted.

On a personal note, I offer a heartfelt thanks to the following for their guidance and assistance: Mark Erickson, for generously taking the time to read the manuscript so carefully; my cousin Peter Albini, for supplying translations whenever—which is to say always—my virtually nonexistent Italian failed; Catherine Daly, director of the American Family Immigration History Center on Ellis Island, who spent extraordinary amounts of time helping me track my grandparents' voyage to the United States; my cousin Don Albino, for sending me family records; Bill Cannon; Rheba Flegelman; Barbara Fasano and Eric Comstock; Kim Kelley; Lynnette Barkley, Brig Berney, and Jan Heise; Nola Safro; Tony DeSare; Ruth Mulhall; Mary Gates; Mimi Lines, my consultant on all matters Italian; Ron and Howard Mandelbaum at Photofest; Katie Gilligan at St. Martin's Press; my publisher, Thomas Dunne; my extraordinary circle of friends, too numerous to mention, for their continual support and forebearance even as I talked incessantly of all matters Italian; Jeanine Basinger; Patti LuPone; and finally, to my pal Craig Sylvester, who inadvertently started this book thirty years ago with his smiling comment: "You're Italian all right—Italian by way of the Taft prep school." It may just be the only comment I remember from my three years in law school.

Notes

1. DON VITO IN HOLLYWOOD

1   "I am willing to sacrifice," Francis Ford Coppola as quoted in Harlan Lebo, *The Godfather Legacy* (New York: Simon & Schuster, 2005), p. 191.

2   "I think you're the only actor," Mario Puzo as quoted in ibid., p. 47.

2   "As president of this company," Stanley Jaffe as quoted in Peter Biskind, "Making Crime Pay," *Premiere*, August 1997.

3   "scared shitless," Harlan Lebo, *The Godfather Legacy*, p. 49.

3   "get a take," Peter Bart, *Infamous Players* (New York: Weinstein Books, 2011), p. 221.

4   "You know those guys," Marlon Brando as quoted in Peter Biskind, "Making Crime Pay," *Premiere*, August 1997.

4   "mean looking," Stefan Kanfer, *Somebody: The Reckless Life and Remarkable Career of Marlon Brando* (New York: Knopf, 2008), p. 238.

5   "the miracle on Mulholland," Peter Bart, *Infamous Players*, p. 221.

5   "He looks Italian," Stefan Kanfer, *Somebody*, p. 238.

5   "Who are ve vatching," Harlan Lebo, *The Godfather Legacy*, p. 50.

5   "backed away," ibid.

2. SPRING 1992

12 "But you know how it is," Bill Tonelli (ed.), *The Italian American Reader* (New York: HarperCollins, 2003), p. xxii.

3. ANCESTRAL VOICES

31 "by learning to be ashamed," Leonard Covello as quoted in Jerre Mangione and Ben Morreale, *La Storia: Five Centuries of the Italian American Experience* (New York: HarperCollins, 1992), p. 222.

31 "There were many times," Gay Talese, *Unto the Sons* (New York: Random House, 1992), p. 51.

32 "Just put down," John D'Agata, "Round Trip," from *Halls of Fame*, as quoted in Bill Tonelli (ed.), *The Italian American Reader*, p. 513.

34 "If my father had said," John Gotti Jr., *60 Minutes*, April 11, 2011.

4. FROM *LA VIA VECCHIA* TO L'AMERICA

39 Gone were the hopes of liberation, ibid., p. 54.

40 "my father, bonarma," Jerre Mangione, *Mount Allegro* (Syracuse, N.Y.: Syracuse University Press, 1942), p. 20.

40 "In effect, the well-to-do," Jerre Mangione and Ben Morreale, *La Storia*, p. 59.

41 the Mezzogiorno, ibid., p. 32.

41 "simply began transferring," ibid., p. 60.

41 The government in Rome kept separate statistics, Mario Puzo, *The Godfather Papers* (New York: Putnam, 1972), p. 194.

42 "the greatest ill afflicting," Jerre Mangione and Ben Morreale, *La Storia*, p. 48.

42 "The Negro is not the man," ibid., p. xv.

43 "Italians are the toughest street fighters," Jackie Mason, *The World According to Me* (New York: Simon and Schuster, 1987).

43 from "mafiosi," Jerre Mangione and Ben Morreale, *La Storia*, p. 51.

43 "In their paranoia," Jerre Mangione and Ben Morreale, *La Storia*, p. 64.

45 "When you see that lady," Ernest Borgnine, *Ernie: The Autobiography* (New York: Citadel Press, 2008), p. 10.

45 in the fifty-year span, Jerre Mangione and Ben Morreale, *La Storia*, p. 32.

46 might begin to require a literacy test, ibid., pp. 100–101.

47 "The American-born children," ibid., p. 160.

48 too late for those immigrants to benefit, ibid., p. 131.

50 "celebrate the existence," Jerre Mangione, *Mount Allegro*, p. 24.

50 did not even possess a word for "privacy," Thomas J. Ferraro, *Feeling Italian: The Art of Ethnicity in America* (New York: New York University Press, 2005), p. 157.

50 the strong family unit found with immigrant Italians, Mario Puzo, *The Godfather Papers*, quoting Nathan Glazer and Daniel Moynihan, *Beyond the Melting Pot* (Cambridge, Mass.: MIT Press, 1963), p. 198.

52 "Then I discovered," Pete Hamill, *Why Sinatra Matters* (New York: Little Brown, 1998), p. 38.

52 "The name is Sinatra," ibid.

52 "such distinguished arbiters," Thomas J. Ferraro, *Feeling Italian*, p. 15.

52 "sneaking and cowardly," Jerre Mangione and Ben Morreale, *La Storia*, p. 211.

53 "a horde of steerage slime," ibid.

53 "There seems to me to be plenty of evidence," James Adams as quoted in ibid., p. 166.

53 "The foreign element excuse," Lincoln Steffens, as quoted in ibid., p. 241.

53 A 1910 study, ibid., p. 138.

54 only eleven possessed even a rudimentary, ibid., p. 166.

54   "None of my relatives," Jerre Mangione, *Mount Allegro*, in Bill Tonelli (ed.), *The Italian American Reader*, p. 474.

56   "changing a man's language," Jerre Mangione and Ben Morreale, *La Storia*, pp. 223–24.

58   "America was absolutely ripe," Francis Ford Coppola, in William Murray, "The *Playboy* Interview," *Playboy*, July 1975.

58   "Prohibition was the dumbest law," Pete Hamill, *Why Sinatra Matters*, p. 74.

60   "they're just a bunch of opera singers," Franklin D. Roosevelt as quoted in Jerre Mangione and Ben Morreale, *La Storia*, p. 25.

60   "great swarming," Henry James as quoted in ibid., p. 217.

61   "All crime could now be blamed," ibid., p. 261.

62   "there is a criminal organization," ibid.

62   had lasted over one year, ibid., pp. 261–62.

63   "a nothing," ibid., p. 262.

63   "largely on his evidence," Christopher Duggan, *Fascism and the Mafia* (New Haven: Yale University Press, 1989), as quoted in ibid.

64   "All the time," Joseph Massino as quoted in "Ex-Mob Boss Tells Jury, Calmly, About Murders," *New York Times*, April 14, 2011.

65   "where would we find," Jerre Mangione and Ben Morreale, *La Storia*, p. 263.

5. THE LURE OF THE CORLEONES

70   over one hundred fifty books, Jerre Mangione and Ben Morreale, *La Storia*, p. 263.

71   over one thousand Socialists, ibid., p. 283.

72   "must learn from the philanthropists," Regina Barreca (ed.), *A Sitdown with the Sopranos* (New York: Palgrave Macmillan, 2002), p. 4.

72   "decent man on the dark side," Mark Seal, "*The Godfather* Wars," *Vanity Fair*, March 2009.

73 75 percent of the money taken in, Gay Talese, *Honor Thy Father* (New York: Fawcett Crest, 1971), p. 127.

74 "It made our life," *New York Times,* October 22, 2010.

74 "I only did," Mark Seal, *"The Godfather* Wars," *Vanity Fair,* March 2009.

74 "seven hundred to one thousand men," Jerre Mangione and Ben Morreale, *La Storia,* pp. 258–59.

75 "The mafia image," ibid., p. 242.

76 "Both the Mafia and America," Francis Ford Coppola as quoted in Stephen Farber, "Coppola and *The Godfather," Sight and Sound* 41, no. 4 (Autumn 1972).

76 "he became nostalgic for," Gay Talese, *Honor Thy Father,* p. 271.

77 "Behind the popularity of the movie," Harlan Lebo, *The Godfather Legacy,* p. 209.

77 "So we beat on," F. Scott Fitzgerald, *The Great Gatsby* (New York: Charles Scribner Sons, 1925), p. 189.

80 "It's about what power does," Harlan Lebo, *The Godfather Legacy,* p. 30.

80 "By the clever and continuous use of propaganda," Steven Bach, *Leni: The Life and Work of Leni Riefenstahl* (New York: Vintage Books, 2008), p. 83.

82 "two sides of the dialectic," Thomas J. Ferraro, *Feeling Italian,* p. 7.

84 "our Dickens or Trollope," *The Godfather Part II: The Coppola Restoration,* Director's Commentary.

86 "the ice-pick of conversation," Fred L. Gardaphe, *From Wiseguys to Wise Men: The Gangster and Italian American Masculinities* (New York: Routledge, 2006), p. 106, citing Frank Lentricchia, *Lucchesi and the Whale* (Durham, N.C.: Duke University Press, 2003).

89 "In dying the way," Shana Alexander, "The Godfather of All Cool Actors," *Life,* March 10, 1972.

90 "[Coppola] wanted the audience to see," Harlan Lebo, *The Godfather Legacy,* p. 92.

91 "It was one of the few," Mario Puzo, *The Godfather* (New York: Putnam, 1969), p. 203.

91   "Vito's mother had been brutally," Vera Dika, "The Representa-
     tion of Ethnicity in *The Godfather*," in Nick Browne (ed.), *Francis
     Ford Coppola's* The Godfather *Trilogy* (New York: Cambridge Uni-
     versity Press, 2000), p. 87.

92   "all left looking for work," Fred L. Gardaphe, *From Wiseguys to
     Wise Men*, p. 39.

93   "Vito kills with," Francis Ford Coppola as quoted in Steve Schap-
     iro, *The Godfather Family Album* (Cologne: Taschen, 2010), p. 371.

6. FOREFATHERS ON FILM

99   "television by then had reared," Jerre Mangione, *Mount Allegro*, p. 301.

104 "In my Chicago neighborhood," Fred L. Gardaphe, "Breaking and
     Entering," in Bill Tonelli (ed.), *The Italian American Reader*, p. 467.

7. GODFATHER CINEMA

111 "I've seen the movie," Peter Bart, *Infamous Players*, p. 218.

111 "It glamorizes the Mob," ibid.

112 "He's a brilliant writer," ibid., p. 209.

112 "I'm fascinated with," Francis Ford Coppola in Stephen Farber, "Cop-
     pola and *The Godfather*," *Sight and Sound* 41, no. 4 (Autumn 1972).

112 "the agonizing religion," Leopardo Sciascia as quoted in Barbara
     Grizzuti Harrison, "*Godfather III*," *Life*, November 1990.

113 "The kid understands," Peter Bart, *Infamous Players*, p. 211.

114 "writer who directs," Harlan Lebo, *The Godfather Legacy*, p. 25.

114 "I want to look at the Mafia," Mark Seal, "*The Godfather* Wars,"
     Vanity Fair, March 2009.

114 "Like America, Michael began," Francis Ford Coppola, in William
     Murray, "The *Playboy* Interview," *Playboy*, July 1975.

114 five times more money selling cigars, Harlan Lebo, *The Godfather Legacy*, p. 3.

114 sell Paramount, Peter Bart, *Infamous Players*, p. 217.

115 "American pride and moral purpose," Vera Dika, "The Representation of Ethnicity in *The Godfather*," Nick Browne (ed.), *Francis Ford Coppola's* The Godfather *Trilogy*, p. 96.

116 ultimately cost Brando," Peter Bart, *Infamous Players*, p. 222.

116 "A runt will not play," Mark Seal, "*The Godfather* Wars," *Vanity Fair*, March 2009.

116 "I'll get you for this," Robert Evans, *The Kid Stays in the Picture* (New York: Hyperion Press, 1994), p. 223.

116 fee of only $35,000, Michael Schumacher, *Francis Ford Coppola: A Filmmaker's Life* (New York: Crown, 1999), p. 118.

117 "asked him if he wanted to finish," Robert Evans, *The Kid Stays in the Picture*, p. 224.

117 "There's no truth to it," Peter Biskind, "Making Crime Pay," *Premiere*, August 1997.

117 "I wrote the script," *The Godfather*, The Coppola Restoration, "Supplements."

118 "thought maybe Diane," Francis Ford Coppola as quoted in Harlan Lebo, *The Godfather Legacy*, p. 54.

118 Paramount spent $420,000, Mark Seal, "*The Godfather* Wars," *Vanity Fair*, March 2009.

119 "The war over casting," Robert Evans, *The Kid Stays in the Picture*, p. 221.

119 "What fucking transformation," Mark Seal, "*The Godfather* Wars," *Vanity Fair*, March 2009.

119 "do anything-say anything," ibid.

119 "I noticed how," Stefan Kanfer, *Somebody*, p. 244.

120 "I was just laughing," Mario Puzo, *The Godfather*, p. 137.

120 "[They all] had to point outward," James Caan as quoted in Peter Biskind, "Making Crime Pay," *Premiere*, August 1997.

121 "A book like *The Godfather*," letter from Italian-American Civil Rights League as cited in Harlan Lebo, *The Godfather Legacy*, p. 42.

122 strong-armed merchants, Mark Seal, "*The Godfather* Wars," *Vanity Fair*, March 2009.

122 "Take some advice," Robert Evans, *The Kid Stays in the Picture*, p. 202.

122 "I want to make," Al Ruddy as quoted in Harlan Lebo, *The Godfather Legacy*, pp. 10–11.

122 "always been able to talk," Nicholas Pileggi, "The Making of *The Godfather*—Sort of a Home Movie," *New York Times*, August 15, 1971.

123 "within 72 hours," Robert Evans, *The Kid Stays in the Picture*, p. 202.

123 "There was an article in the *Wall Street Journal*," Al Ruddy as quoted in Peter Biskind, "Making Crime Pay," *Premiere*, August 1997.

124 "a monstrous insult," *New York Times*, March 23, 1971.

124 "makes it look like," "Damone Drops Role in *Godfather* Film," *New York Times*, August 15, 1971.

124 "hypocritical, craven act," Michael Schumacher, *Francis Ford Coppola*, p. 105.

124 "There would have been pickets," Al Ruddy as quoted in Harlan Lebo, *The Godfather Legacy*, p. 97.

125 "You didn't bullshit us," ibid., pp. 96, 98.

125 "the first organization in the world," "Damone Drops Role," *New York Times*, August 15, 1971.

125 "pointed to [league] members," Jenny M. Jones, *The Annotated Godfather* (New York: Black Dog & Levanthal, 2007), p. 71.

125 most notably Carmine "The Snake" Persico, Nicholas Pileggi, "The Making of *The Godfather*—Sort of a Home Movie," *New York Times*, August 15, 1971.

126 "of this marvelous old world stuff," James Caan as quoted in ibid.

126 "several members of the crew," Marlon Brando with Robert Lindsey, *Songs My Mother Taught Me* (New York: Random House, 1994), p. 407.

126 "reputed capo," Mark Seal, "Meadow Soprano on Line One," *Vanity-Fair.com*, February 26, 2009, citing *New York Times*.

126 "a self-described," ibid.

126 "on July 16, 1972," ibid.

128 cumulative worldwide gross of one billion dollars, Harlan Lebo, *The Godfather Legacy*, p. 125.

128 "You're not using," Peter Bart, *Infamous Players*, p. 225.

129 Coppola's response was to lift, Michael Schumacher, *Francis Ford Coppola*, p. 210.

129 Coppola fell to the ground, ibid., p. 100.

129 "I can't understand Brando," Peter Bart, *Infamous Players*, p. 225.

130 "wouldn't cut," Jon Lewis, *The Godfather* (London: Palgrave Macmillan, 2010), p. 55.

130 "wasn't up to the job," Peter Bart, *Infamous Players*, p. 226.

130 "So on that Thursday," Francis Ford Coppola as quoted in Peter Biskind, "Making Crime Pay," *Premiere*, August 1997.

130 "If you fire Francis," Marlon Brando with Robert Lindsey, *Songs My Mother Taught Me*, p. 409.

130 "Brando saved my neck," Harlan Lebo, *The Godfather Legacy*, p. 123.

130 "I think they [Paramount] decided," Francis Ford Coppola in Stephen Farber, "Coppola and *The Godfather*," *Sight and Sound* 41, no. 4 (Autumn 1972).

130 "Because I can read them," Peter Bart, *Infamous Players*, p. 227.

131 "kind of bright Kodachrome," Peter Manso, *Brando: The Biography* (New York: Hyperion, 1994), pp. 725–26.

134 "bounced into diffusing frames," Harlan Lebo, *The Godfather Legacy*, p. 157.

134 "It put his eye sockets," Gordon Willis as quoted in Peter Biskind, "Making Crime Pay," *Premiere*, August 1997.

134 "Point, counterpoint," Harlan Lebo, *The Godfather Legacy*, p. 157.

134 "like making a Xerox," *The Godfather*, The Coppola Restoration, "Supplements."

136   "Every piece of shit," Mario Puzo, *The Godfather*, p. 150.

137   "beautiful piece of misdirection," Jenny M. Jones, *The Annotated Godfather*, p. 75.

140   "The art of making art," "Putting It Together," from *Sunday in the Park with George*, music and lyrics by Stephen Sondheim.

144   "Powerful people don't need to shout," Mark Seal, "*The Godfather* Wars," *Vanity Fair*, March 2009.

144   "after I had read the book," Marlon Brando with Robert Lindsey, *Songs My Mother Taught Me*, p. 411.

144   "I had a great deal of respect," ibid.

144   "The story is about," Stefan Kanfer, *Somebody*, p. 237.

144   "The key phrase in the story," Mark Seal, "*The Godfather* Wars," *Vanity Fair*, March 2009.

144   "At the time we made the film," Marlon Brando with Robert Lindsey, *Songs My Mother Taught Me*, p. 413.

145   "What's the difference," Francis Ford Coppola, in William Murray, "The *Playboy* Interview," *Playboy*, July 1975.

145   "I wonder what would happen," Marlon Brando with Robert Lindsey, *Songs My Mother Taught Me*, p. 413.

145   "was drinking heavily," Peter Bart, *Infamous Players*, p. 226.

147   "Partly I did Francis," Al Pacino, Lawrence Grobel, "The *Playboy* Interview,"*Playboy*, December 1979.

148   "an instant classic," Charles Champlin, *Los Angeles Times*, as quoted in Jenny M. Jones, *The Annotated Godfather*, p. 247.

148   "If ever there was an example," Pauline Kael, *The New Yorker*, as quoted in ibid.

148   "They have put pudding," Stanley Kauffman, *The New Republic*, as quoted in Stefan Kanfer, *Somebody*, p. 257.

148   "dynastic sweep," *Time* as quoted in Harlan Lebo, *The Godfather Legacy*, p. 204.

148   "the defense of a narrow place," W. P. Ker as quoted in Maureen Dowd, *New York Times*, October 10, 2010.

149 "investing more money," Harlan Lebo, *The Godfather Legacy*, p. 210.
150 a former "Miss Vampire of 1970," Stefan Kanfer, *Somebody*, p. 266.
150 "Littlefeather's heritage," ibid.
150 "The game has taken the work," ibid., p. 305.
151 "When I saw *The Godfather* the first time," Marlon Brando with Robert Lindsey, *Songs My Mother Taught Me*, p. 418.

8. FRANK SINATRA

154 "I would hate myself for laughing," Pete Hamill, *Why Sinatra Matters*, p. 49.
154 "I never heard an Italian singing," Mario Puzo as quoted in Harlan Lebo, *The Godfather Legacy*, pp. 1–2.
155 "In his youth," Thomas J. Ferraro, *Feeling Italian*, p. 101.
156 "soundtrack to which we choreograph," ibid., p. 205.
156 "Francis, I'd play the Godfather for you," Mario Puzo, *The Godfather Papers*, p. 50.
156 Given Sinatra's decree, Michael Schumacher, *Francis Ford Coppola*, p. 99.
156 "It's up to you, pal," Vic Damone, *Singing Was the Easy Part* (New York: St. Martin's, 2009), p. 102.
156 "even offered," Mia Farrow, *What Falls Away* (New York: Bantam, 1997), p. 307.
157 "he's the secret idol," Mario Puzo, *The Godfather Papers*, pp. 190–91.
158 "in it I saw myself," Nancy Sinatra, *Frank Sinatra: An American Legend* (Santa Monica, Calif.: General Publishing Group, 1995), p. 106.
159 "You know who's right," ibid., p. 115.
159 the singer had a disagreement, Vic Damone, *Singing Was the Easy Part*, p. 30.
159 "I just read a book," Phyllis McGuire as quoted in Mark Seal, "*The Godfather* Wars," *Vanity Fair*, March 2009.

160 "future earnings, the money we could have made," Mark Seal, *"The Godfather* Wars," *Vanity Fair,* March 2009.

160 "He came back when," Harlan Lebo, *The Godfather Legacy,* p. 98.

160 "called Angelo Bruno," Mark Seal, *"The Godfather* Wars," *Vanity Fair,* March 2009.

160 "I had to step on some toes," ibid.

160 claiming that he had been ostracized, ibid.

162 "The next thing I know," Harlan Lebo, *The Godfather Legacy,* p. 28.

162 "But I owe," Peter Bart, *Infamous Players,* p. 112.

162 "Get out of my," ibid, p. 113.

162 "I ought to break you legs," Mark Seal, "The Godfather Wars," *Vanity Fair,* April 2009.

162 "a pimp," Mario Puzo, *The Godfather Papers,* p. 49.

162 "What hurt," ibid.

163 "You would have been better for the part," Victor Gold, "Letters to the Editor," *Vanity Fair,* May 2009.

163 a staggering one billion dollars, *Frank Sinatra Memorial DVD,* Passport Productions, 1999.

164 "Oh, I just wish," Shirley MacLaine, *My Lucky Stars* (New York: Bantam Publishing 1996), p. 87.

164 the company was called Reprise, Stan Cornyn, The Reprise Years-UMG Borset, Liner notes, p. 1.

165 " 'You like people,' " Pete Hamill, *Why Sinatra Matters,* p. 180.

9. *LA FAMIGLIA* (DI SANTOPIETRO, CORLEONE *E* COPPOLA)

171 "Television, two-career families," Robert D. Putnam, *Bowling Alone: The Collapse and Revival of American Community* (New York: Simon and Schuster, 1995).

175 "Italian eyes are all dark," George Panetta, "Suit" from *Viva*

Madison Avenue in Bill Tonelli (ed.), *The Italian American Reader,*
p. 495.

176 "god is in the details," Stephen Sondheim, *Finishing the Hat* (New
York: Knopf, 2010).

176 "Gangsters don't brown," Harlan Lebo, *The Godfather Legacy*, p. 30.

179 "scared of what," George Panetta in Bill Tonelli (ed.), *The Italian
American Reader*, p. 498.

179 "a romance about a king," Francis Ford Coppola, in William Mu-
ray, "The *Playboy* Interview," *Playboy,* July 1975.

180 "you left only when it was impossible," Jerre Mangione, *Mount Allegro,* p. 227.

180 "talked to a few people," Mark Seal, "The Godfather Wars," *Vanity
Fair,* March 2009.

181 "Ruddy fell in love with it," Jennifer Gould Keil, "Staten Island
House in 'The Godfather' Up for Sale," *New York Post,* December 3,
2010.

181 "I could have gotten them much more money," ibid.

181 "His wife and kids were second," John Gotti Jr. speaking on *60
Minutes,* April 11, 2010.

183 "the ultimate value," Nick Browne (ed.), *Francis Ford Coppola's* The
Godfather *Trilogy,* p. 60.

183 "comes down to huddling," *The Godfather Part II,* The Coppola Restoration, Director's Commentary.

185 "The final cut was Francis's," Al Ruddy as quoted in Harlan Lebo,
The Godfather Legacy, p. 200.

185 "eighteen hour days," Peter Bart, *Infamous Players,* p. 229.

185 the final 175-minute version simply restored, Mark Seal, "The Godfather Wars," *Vanity Fair,* March 2009.

185 "Francis and I," Robert Evans, *The Kid Stays in the Picture,* p. 227.

188 "biggest home movie in history," *The Godfather,* The Coppola Restoration, "Supplements."

188 "films about a family," *The Godfather*, The Coppola Restoration, Director's Commentary.

189 "Michael's relationship with his sister," *The Godfather: Part III*, The Coppola Restoration, Director's Commentary.

189 "the family," Maureen Orth, "Godfather of the Movies," *Newsweek*, November 25, 1974.

190 "important beyond fame and wealth," *The Godfather: Part III*, The Coppola Restoration, Director's Commentary.

10. THE GODFATHER: PART II

194 "would have zero to do with it," Michael Schumacher, *Francis Ford Coppola: A Filmmaker's Life*, p. 154.

194 "Charlie Bluhdorn talked me," Francis Ford Coppola in Stephen Farber, "They Made Him Two Offers He Couldn't Refuse," *New York Times*, December 22, 1974.

194 "I was making," Michael Schumacher, *Francis Ford Coppola: A Filmmaker's Life*, p. 163.

195 "about $15,000," Al Pacino as quoted in Lawrence Grobel, "The *Playboy* Interview," *Playboy*, December 1979.

195 "the night before we were going to shoot," Michael Schumacher, *Francis Ford Coppola: A Filmmaker's Life*, p. 163.

195 "quick $100,000 in cash" Peter Manso, *Brando: The Biography*, p. 753.

196 "The movies," John Gotti Jr. on *60 Minutes*, April 11, 2010.

197 "very Italian-American," Francis Ford Coppola in Barbara Grizzuti Harrison, "*Godfather III*," *Life*, November 1990.

197 "Suspicion runs high," Harlan Lebo, *The Godfather Legacy*, p. 227.

198 "not only the mirror image," Francis Ford Coppola, "The *Playboy* Interview," *Playboy*, July 1975.

200 "In a period film," Dean Tavoularis as quoted in Harlan Lebo, *The Godfather Legacy*, pp. 69, 74.

201 "may seem like a long time," Francis Ford Coppola, "The *Playboy* Interview," *Playboy*, July 1975.

203 ranked *The Godfather* third on the list, American Film Institute (AFI).com.

203 placed the first two *Godfather* movies, British Film Institute (BFI). org.uk.

11. PATRIARCHY

205 "She wielded power," Mario Puzo as quoted in Peter Biskind, "Making Crime Pay," *Premiere*, August 1997.

206 eight out of ten, Tom Matlack "Mammoni: Good Men or Lazy-Asses," October 7, 2007. goodmenproject.com, July 20, 2011.

206 "*mammoni*," *60 Minutes*, CBS Television, March 4, 2001.

206 "Let's get these big babies," Tornasso Padou-Schnoppa, goodmenproject.com, July 20, 2011.

208 "filled with hope," Mario Puzo, *The Fortunate Pilgrim* (New York: Random House, 1965), p. 7.

208 "members of a different race," ibid.

208 "If you were raised," Francis Ford Coppola in Stephen Farber, "Coppola and *The Godfather*," *Sight and Sound*, Autumn 1972.

224 "Could it be that," Guy Talese as quoted in Fred L. Gardaphe, *From Wiseguys to Wise Men*, pp. 49–50.

225 "a spoiled pain-in-the-ass," Mark Seal, "*The Godfather* Wars," *Vanity Fair*, March 2009.

12. RELIGION, DEATH, AND GRIEF

236 "Closure is a word," John Gotti Sr. as seen on *60 Minutes*, April 11, 2010.

13. THE GODFATHER: PART III

243　"Paramount spent almost $800,000," Michael Schumacher, *Francis Ford Coppola*, p. 413.

244　until Paramount offered him, ibid.

244　Six million dollars to write and direct, ibid., p. 416.

244　Coppola used *King Lear*, ibid., p. 417.

245　"Duvall, angered over," ibid., p. 422.

245　helped Sindona acquire, Nick Browne (ed.), *Francis Ford Coppola's The Godfather Trilogy*, p. 51.

245　"According to Bart," ibid.

246　convicted on sixty-five counts, Mark Seal, "*The Godfather* Wars," *Vanity Fair*, March 2009.

246　the murder of attorney Giorgio Ambrosoli, Jon Lewis, *The Godfather*, p. 88.

246　"under mysterious circumstances," Mark Seal, "*The Godfather* Wars," *Vanity Fair*, March 2009.

246　"[It is a] story of," Francis Ford Coppola in Steve Schapiro, *The Godfather Family Album*, p. 393.

248　"bit," *The Godfather*, The Coppola Restoration, "Supplements."

249　"Coppola is the inheritor," Pauline Kael as quoted in Michael Schumacher, *Francis Ford Coppola*, p. 179.

249　"opera is always about transgressions," Cathereine Clement, *Opera; or, The Undoing of Women* (Minneapolis: University of Minnesota Press, 1988), cited in Naomi Greene, "Family Ceremonies," Nick Browne (ed.), *Francis Ford Coppola's The Godfather Trilogy*, p. 148.

251　"She's there," *The Godfather: Part III*, The Coppola Restoration, The Director's Commentary.

251　"They shot bullets at Sofia," ibid.

252　"My gut feeling was," Talia Shire as quoted in Michael Schumacher, *Francis Ford Coppola*, p. 429.

253 "matters of heart and soul," *The Godfather: Part* III, The Coppola Restoration, Director's Commentary.

254 "There are no good guys," Joe Mantegna as quoted in Barbara Grizzuti Harrison, *"Godfather III," Life,* November 1990.

255 "did the unthinkable," Don De Lilo, *Underworld* (New York: Scribner 1997), p. 204.

255 "living corpse," Francis Ford Coppola, "The *Playboy* Interview," *Playboy,* July 1975.

255 "the most successful Italian man," Mario Puzo, *The Godfather Papers,* p. 18.

256 "So when it sinks in," Peter Travers, *Rolling Stone,* December 25, 1990.

14. THE SHADOW OF *THE GODFATHER*

260 "This focus on image," Fred L. Gardaphe, *From Wiseguys to Wise Men,* p. 56.

261 "the Italian *Star Wars,*" *The Godfather,* The Coppola Restoration, "Supplements."

262 "because the state of grace," Franco La Cecla as quoted in Fred L. Gardaphe, *From Wiseguys to Wise Men,* p. 69.

263 "denigrating . . . Most Italian-American characters," Jerre Mangione and Ben Morreale, *La Storia,* p. 219.

263 0.00782% of Italian-Americans, Rosario A. Iaconnis, "Letters to the Editors," *Vanity Fair,* May 2009.

264 "The Italians are damned well," Paul O'Dwyer as cited in Harlan Lebo, *The Godfather Legacy,* p. 41.

264 Her response to the show's vociferous critics, *Popeater.com,* February 17, 2010.

265 "Being tan," "Snooki's Advice to Rutgers Students: Study Hard but

Party Harder," *New Jersey Star Ledger*, March 31, 2011, www.nj.com
/starledger.

265 "I don't see nothing" Nick Pisa and Ginger Adams Otis, "Florence
Rips 'Jersey Shore' Supercafoni," *New York Post*, May 29, 2011.

265 "There are many more," Bill Tonelli (ed.), *The Italian American
Reader*, p. xxv.

266 "He dumped the fight," Pete Hamill, *Why Sinatra Matters*, p. 18.

Bibliography

BOOKS

Barreca, Regina (ed.). *A Sitdown with the Sopranos*. New York: Palgrave Macmillan, 2002.

Bart, Peter. *Infamous Players: A Tale of Movies, The Mob (and Sex)*. New York: Weinstein Books, 2011.

Brando, Marlon, with Robert Lindsey. *Songs My Mother Taught Me*. New York: Random House, 1994.

Browne, Nick (ed.). *Francis Ford Coppola's* The Godfather *Trilogy*. New York: Cambridge University Press, 2000.

Chown, Jeffrey. *Hollywood Auteur: Francis Coppola*. New York: Praeger, 1988.

Damone, Vic. *Singing Was the Easy Part*. New York: St. Martin's, 2009.

Evans, Robert. *The Kid Stays in the Picture*. New York: Hyperion, 1994.

Ferraro, Thomas J. *Feeling Italian: The Art of Ethnicity in America*. New York: New York University Press, 2005.

Gardaphe, Fred L. *From Wiseguys to Wise Men: The Gangster and Italian American Masculinities*. New York: Routledge, 2006.

Glazer, Nathan, and Daniel Moynihan. *Beyond the Melting Pot*. Cambridge, Mass.: MIT Press, 1963.

Hamill, Pete. *Why Sinatra Matters*. New York: Little Brown, 1998.

Jones, Jenny M. *The Annotated Godfather*. New York: Black Dog & Leventhal, 2007.

Kanfer, Stefan. *Somebody: The Reckless Life and Remarkable Career of Marlon Brando*. New York: Knopf, 2008.

Lebo, Harlan. *The Godfather Legacy*. New York: Simon and Schuster, 2005.

Lewis, Jon. *The Godfather*. London: Palgrave Macmillan, 2010.

————. *Whom God Wishes to Destroy . . . Francis Coppola and the New Hollywood*. Durham, N.C.: Duke University Press, 1995.

Mangione, Jerre. *Mount Allegro: A Memoir of Italian American Life*. Syracuse, N.Y.: Syracuse University Press, 1942.

Mangione, Jerre, and Ben Morreale. *La Storia: Five Centures of the Italian American Experience*. New York: HarperCollins, 1992.

Manso, Peter. *Brando: The Biography*. New York: Hyperion, 1994.

Putnam, Robert D. *Bowling Alone: The Collapse and Revival of American Community*. New York: Simon and Schuster, 1995.

Puzo, Mario. *The Godfather*. New York: Putnam, 1969.

————. *The Godfather Papers and Other Confessions*. New York: Putnam, 1972.

Raab, Selwyn. *Five Families: The Rise, Fall, and Resurgence of America's Most Powerful Mafia Empires*. New York: St. Martin's Press: 2006.

Schapiro, Steve (photographer). *The Godfather Family Album*. Cologne: Taschen, 2010.

Schumacher, Michael. *Francis Ford Coppola: A Filmmaker's Life*. New York: Crown, 1999.

Sinatra, Nancy. *Frank Sinatra: An American Legend*. Santa Monica, Calif.: General Publishing Group, 1995.

Tonelli, Bill (ed.). *The Italian American Reader*. New York: HarperCollins, 2003.

Warshow, Robert. *The Immediate Experience: Movies, Comics, Theatre, and Other Aspects of Popular Culture*. Cambridge: Harvard University Press, 2002.

Zuckerman, Ira. *The Godfather Journal*. New York: Manor Books, 1972.

ARTICLES

Life, March 10, 1972, Shana Alexander, "The Godfather of All Cool Actors"; November 1990, Barbara Grizzuti Harrison, *"Godfather III."*

New Jersey Star Ledger, March 31, 2011, www.nj.com/starledger, "Snooki's Advice to Rutgers Students: Study Hard but Party Harder."

Newsweek, Novermber 25, 1974, Maureen Orth, "Godfather of the Movies"; May 25, 1998, Bill Zehme,"The Final Curtain."

New York Post, May 29,2011, Nick Pisa and Ginger Adams Otis, "Florence Rips 'Jersey Shore' Supercafoni"; December 3, 2010, Jennifer Gould Keil, Perry Chiaramonte, and Tim Perone, "Staten Island House in 'The Godfather' up for Sale."

New York Times, March 20, 1971, "Godfather Films Won't Mention Mafia"; April 5, 1971, "Damone Drops Role in *Godfather* Film; August 15, 1971, "The Making of *The Godfather*—Sort of a Home Movie"; June 8, 1972, "Sinatra to Shun Inquiry on Crime"; July 24, 1972, Frank Sinatra, "We Might Call This the Politics of Fantasy"; October 10, 2010, Maureen Dowd, "Lord of the Internet Rings"; November 10, 2010, Michael Cieply, "The Older Side of Hollywood Gets Its Due"; February 22, 2011, "Little Italy: Littler by the Year"; April 13, 2011, "A Mafia Boss Breaks a Code in Telling All"; April 14, 2011, "Ex-Mob Boss Tells Jury, Calmly, About Murders."

New York Daily News, September 22, 1998, "Godfather Sinatra."

Playboy, July 1975, William Murray, "The *Playboy* Interview: Francis Ford Coppola"; December 1979, Lawrence Grobel, "The *Playboy* Interview: Al Pacino."

Premiere, August 1997, Peter Biskind, "Making Crime Pay."

Show, September 1971, "Al Pacino: An Actor Who Believes in Taking Chances."

Sight and Sound 41, no. 4, (Autumn 1972), Stephen Farber, "Coppola and *The Godfather.*"

Time, March 13, 1972, "The Making of *The Godfather.*"

Vanity Fair, June 1990, Peter Boyer, "Under the Gun"; March 2009, Mark Seal, "*The Godfather* Wars"; May 2009, "Letters to the Editors."

VanityFair.com, February 26, 2009, Mark Seal, "Meadow Soprano on Line One."

World Journal Telegram, May 3, 1967, Hy Gardner, "Sinatra to Head US-Italian ADL"; May 4, 1967, "Sinatra Vows Active Bias Fight."

ARCHIVES

Billy Rose Theatre Collection, Lincoln Center Library for the Performing Arts, New York.

The Paley Center for Media, New York.

Index

Academy Awards
  Brando and, 143
  Brando's refusal of, 150
  The Godfather: Part II and, 202
  The Godfather: Part III and,
    256
  The Godfather and, 149–50
  musical score and, 142–43
  Pacino and, 147
Adams, James, 53
Adams, Kay (character), 33, 184–86,
  254
Adler, Buddy, 158
advertising, 103
African-Americans, 230–31
Agnew, Spiro, 162
Albini, Mario, 238–39
Albini, Raymond, 238
Albini, Salvatore, 238
Albino, Carmine, 170, 210–14
Albino, Donald, 213–14
Albino, Emma, 209–11
Alexander, Shana, 89
Allen, Woody, 156
Ambrosoli, Giorgio, 246

America
  Corleone, Michael, as metaphor
    for, 75
  identity, 30–33, 83–84
  Italianization of, 82–83, 282
  Mafia in, 58
  unraveling of, 107
American Bar Association Journal, 270
American dream, 6–7, 34
  Coppola, Francis Ford, and, 7, 282
  cynicism and, 284
  mother/son dynamic and, 208
  Sicilian immigration and, 45
  souring of, 57
American Film Institute, 202–3
American Zoetrope, 112, 189, 244
Analyze That, 268
Analyze This, 268
Andolini, Vito. *See* Corleone, Vito
The Annotated Godfather (Jones), 129
antidefamation organizations,
  120–21
antiheroes, 99
Aubrey, James, 116
Avakian, Aram, 130

Baldini, Oreste, 20
Ballard, Jack, 130
Barone, Marie (character), 263
Bart, Peter, 70, 112, 129, 162, 185, 245
Basciano, Vincent, 64
Batista, Fulgencio, 81
Battle of the Somme, 22–23
"Be My Baby" (Ronettes), 261
Bellino, Giovannina, 126
The Bells of St. Mary's, 230
Benny, Jack, 162–63
Bergman, Ingrid, 230
Beyond the Melting Pot (Moynihan & Glazer), 50
Bluhdorn, Charles, 5, 114–15, 123–24, 194, 245
Bonanno, Bill, 76
Bonanno crime family, 64, 76
Bonasera, Amerigo (character), 56–57, 85–86
Bonnie and Clyde, 99, 107
bootlegging, 59
Borgnine, Ernest, 2, 45
Bowling Alone (Putnam), 171
Boyd, Franklin, 170
Brando, Marlon, 151
    Academy Awards and, 143
    Bufalino and, 126–27
    casting of, 1–3, 115
    Eboli and, 126
    The Freshman and, 150
    makeup for, 134, 143–44
    makeup test of, 3–5
    as paterfamilias, 127
    politics of, 144–45
    refusal of Academy Award by, 150
    salary of, 115–16

    support of Coppola, Francis Ford, by, 130
Brasi, Luca (character), 117, 137
Bronson, Charles, 63
A Bronx Tale, 269–70
Brooklyn, 266
Brooks, Richard, 111
The Brotherhood, 115, 268
Brown, James, 225
Browning, Robert, 283
Bruno, Angelo, 160
Bufalino, Joe, 126–27
Bufalino, Russ, 160
business, 76, 135–36

Caan, James, 118–20, 125–26
Cabaret, 149
Cage, Nicolas, 266
Cagney, James, 101
Camino Real (Williams), 159
Camon, Alessandro, 183
capitalism, 71, 93–94
    The Godfather as indictment of, 60
    Mafia and, 76
    Mafia as metaphor for, 82
    Scarface (1983) and, 273
Capitol Records, 164
Capone, Al, 59, 74–75, 100
caporegiemes, 74
Capra, Frank, 99
Caridi, Carmine, 118–19
Casino, 261
Castellano, Richard, 175, 195
Catholic church, 18–19
    Mafia and, 44
    rituals of, 229–30
Cavalleria rusticana (Mascagni), 249–50

cemeteries, 236–37
Cerf, Bennett, 162–63
Champlin, Charles, 148
charity, 161
Chase, David, 207, 262, 271
chauvinism, 224
Cher, 266
Chianese, Dominic, 271
Christmas, 218–19
Ciccio, Don (character), 91–92
Cinecitta Studios, 244–45
cinematography, 77, 134, 199
cities, 48–49, 106–7
Citizen Kane, 203
Clement, Catherine, 249
closure, 236
Clymer, Warren, 140
code of honor, 79, 85–86, 196
code of silence, 63–65. *See also*
    omerta
Cohn, Harry, 159
Colombo, Joseph, 121–25, 180
Columbia Pictures, 159
community work, 221
Como, Perry, 164
Congress of Vienna, 39
consiglieres, 74
cooking, 217–18. *See also* food
Coolidge, Calvin, 79
Coppola, Carmine, 142–43, 188–89,
    250
Coppola, Francis Ford
    American dream and, 7, 282
    Brando, casting of, and, 1–2
    Brando makeup test and, 3–5
    conditions for producing *The
        Godfather: Part II*, 193–94
    Coppola, Sofia, and, 251–52

on Corleone, Vito, 21
death of Corleone, Vito, and, 89
determination of, 1–2
directorial style of, 137–38
doubts about, 128–30
ending of *The Godfather* and, 185
Evans and, 112
la famiglia and, 189–90
The Godfather: Part IV and, 277–78
hiring of, 111–13
Mafia in America and, 58
Martino and, 160
Pacino and, 147
as paterfamilias, 189
politics of, 145
power and, 80
salary for *The Godfather: Part II*,
    194
Sinatra, Frank, and, 156–57
Tetro and, 279
violence and, 128, 138
on violence's effect, 188–89
visual imagery of, 131–32
Willis and, 139
writing of *The Godfather: Part III*
    and, 243–44
Youth Without Youth and, 279
Coppola, Sofia, 188, 251–52
"The Coppola Restoration" (DVD),
    277–79
Corleone, Anthony (character), 183,
    187
Corleone, Connie (character)
    education and, 30
    evolution of, 225–26
    wedding reception of, 131–32
Corleone, Fredo (character), 93,
    186–87, 198

Corleone, Kay. *See* Adams, Kay

Corleone, Mama (character), 207–8, 233

Corleone, Mary (character), 187–88, 234, 255–56

Corleone, Michael (character)
  aging of, 252–53
  American identity and, 32–33
  ascendance of, 137–38
  business and, 135–36
  capitalism and, 93–94
  characterization of, 145–47
  confession of, 208
  conscience of, 249
  corruption of, 33–34
  death and, 233–34
  death of Corleone, Fredo, and, 198
  demise of, 256–57
  embracing of Italian identity of, 34
  exile of, 92
  as icon, 71
  investigation of, 62
  lies of, 185–86
  as metaphor for America, 75
  as paterfamilias, 186
  repentance of, 253–54
  revenge and, 92–93
  self-identity and, 248
  Società General Immobiliare and, 233
  transfer of power to, 182–83

Corleone, Sonny (character)
  business and, 136
  casting of, 118–20
  death of, 107
  The Godfather: Part IV and, 278
  Mancini, Lucy, and, 225

Corleone, Vito (character), *14, 38*
  authority of, 21
  code of honor and, 85–86
  corruption and, 72–73
  creation of, 205–6
  cultural impact of, 150–51
  death of, 89
  emigration of, 15–16
  The Godfather: Part IV and, 278
  as icon, 71
  imitations of, 6
  parody of, 150
  revenge and, 91–92
  rise of, 49
  souring of American dream and, 57
  violence and, 87–88
  voice of, 144
  wisdom of, 86–87
  young life of, 91

Corleone compound, 179–81

corruption, 72–73
  of Corleone, Michael, 33–34
  ubiquity of, 80–81

Corsitto, Salvatore, 56

cosa nostra, 63. *See also* Mafia

Costello, Frank, 144

The Cotton Club, 244

coupons, 220

Covello, Leonard, 30

crime
  Italian immigrants and, 53
  organized, 65
  Prohibition and, 59
  in Scorsese films, 261–62

Crosby, Bing, 164, 230

Cuba, 81

cynicism, *35,* 284

D'Agata, John, 32
Damone, Vic, 156, 159–60, 262
D'Angelo, Franny, 159
D'Angelo, Johnny, 159
Dante, 25
Dante Alighieri, 45
The Dark Arena (Puzo), 69, 154
Day, Doris, 51
The Dead (film), 113
death, 233–34
    of Corleone, Fredo, 198
    of Corleone, Mary, 187–88, 234,
        255–56
    of Corleone, Sonny, 107
    of Corleone, Vito, 89
    Godfather murder montage and,
        231–32
    Italian immigrants and, 236–38
DeLillo, Don, 255
Dementia 13, 4
DeNiro, Robert, 118
    A Bronx Tale and, 269
    in *The Godfather: Part II*, 196–97
    Mean Streets and, 262
    Raging Bull and, 266
    Shark Tale and, 269
Department of Justice, 65
Depression, 25–26, 29–30, 59, 210
il destino, 46
Dika, Vera, 91, 115
DiMaggio, Joe, 60
Dirty Harry, 107–8
discrimination
    of Italian immigrants, 54
    of Sicilians, 42
    in World War II, 60
The Divine Comedy (Dante), 25
Division Street, 9–12, 17–18

Donahue, Troy, 186
Donnie Brasco, 268
Douglas, Kirk, 115, 268
Draper, Don (character), 224–25
DreamWorks, 269
drugs, 73
Duggan, Christopher, 63
Duvall, Robert, 118, 245

Eastwood, Clint, 107, 149–50
Easy Rider, 107
Eboli, Pasquale "Patsy Ryan," 126
editing, 141, 201–2
education, 24–25, 29–30, 33
Ellis Island, 16, 283–84
English class system, 22–23
Ephron, Nora, 270–71
Episcopal church, 19
Evans, Robert, 69–70, 114–15,
        193–94, 268
    Brando makeup test and, 4–5
    Caan and, 118–19
    Colombo and, 122
    Coppola, Francis Ford, and, 112
    ending of *The Godfather* and, 185
    Pacino and, 116–17
    Rota and, 141–42
    Zinner and, 130
Everybody Loves Raymond (television
        show), 263

factories, 48–49, 53–54
Falco, Ed, 261
Falco, Edie, 271
la famiglia, 50, 133–34
    Adams, Kay, and, 184–86
    Coppola, Francis Ford, and,
        189–90

la famiglia (*continued*)
  gatherings of, 172–73
  in *The Godfather*, 181–82
family
  closeness, 50, 174
  protection of, 255
  relationships, 183–84, 207–8
"Family Ceremonies" (Greene, N.),
    249–50
The Family Corleone (Falco, Ed), 261
Fanucci, Don (character), 87–88
Farrow, Mia, 156
fascism, 54–55
fate, 46
FBI. *See* Federal Bureau of
    Investigation
Feast of San Gennaro, 78
Federal Bureau of Investigation
    (FBI), 55–56, 61
Feeling Italian (Ferraro), 52, 82
Ferraro, Thomas, 50, 52, 155
Ferraro, Thomas J., 82
Fiddler on the Roof, 173
filming locations, 179–81
Finian's Rainbow, 4, 193
Fitzgerald, F. Scott, 77–78
Five Easy Pieces, 107
Flowers, A. D., 120
Fontane, Johnny (character), 73, 153
  casting of, 159–60
  Sinatra, Frank, and, 156–58
food
  cooking and, 217–18
  in *The Godfather*, 175–76
  holidays and, 218–19
  Italian-Americans and, 174–75
  Sunday dinner and, 172–75
Ford, John, 158

The Fortunate Pilgrim (Puzo), 69, 154,
    208
Fortunella, 142
Fosse, Bob, 149
Frederickson, Gray, 180
The Freshman, 127, 150
Freud, Sigmund, 177
friendship, 86
From Here to Eternity, 153, 157–59
From Wiseguys to Wise Men
    (Gardaphé), 260
funeral homes, 237–39

Gallo, "Crazy Joe," 125
Gambino, Carlo, 206
Gambino crime family, 245
gambling, 73
Gance, Abel, 143
Gandolfini, James, 271
The Gang That Couldn't Shoot Straight,
    116
"The Gangster as Tragic Hero"
    (Warshow), 82
gangster films
  popularization of, 100–102
  post-World War II, 104–5
  redefinition of, 148–49
  Scorsese and, 261–62
Garcia, Andy, 226, *276*
Gardaphé, Fred, 104, 260
Gardner, Ava, 157–59
Garibaldi, Giuseppe, 40–41
Gary, Norman, 115–16
Gazzo, Michael V., 195–96
Gekko, Gordon (character), 93
Genovese, Vito, 206
Genovese crime family, 126
ghettos, 49–50

Giancana, Sam, 61, 159
Giuliani, Rudolph, 62
glamour, 259
Glazer, Nathan, 50
The Godfather (film)
  Academy Awards for, 149–50
  American dream and, 6–7
  American identity in, 32–33
  Brando, casting of, 1–2
  cinematography of, 77
  Corleone compound in, 179–81
  corruption in, 72–73
  cultural appeal of, 84–85
  curse words in, 27–28
  editing of, 141
  ending of, 184–85
  la famiglia in, 181–82
  family relationships in, 183
  filming locations, 179–81
  filming of, 128
  food in, 175–76
  heroism, 79
  humanizing of Mafia in, 89–90
  iconic status of, 262–63
  as indictment of capitalism, 60
  Italianization of America in,
    82–83
  legacy of, 202–3
  Mafia as capitalist metaphor in, 82
  Mafia on set of, 125–26
  marketing of, 149
  mother/son dynamic in, 207–8
  murder montage in, 231–32
  musical score of, 141–43
  mythologizing of, 35–36
  Old World in, 66
  oranges in, 177
  Pacino in, 145–47

patriarchy and, 223–24
potential directors of, 111–12
production design of, 139–41
profundity of, 281–82
protests against, 121–23
public reception of, 5–6
publicity campaign for, 5
religious imagery in, 231–32
restoration of, 134–35
reviews of, 147–48
sensationalism of violence in, 197
in *The Sopranos*, 272–73
sound design, 143
themes of, 34
transfer of power in, 182–83
viewing of by Sinatra, Frank,
    162–63
wedding reception scene in,
    131–32
The Godfather: Part II, 15–16
  Academy Awards and, 202
  casting of, 195–97
  cinematography of, 77, 199
  conditions for producing, 193–94
  Cuba and, 81
  cynicism in, 35
  DeNiro in, 196–97
  editing in, 201–2
  legacy of, 202–3
  lies in, 185–86
  Little Italy in, 26, 200
  musical score of, 142–43
  oranges in, 177
  Pacino in, 198–99
  parallel storylines in, 201–2
  production design of, 199–201
  violence in, 87
  writing of, 194

The Godfather: Part III, 35
  Academy Awards and, 256
  casting controversies of, 251–52
  Catholic church and, 44
  Corleone, Connie, in, 226
  death of Corleone, Mary, in, 187–88
  music as character in, 250
  musical score of, 143
  oranges in, 177
  plot of, 246–49
  poignancy of, 256
  poor box office of, 94
  public distaste for, 250–53
  religious imagery in, 232–33
  salaries, 244–45
  Sinatra, Frank, and, 163
  women in, 225–26
  writing of, 243–44
The Godfather: Part IV, 277–79
The Godfather (novel)
  appeal of, 70–71
  film rights of, 69–70
  impact of, 73–74
  patriarchy and, 223–24
  publication of, 70
  themes of, 71–72
The Godfather (video game), 150
godfather (term), 74
The Godfather Legacy (Lebo), 77, 160
The Godfather Returns (Winegardner), 260–61
Gold, Victor, 162–63
Goodfellas, 261
Gotti, John, 127, 181, 236, 259–60
Gotti, John, Jr., 34, 181
government
  distrust of, 58

  hypocrisy in, 80–81
  in Italy, 42–43
The Graduate, 107
Grasso, Ella, 217
Gravano, Karen, 64
Gravano, Salvatore "Sammy the Bull," 64, 74
Greeley, Horace, 106
Greene, Moe (character), 146–47
Greene, Naomi, 249–50
Growing Up Gotti (television show), 260
Gulf & Western, 1, 114, 149

Hagen, Tom (character), 161
Haiphong Harbor, 133
Hamilton, George, 245, 251
Harris, Robert, 134–35
Hawks, Howard, 101–2
Hays Code, 102–3
Hecht, Ben, 102
heroism, 79
Hitler, Adolf, 80
holidays, 218–19
honor. *See* code of honor
Honor Thy Father (Talese), 73, 76
Hoover, J. Edgar, 61
Hope and Glory, 25
"The House I Live In" (song), 167
Huston, John, 113, 261
hypocrisy, 80–81

"If History Has Taught Us Anything" (Lewis), 245–46
illiteracy, 46
immigration, 34, 44–48, 83. *See also* Italian immigrants
Immigration Act of 1924, 54

It Happened in Brooklyn, 167
Italian American Reader (Tonelli),
      60
Italian identity, 6, 15
   embracing of, 34
   shame over, 27–28, 30–31
   shedding of, 32
   of Sinatra, Frank, 166–67
Italian immigrants. *See also*
      immigration
   assimilation of, 47–49
   crime and, 53
   death and, 236–38
   discrimination against, 54
   education and, 29–30
   family closeness of, 50
   in ghettos, 49–50
   labor quotas on, 53–54
   lynching of, 52–53
   patriarchy and, 223–24
   physical labor and, 214
   prejudice towards, 51–52
   storytelling and, 97
   women, 208–9
Italian language, 26–28, 197
Italian-American Civil Rights
      League, 121
Italian-American Unity Day, 125
Italian-Americans
   antidefamation organizations,
      120–21
   caricatures of, 101–3
   food and, 174–75
   Jersey Shore and, 264–65
   in movies, 99, 266–71
   public perception of, 263
   self-identity of, 83
   self-image of, 263–64

   Sinatra, Frank, and, 155
   in *The Sopranos*, 271–72
   stereotypes, 154, 263–65
   as storytellers, 98–99
   World War II and, 60–61
   as writers, 98
Italic Institute of America, 263
Italy
   discrimination in, 42
   distrust of government in,
      42–43
   fascism in, 54–55
   immigration from, 45–48
   states of, 39–40
   unification of, 40–41
"It's a Man's, Man's World" (Brown),
      225

Jaffe, Stanley, 2–3, 4–5
James, Henry, 60
Japanese society, 77
Japanese-Americans, 60
Jasper, Richard, 64
Jersey Shore (television show),
      264–65
John Paul I, Pope, 246, 253
Johnson, Jerome, 125
Johnstone, Anna Hill, 140
Jones, Jenny, 129
Journey's End (Sheriff), 23
Joyce, James, 113
judicial system, 56–57
JWoww, 265

Kael, Pauline, 107, 148, 249
Karloff, Boris, 102
Kauffman, Stanley, 148
Kazan, Elia, 129

Keaton, Diane, 254
  casting of, 118
  salary for *The Godfather: Part III*,
    245
Kefauver, Estes, 61–62, 144
Keitel, Harvey, 261–62
Kennedy, John, 157
Kennedy, Joseph P., 59
Kennedy, Robert F., 61
Kennedy family, 179–80
Ker, W. P., 148
Kerkorian, Kirk, 116–17
The Kid Stays in the Picture (Evans),
  119
The Kid Stays in the Picture (film), 268
King, Morgana, 126
King Lear (Shakespeare), 244
Koch, Howard, 150
Korshak, Sidney, 116–17, 123
Kurosawa, Akira, 107

La Motta, Jake, 266
*La Storia: Five Centuries of the Italian
    American Experience*
    (Mangione), 43
labor quotas, 53–54
Lamberto, Cardinal (character), 253
Lancaster, Burt, 2
The Last Don (Puzo), 65, 260
Lawford, Peter, 165
Lazarus, Emma, 31–32
Le Cecla, Franco, 262
Lebo, Harlan, 77, 149, 160
Lentricchia, Frank, 86
Lettieri, Al, 126
Lewis, Jon, 245–46
lies, 185–86
Life with Luigi (radio show), 154, 270

lighting, 134–35
Little Caesar, 59, 99–101
Little Italy, 77–79, 141
  The Godfather: Part II and, 26, 200
Littlefeather, Sacheen, 150
Lodge, Henry Cabot, 52
Loew's Poli Theatre, 210
The Los Angeles Times, 148
Love Story, 115
Lovers and Other Strangers, 118
Lucas, George, 176
Lucchesi and the Whale (Lentricchia),
  86
Luciano, Charlie "Lucky," 99–100
lynchings, 52–53

Mad Men (television show), 224–25
Mafia
  activities of, 73
  in America, 58
  Americanization of, 99–100
  capitalism and, 76
  as capitalism metaphor, 82
  caricatures of, 268
  Catholic church and, 44
  code of silence of, 63–65
  coining of, 74–75
  development of, 43
  filming of *The Godfather* and,
    125–26
  glamour and, 259
  Hoover and, 61
  humanizing of, 89–90
  Martino and, 159–60
  McClellan investigation of, 63
  in novels, 260–61
  oppression by, 43–44
  Prohibition and, 58–59

prosecution of, 61–62
Senate hearings on, 61–62
in Sicily, 40
Malkin, Barry, 202, 234
mammoni, 206
The Man Who Knew Too Much, 250
The Man Who Shot Liberty Valence, 158
Mancini, Lucy (character), 225
Mancini, Vincent (character), 226, 232–33, 245, 248
Mancuso, Frank, 245
Mangione, Jerre, 40–41, 43, 50, 54, 61, 180
Mantegna, Joe, 254–55, 261
Maranzano, Salvatore, 99
Marchi, John, 124
marketing, 149
Married to the Mob, 270
Martin, Steve, 270–71
Martino, Al, 159–60, 262
Marx, Chico, 99
Mascagni, Pietro, 249–50
Mason, Jackie, 43
Massara, Giuseppe, 42
Masseria, Joe "The Boss," 99, 146
Massino, Joseph C., 64
material success, 34
McCartt, Bettye, 122
McClellan, John, 63
McGraw, Ali, 122
McGuire, Phyllis, 159
Mean Streets, 188, 261–62
Meese, Edwin, 75
Mezzogiorno, 41
MGM, 116
military, 42–43
Million Dollar Baby, 149–50

Minnelli, Vincent, 99
Mitchell, John, 65
Mob Wives (television show), 64
Modine, Matthew, 270
Mogambo, 158
money
    cynicism and, 284
    as power, 79–80
    thriftiness and, 219–21
Montana, Lenny, 117
Montana, Tony (character), 273
Moonstruck, 266
Morreale, Ben, 40–41, 61
Morrison, Toni, 264
mother/son dynamic, 207–8
Mount Allegro (Mangione), 40, 54
Mount Holyoke College, 217
movies. *See also* gangster films
    Italian-Americans in, 99, 261–71
    violence in, 107
    Westerns, 103, 105
Moynihan, Daniel, 50
Muni, Paul, 96, 100, 102
Murder Inc. trial, 62–63
murder montage, 231–32
Murray, Albert, 156
music, as character, 250
musical score, 141–43
Mussolini, Benito, 72
My Blue Heaven, 268, 270–71
My Cousin Vinnie, 270
"My Way" (song), 86, 166

Naish, J. Carrol, 154, 270
Napoléon, 143
National Italian-American Federation (NIAF), 121
Native Americans, 103

Nazi Party, 80
New Orleans, 48, 52–53
The New Republic, 148
New York City, 48
New York Post, 260
New York Times, 52–53, 70, 123
NIAF. *See* National Italian-American
    Federation
Nichols, Mike, 114
Nitti, Frank, 100
Nixon, Richard, 65, 133, 157,
    177–78
Norton Anthology, 98
novels, 69, 260–61

Oceania, 283
O'Dwyer, Paul, 264
Old World, 66
omerta, 63–65, 196
Omerta (Puzo), 260
opera, 249–50
Opera; or, the Undoing of Women
    (Clement, ed.), 249
oranges, 176–77
organized crime, 65. *See also* Mafia
otherness, 28–30
    Italian-American caricatures and,
        103
    in *Moonstruck*, 266
    popularization of, 104–5
    in *The Sopranos*, 272

Pacino, Al
    Academy Awards and, 147
    casting of, 116–17
    Coppola, Francis Ford, and, 147
    doubts about, 145–46
    Eboli and, 126

Evans and, 116–17
    performance in *The Godfather*,
        145–47
    performance in *The Godfather:
        Part II*, 198–99
    salary for *The Godfather: Part II*,
        195
    salary for *The Godfather: Part III*,
        245
    Scarface (1983) and, 273
    Serpico and, 267
Padoa-Schioppa, Tomasso, 206
paesanos, 27–28
Palminteri, Chazz, 269
Panetta, George, 175, 178–79
Paramount Pictures
    Bluhdorn and, 114–15
    Brando, casting of, 1–2
    Colombo and, 121–22
    conditions for producing *The
        Godfather: Part II*, 193–94
    doubts of Coppola, Francis Ford,
        by, 129–30
    Società General Immobiliare and,
        245–46
    writing of *The Godfather: Part III*
        and, 243–44
Parker, Helen Sarah Norton, 28
Parker, Nancy Edge, 18, *204*, 221–23,
    240
Parker, Thomas, 23, 283
paterfamilias, 255
    Brando as, 127
    Coppola, Francis Ford, as, 189
    Corleone, Michael, as, 186
    Soprano, Tony, as, 225
patriarchy, 223–24
peasants, 41–42

Peckinpah, Sam, 107
Penn, Arthur, 107, 111
Pentangeli, Frankie (character),
195–96
People, 65
Perisco, Carmine "The Snake,"
125–26
Pesci, Joe, 270
physical labor, 214
Pianti, Romano, 197
Pileggi, Nicholas, 122, 125
Playboy, 189
Polizzi, Nicole "Snooki," 264–65
Pontelandolfo, Italy, 16, 170
poverty, 25–26, 46–47
power, 79–80
    friendship as, 86
    transfer of, 182–83
The Pride and the Passion, 157
Prizzi's Honor, 113, 261
procreation, 255
production design, 139–41, 199–201
Profaci, Joe, 206
profanity, 27–28
Prohibition, 58–59
propaganda, 80
Public Enemy, 101
Putnam, Robert D., 171
Putnam & Co., 69–70
Puzo, Mario, 65, 208
    American dream and, 6–7
    Brando, casting of, 1–2
    business and, 76
    Coppola, Francis Ford, and, 113
    creation of Corleone, Vito, and,
    205–6
    early books of, 69
    Evans and, 69–70

Italian-American stereotypes and,
154
Mafia and, 260
power and, 80
research of, 71
Sinatra, Frank, and, 157, 162
socialism and, 71–72
writing of *The Godfather: Part III*
and, 244

Quinn, Anthony, 2

racial slurs, 51–52
Raft, George, 102
The Rain People, 4, 193
Rand, Ayn, 47
Reagan, Ronald, 81, 157, 178
Reaganomics, 246
reality television, 64, 264
redemption, 34
reincarnation, 22
reinvention, 34
religion, 18–19
    imagery and, 231–33
    themes of, 229–30
"The Representation of Ethnicity in
    The Godfather" (Dika), 91
Reprise Records, 164
revenge, 72, 91–93
Reynolds, William, 141
Rickles, Don, 119
Riefenstahl, Leni, 80
Rigoletto (Verdi), 249
Ritt, Martin, 115
Rizzo, Jilly, 162–63
Robinson, Amy, 262
Robinson, Edward G., 99
Rocky, 266

Rolling Stone, 256
The Ronettes, 261
Roosevelt, Franklin D., 60
Ross, Herbert, 271
Rota, Nino, 141–42
"Round Trip" (D'Agata), 32
Royal Welch Fusiliers, 23
Ruddy, Al, 113, 117, 193
    Academy Awards and, 149–50
    Brando makeup test and, 4–5
    Colombo and, 122–24
    ending of *The Godfather* and,
        185
    Sinatra, Frank, and, 162
Rules of the Game, 203
Russo, Gianni, 126, 128, 180
Rutgers University, 264
Ryder, Winona, 251

Sacco, Nicola, 55–56
San Francisco, 48
Santopietro, Andrew, 8, 61, 169, *204*
Santopietro, Maria Valletta, 174, *204*,
        215–16, 234–36
Santopietro, Olindo Oreste, 8, 18, 21,
        204
    American identity and, 30–31
    FBI and, 55–56
    thriftiness of, 219–21
    in World War II, 61
Santopietro, Orazio, 16, *204*, 234–35,
        283–84, *286*
Sato, Tadao, 77
Saturday Night Fever, 267–68
Scarface (1932), 59, *96*, 100–102
Scarface (1983), 273
Scent of a Woman, 147
Schaffner, Franklin, 111

Scorsese, Martin, 188
    crime trilogy of, 261–62
    The Godfather: Part II and, 193
    Raging Bull and, 266
Senate hearings, 61–62
Serpico, 267–68
Shakespeare, William, 244
Shark Tale, 269
Sheriff, R. C., 23
Shire, Talia, 188–89
    casting of, 127–28
    Coppola, Sofia, and, 252
    on Corleone, Connie, 225–26
    on Corleone, Vito, 72
The Sicilian (Puzo), 260
Sicily
    Corleone, Michael, in, 92
    DeNiro in, 197
    discrimination in, 42
    history of, 40–41
    immigration from, 44–47
Sight and Sound, 203
Sinatra, Frank, 2, 51–52, 86, 153–54,
        262
    acting career of, 154–56
    Coppola, Francis Ford, and, 156–57
    Fontane and, 156–58
    From Here to Eternity and, 157–59
    The Godfather: Part III and, 163
    Italian identity of, 166–67
    Prohibition and, 58–59
    Puzo and, 157, 162
    street credibility of, 164
    temperament of, 163–64
    viewing of *The Godfather*, 162–63
Sinatra, Frank, Jr., 251
Sinatra, Martin, 52
Sindona, Michele, 245–46

Sirica, John J., 65
60 Minutes (television show), 206
Slocum Grammar School, 26
slums, 106–7
Smith, Dick, 143–44
Smith, Philip, 140
social status, 86
socialism, 55–56, 71–72
Società General Immobiliare, 233, 245–46
Sondheim, Stephen, 140, 176
Songs My Mother Taught Me (Brando), 151
Soprano, Carmella (character), 273–74
Soprano, Tony (character), 225, 262, 273
The Sopranos (television show), 136, 207, 225, 262, 271–75
sound design, 143
Stallone, Sylvester, 267
Staten Island, 180–81
Statue of Liberty, 16, 31–32, 45, 282
Stefanelli, Simonetta, 118
stereotypes, 104, 154, 263–65
storytelling, 97–99
street credibility, 164
Sunday dinner, 172–75

Talese, Gay, 31–32, 73, 76, 98, 224
Targ, William, 70
Tavoularis, Dean, 90, 139–41, 177, 199–201
television, 99
    Italian-American portrayals on, 271
    reality, 64, 264
    stereotypes on, 104
Teresa, Vincent, 63

Tessio, Salvatore (character), 135–36
Tetro, 279
thriftiness, 219–21
Till the Clouds Roll By, 236
To Kill a Mockingbird, 118, 270
Tolstoy, Leo, 25
Tomei, Marisa, 270
Tonelli, Bill, 11–12, 60, 265–66
Tony n' Tina's Wedding, 24
Towne, Robert, 182
tradition, 173
Trave, 283
Travers, Peter, 256
Travolta, John, 267
Tucker: The Man and His Dream, 244
Tufts University, 31
Turkus, Baron, 62
Twelve Angry Men, 270

Underworld (DeLillo), 255
UNICO, 121
unions, 72–73
Unto the Sons (Talese), 31–32
The Untouchables (television show), 104
U.S. Immigration Commission, 53–54

Valachi, Joseph, 63
The Valachi Papers, 63
Vale, Jerry, 262
Vallone, Raf, 253
Van Runkle, Theadora, 199
Vanity Fair, 251–52
Vanzetti, Bartolomeo, 55–56
Variety, 70
Vatican Bank, 245–46
Ventura, Simona, 265

Verdi, Giuseppe, 249
Vertigo, 203
la via vecchia, 33, 48
video games, 150
Vietnam War, 35, 75
Vigoda, Abe, 114
violence, 35, 128
    Coppola, Francis Ford, and, 128, 138
    Corleone, Vito, and, 87–88
    effect of, 188–89
    friendship and, 86
    in *The Godfather: Part II*, 86
    justification of, 90
    in movies, 107
    sensationalism of, 197
visual imagery, 131–32, 231–33
Viva Madison Avenue! (Panetta), 178–79

Wall Street, 93
Wall Street Journal, 123
Wallace, Henry, 81
Wallach, Eli, 159, 163
War and Peace (Tolstoy), 25
Warner Bros., 112
Warshow, Robert, 82
Washington, Booker T., 42
Waterbury, Connecticut, 9–11

Waterbury Country Club, 20
Watergate scandal, 35
Westerns, 103, 105
White Defense Mob, 52
The Wild Bunch, 107
Williams, Tennessee, 159
Willis, Gordon, 77, 128–29, 131, 134, 139
    The Godfather: Part II and, 199
    symbolism of, 177
Winegardner, Mark, 260–61
Woltz, Jack (character), 73, 87, 161
women
    in *The Godfather: Part III*, 225–26
    Italian immigrant, 208–9
    mother/son dynamic and, 207–8
World War I, 22–24
World War II, 60–61
writers, 98

Yates, Peter, 111
You're a Big Boy Now, 4
Youth Without Youth, 279

Zasa, Joey (character), 232–33
Zinnemann, Fred, 111, 158
Zinner, Peter, 130, 141
Zogby poll, 263